Media
Unlimited

TODD GITLIN

Media Unlimited

HOW THE TORRENT OF IMAGES AND SOUNDS OVERWHELMS OUR LIVES

METROPOLITAN BOOKS

Henry Holt and Company | New York

Metropolitan Books
Henry Holt and Company, LLC
Publishers since 1866
115 West 18th Street
New York, New York 10011

Metropolitan Books™ is a registered
trademark of Henry Holt and Company, LLC.

Library of Congress Cataloging-in-Publication Data

Gitlin, Todd.
    Media unlimited : how the torrent of images and sounds
    overwhelms our lives / Todd Gitlin.—1st ed.
        p.   cm.
    Includes index.
    ISBN 0-8050-4898-7 (hb)
    1.   Mass media.   I. Title.
P90.G4778   2002
302.23—dc21

                                          2001039838

Henry Holt books are available for special promotions and
premiums. For details contact: Director, Special Markets.

First Edition 2001

Printed in the United States of America

10 9 8 7 6 5 4 3 2 1

Again to Laurel
and to Shoshana,
Justin, and Fletcher

Contents

Introduction

Every book begins with a dissatisfaction, a hope, and a gamble. The dissatisfaction first. Truth is, I got tired of what I knew, or thought I knew, or sounded as though I knew, about media, and dissatisfied, too, with what others were writing and saying. I was trapped in a tree-forest imbalance. The more trees I identified, the less forest I saw. But the nature of the forest, the hugeness and weirdness of it, was exactly what mattered.

I have been reading and writing about media for more than twenty-five years now, from varying angles, in different moods, modes, and styles, in scholarly studies and popular magazines, coolly and not so coolly, rethinking here and there but persuaded in general that media matter greatly, that it takes effort to work out just how they matter, and that, if properly understood, they cast light on how our world works, though not necessarily as the engineers, proprietors, or users may have intended.

For me, it began with awareness of a considerable discrepancy between media images and what I was pleased (or displeased) to call reality. This discrepancy came to me as a revelation and something of a shock. I tried to analyze, in some detail, how it happened that the world I had known in the New Left movement of the 1960s had been processed by the news industry into pictures and slogans that seemed quite different from, even contrary to, what I knew with my own senses; and how this manufactured impression, like some ghostly emanation, produced a strong and eerie impact on the movement itself. I wrote a book called *The Whole World Is Watching*, extrapolating from this episode to show and explain how the media are, in relation to social reality, fun-house mirrors, selective in their appetites, skewed in their imagery. The news is not in any simple way a "mirror" on the world; it is a conduit for ideas and symbols, an industrial product that promotes packages of ideas and ideologies, and serves, consequently, as social ballast, though at times also a harbinger of social change. The news is a cognitive warp. The world is this way; the media make it appear that way. I wanted to know why and what difference it made.

Curiosity then drew me to the entertainment industry, another apparatus that systematically produces versions of reality. I started out by wondering how Hollywood digested social turmoil into television fictions, then realized that in order to work out how political controversy got domesticated, I would have to discover how all kinds of programs got packaged, and what got left out and why. Accordingly, I spent months in Hollywood and wrote a book called *Inside Prime Time*, an analysis of the network television business, tracing the corporate and cultural forces that churn out programs.

To a hammer, they say, the whole world looks like nails. Occupationally, I had somehow become a "media sociologist" and "media critic," though my interest in media was precisely in the light they cast on a whole society and culture. Over the years, as I resisted narrowness and worked on other projects, I kept being drawn back to the subject of media and their place in the contemporary world. I followed the scholarly literature as much as a single individual can in an age of academic overflow. I wrote dozens upon dozens of articles on media subjects: happy-talk news, Ronald Reagan and the so-called Teflon effect, sound bites and politics, the treatment of campaigns as horse races, TV's depiction of the Cold War, the Gulf War, earthquakes, and anniversaries, car commercials, MTV, *Survivor*, television's corps of pundits, its treatment of gays and African-Americans, of Internet hype and dot-com mania, moralism and politics in the movies, media violence, conglomerate mergers, college students' taste in documentary films, the export of American popular culture, O. J. Simpson, Princess Diana, Monica Lewinsky. . . . Each time, I started with a subject of some currency and hoped to see it as part of a whole field. Except: Where was that whole field?

Which brings me to a parable.

TRUCKS

A customs officer observes a truck pulling up at the border. Suspicious, he orders the driver out and searches the vehicle. He pulls off panels, bumpers, and wheel cases but finds not a single scrap of contraband, whereupon, still suspicious but at a loss to know where else to search, he waves the driver through. The next week, the same driver arrives. Again the official searches, and again finds nothing illicit. Over the years, the official tries full-body searches, X rays, and sonar, anything he can think of, and each week the same man drives up, but no mysterious cargo ever appears, and each time, reluctantly, the customs man waves the driver on.

Finally, after many years, the officer is about to retire. The driver pulls up.

"I know you're a smuggler," the customs officer says. "Don't bother denying it. But damned if I can figure out what you've been smuggling all these years. I'm leaving now. I swear to you I can do you no harm. Won't you please tell me what you've been smuggling?"

"Trucks," the driver says.

The media have been smuggling the habit of living with the media. The swarming enormity of American popular culture ought to be obvious, for never have so many communicated so much, on so many screens, through so many channels, absorbing so many hours of irreplaceable human attention, about communications. Whenever strangers wish to feel out common ground and establish that they are not altogether alien to one another, they compare notes on stars and shows, declare thumbs up or thumbs down, deploy the latest catch phrases, indicate that they are *West Wing*, *South Park*, Oprah, Howard Stern, World Wrestling Federation, or Rush Limbaugh types of people. In all their bits and chunks, the media are major subjects of the media themselves, glutted as they are with reviews, profiles, commentaries, gossip, trivia, and bulletins about hits and celebrities, rising and falling stars, blazing and cooling fads, trends and gadgets, the ebb and flow of executive careers in the media, the latest in media corporate acquisitions of other media corporations. Entertainment writers and talking heads are legion. The *New York Times*'s weekly section "Circuits," devoted to new communications technology, has been emulated elsewhere. Claims of "media effects" are legion, and many of them, or at least their authors, circulate through television, newspaper columns, and the Internet. Organizations galore sponsor conferences galore on violence and profanity in the media. Books and journals about the media stream off the presses.

Yet for all the talk and the talk about the talk, the main truth about the media slips through our fingers. Critics and commentators look for contraband but miss the truck—the immensity of the experience of media, the sheer quantity of attention paid, the devotions and rituals that absorb our time and resources. The obvious but hard-to-grasp truth is that living with the media is today one of the main things Americans and many other human beings do.

INFORMATION? PLEASE

The centrality of media is disguised, in part, by the prevalence of that assured, hard-edged phrase *information society*, or even more grandly, *information age*. Such terms are instant propaganda for a way of life that is also a way of progress. Who in his right mind could be against information or want to be without it? Who wouldn't want to produce, consume, and accumulate more of this useful stuff, remove obstacles to its spread, invest in it, see better variants of it spring to life? Even today's Luddites want to obtain speedier Internet access, put up more Web sites, promote more extensive listservs, publish more tracts, and otherwise diffuse more information about the dangers of high technology. *Information society* glows with a positive aura. The very term *information* points to a gift—specific and ever replenished, shining forth in the bright light of utility. Ignorance is not bliss; information is.

But we diminish the significance of media and our reliance on them in everyday life by classifying them as channels of information. Media today are occasions for and conduits of a way of life identified with rationality, technological achievement, and the quest for wealth, but also for something else entirely, something we call *fun, comfort, convenience,* or *pleasure*. We have come to care tremendously about how we feel and how readily we can change our feelings. Media are means. We aim, through media, to indulge and serve our hungers by inviting images and sounds into our lives, making them come and go with ease in a never-ending quest for stimulus and sensation. Our prevailing business is the business not of information but of satisfaction, the feeling of feelings, to which we give as much time as we can manage, not only at home but in the car, at work, or walking down the street. We seek and sometimes find a laugh from a sitcom joke, an erotic twinge from an underwear ad, a jolt of rhythm from a radio playlist, a sensation of moving with remarkable speed through a video game. Even the quest for information includes the quest for the delight to be found in retrieving it—a quest, that is, for a feeling. Even on and after the infamous day of September 11, 2001, people turned to television not only for facts but for rituals of shared horror, grief, sympathy, reassurance, and the many forms of solidarity.

In a society that fancies itself the freest ever, spending time with communications machinery is the main use to which we have put our freedom. All human beings play, but this civilization has evolved a particular form of play: wedding fun to convenience by bathing ourselves in images and sounds. The most important thing about the communications we live among is not that they deceive (which they do); or that they broadcast a limiting ideology (which they do); or emphasize sex and violence (which they do); or convey diminished images of the good, the true, and the normal (which they do); or corrode the quality of art (which they also do); or reduce language (which they surely do)—but that with all their lies, skews, and shallow pleasures, they saturate our way of life with a promise of feeling, even if we may not know exactly how we feel about one or another batch of images except that they are *there*, streaming out of screens large and small, or bubbling in the background of life, but always coursing onward. To an unprecedented degree, the torrent of images, songs, and stories streaming has become our familiar world.

Accordingly, supersaturation is the subject of chapter 1 and the speed of the media torrent the subject of chapter 2.

THE TRUTH OF A GRAMMATICAL ERROR

Obliquely and unintentionally, we allude to the biggest truth about media with a grammatical error. We commonly speak of "the media" in the singular. Grammatical sticklers (like this writer) cringe when the media themselves or college students reared on them (or it) speak of "the media" as they might speak of "the sky"—as if there were only one. There is, however, a reason for this error other than grammatical slovenliness. Something in our experience makes us want to address media as "it." We may be confused about whether "the media" are or "is" technologies or cultural codes—whether "television" is an electronic system for bringing images into the home, or the sum of Oprah, Dan Rather, Jerry Springer, and MTV; whether "the media" includes alternative rock or the Internet. But through all the confusion we sense something like a unity at work. The torrent is seamless: a collage of back-to-back stories, talk show banter, fragments of ads, soundtracks of musical snippets. Even as we click around, something *feels* uniform—a relentless pace, a pattern of interruption, a pressure toward unseriousness, a readiness for sensation, an anticipation of the next new thing. Whatever the diversity of texts, the media largely share a texture, even if it is maddeningly difficult to describe—real and unreal, present and absent, disposable and essential, distracting and absorbing, sensational and tedious, emotional and numbing.

This book is an attempt to get at the maddening difficulty.

WHAT THIS BOOK IS NOT ABOUT

Overwhelmed by the immensity and ubiquity of the media, we prefer to concentrate on their "effects." Considering the vast cornucopia of the items on offer, the cars, toys, beers, running shoes, weight reducers, muscle tighteners, and so on, do media make us value material goods more than we otherwise would? Does the shapeliness of the models promoting the cars and taco chips make us want to be thinner, more muscular, or implanted with silicone? Have the commercials for prescription drugs made us reliable customers for pharmaceutical blockbusters like Viagra and Claritin? Do the shoot-ups and gore make us more aggressive and murderous, the high-velocity vehicle chases more prone to speed and mayhem? Has the bare flesh on screen made us sex crazed? Have the pace and discontinuity of the media put deficits in our attention? Does the time we spend watching make us obese? Considering the pleasures of private immersion, have we become less sociable—indeed, less democratic?

Surely media have effects on behaviors and ideas, not so much because any single exposure is powerful but because they repeat. And repeat. And repeat. There is ample evidence that the answer to each of the questions above is, largely, yes—with the important qualification that more aggressive is not the same as more murderous. (For this link in the logical chain to be forged, guns must be freely available.) Still, as the industries that circulate images and sounds like to remind us—some things are true even if profiteers say so—they do not bind unwilling victims in their coils. We are regaled by choices. Everywhere we look, we are offered an index, an inventory, a menu, a guide. The media are not only performances but promises. We return for more. Crucially, the machines can be turned on and off; in fact, the on-off switches, mute buttons, channel changers, remote control clickers are part of their essence, part of what's so appealing about them. The programs, ads, songs, and stories exist in passing. One by one, they can be taken lightly. They are *made* to be taken lightly, to fill their moments in time but yield gracefully to their successors. The morals on offer can be endorsed, disputed, or shrugged off according to the social experience, disposition, or plain idiosyncrasy of the customers.

To put this another way: alongside specific effects, much of the time the everyday noise of media is the buzz of the inconsequential, the *just there*. This is neither the media's downside nor their saving grace. The buzz of the inconsequential is the media's essence. This pointlessness is precisely what we are, by and large, not free *not* to choose.

Then are we, as William Gass once suggested, "no more than the vanishing cross-hatch where the media intersect"? To answer in the affirmative would be to look for another wrong sort of contraband. We have not vanished, and we are not helpless. Everyone struggles to cope, devising commonplace stratagems to tame the onrush. These stratagems—becoming fans, critics, paranoids, exhibitionists, ironists, jammers, secessionists, and abolitionists—are the subject of chapter 3. They help us navigate, but they are also means by which we evade the immense facts of saturation and speed. Collectively, the main "effect" of media saturation is that we live—we have no other choice—in societies whose people while away countless hours watching television, listening to recorded music, playing video games, connecting to the Internet, and so on unto the next wave of technologies.

Moreover, the "we" who live in the torrent are not only Americans. The saturation is increasingly global, though not irresistibly so. The United States is the world capital of tinsel and celebrity, the homeland for the manufacture of images and soundtracks in unprecedented numbers and at unprecedented velocity. How it came to pass that American media are so exportable is the subject of chapter 4.

One caution: the swarming enormity of popular culture cannot be comprehended by calling it, in the current academic mode, *meaning-making*. Dignified as the term may sound, people do not necessarily "make meaning" from the images and sounds that they take in or sift through or that sift through them. We do not necessarily interpret (although we are more likely to do so when a researcher asks), and even when we may, under pressure, find words to express what we like or dislike about a media moment, the interpretation or judgment is not the only or even the main thing under way. We are watching, listening, feeling. We may well be escaping from meaning. We are living a life with media, undergoing an experience that is not reducible to the celebrities or shows we "like" or "dislike." Sometimes the stuff of media does "mean" something to us, like our consumer goods, our dwellings, cars, and fashions, all the labels that serve as markers of status or badges of identity. But in any event, what happens in the process of living with media is both more and less than getting a label. It is *being with media*.

Neither are the media themselves messages—that is, statements about the world. Marshall McLuhan's glib formulation turns out to mean next to nothing. This is partly because he was not clear or convincing about just what he meant by a medium—a television set? a commercial channel? a sitcom? But McLuhan was not precise either in his use of the word *message*. Media do not simply deliver information. An image or a soundtrack is not simply a set of abstract signs that describe, point to, or represent realities standing elsewhere. Not only do they point; they *are*. They are wraparound presences with which we live much of our lives. McLuhan was closer to the truth when, in a playful mood, he titled one of his later books *The Media Is the Massage*.

Experience is not a message, though it takes in messages. In the presence of media, we may be attentive or inattentive, aroused or deadened, but it is in symbiotic relation to them, their pictures, texts, and sounds, in the time we spend with them, the trouble we take to obtain, absorb, repel, and discuss them, that much of the world happens for us. Media are occasions for experiences—experiences that are themselves the main products, the main transactions, the main "effects" of media. This is the big story; the rest is details.

Which takes me to the gamble of this book. Instead of stringing together piecemeal analyses, arguments, complaints, and fulminations about media, I thought this was the time, at least for me, to leave behind the more manageable questions and head toward the baffling media totality itself. The larger the ambition, of course, the chancier the book and the more conspicuous the author's limitations. I was searching for the right way to ask the reader's indulgence when I discovered that one of the great cultural historians of the twentieth century, the Dutchman Johan Huizinga, had already said what I wanted to say in the foreword to his masterwork, *Homo Ludens: A Study of the Play Element in Culture:*

> The reader of these pages should not look for detailed documentation of every word. In treating of the general problems of culture one is constantly obliged to undertake predatory incursions into provinces not sufficiently explored by the raider himself. To fill in all the gaps in my knowledge beforehand was out of the question for me. I had to write now, or not at all. And I wanted to write.

1 | Supersaturation, or, The Media Torrent and Disposable Feeling

On my bedroom wall hangs a print of Vermeer's *The Concert*, painted around 1660. A young woman is playing a spinet. A second woman, probably her maid, holds a letter. A cavalier stands between them, his back to us. A landscape is painted on the raised lid of the spinet, and on the wall hang two paintings, a landscape and *The Procuress*, a work by Baburen, another Dutch artist, depicting a man and two women in a brothel. As in many seventeenth-century Dutch paintings, the domestic space is decorated by paintings. In wealthy Holland, many homes, and not only bourgeois ones, featured such renderings of the outer world. These pictures were pleasing, but more: they were proofs of taste and prosperity, amusements and news at once.

Vermeer froze instants, but instants that spoke of the relative constancy of the world in which his subjects lived. If he had painted the same room in the same house an hour, a day, or a month later, the letter in the maid's hand would have been different, and the woman might have been playing a different selection, but the paintings on the far wall would likely have been the same. There might have been other paintings, etchings, and prints elsewhere in the house, but they would not have changed much from month to month, year to year.

In what was then the richest country in the world, "everyone strives to embellish his house with precious pieces, especially the room toward the street," as one English visitor to Amsterdam wrote in 1640, noting that he had observed paintings in bakeries, butcher's shops, and the workshops of blacksmiths and cobblers. Of course, the number of paintings, etchings, and prints in homes varied considerably. One tailor owned five paintings, for example, while at the high end, a 1665 inventory of a lavish patrician's house in Amsterdam held two maps and thirteen paintings in one grand room, twelve paintings in his widow's bedroom, and seven in the maid's room. Still, compared with today's domestic imagery, the grandest Dutch inventories of that prosperous era were tiny. Even in the better-off households depicted by Vermeer, the visual field inhabited by his figures was relatively scanty and fixed.

Today, Vermeer's equivalent, if he were painting domestic scenes, or shooting a spread for *Vanity Fair*, or directing commercials or movies, would also display his figures against a background of images; and if his work appeared on-screen, there is a good chance that he would mix in a soundtrack as well. Most of the images would be portraits of individuals who have never walked in the door—not in the flesh—and yet are recognized and welcomed, though not like actual persons. They would rapidly segue into others—either because they had been edited into a video montage, or because they appear on pages meant to be leafed through. Today's Vermeer would discover that the private space of the home offers up vastly more impressions of the larger world than was possible in 1660. In seventeenth-century Delft, painters did not knock on the door day and night offering fresh images for sale. Today, though living space has been set apart from working space, as would have been the case only for the wealthier burghers of Vermeer's time, the outside world has entered the home with a vengeance—in the profusion of media.

The flow of images and sounds through the households of the rich world, and the richer parts of the poor world, seems unremarkable today. Only a visitor from an earlier century or an impoverished country could be startled by the fact that life is now played out against a shimmering multitude of images and sounds, emanating from television, videotapes, videodiscs, video games, VCRs, computer screens, digital displays of all sorts, always in flux, chosen partly at will, partly by whim, supplemented by words, numbers, symbols, phrases, fragments, all passing through screens that in a single minute can display more pictures than a prosperous seventeenth-century Dutch household contained over several lifetimes, portraying in one day more individuals than the Dutch burgher would have beheld in the course of years, and in one week more bits of what we have come to call "information" than all the books in all the households in Vermeer's Delft. And this is not yet to speak of our sonic surroundings: the music, voices, and sound effects from radios, CD players, and turntables. Nor is it to speak of newspapers, magazines, newsletters, and books. Most of the faces we shall ever behold, we shall behold in the form of images.

Because they arrive with sound, at home, in the car, the elevator, or the waiting room, today's images are capable of attracting our attention during much of the day. We may ignore most of them most of the time, take issue with them or shrug them off (or think we are shrugging them off), but we must do the work of dispelling them— and even then, we know we can usher them into our presence whenever we like. Iconic plenitude is the contemporary condition, and it is taken for granted. To grow up in this culture is to grow into an expectation that images and sounds will be there for us on command, and that the stories they compose will be succeeded by still other stories, all bidding for our attention, all striving to make sense, all, in some sense, *ours*. Raymond Williams, the first analyst to pay attention to the fact that television is not just pictures but flow, and not just flow but drama upon drama, pointed out more than a quarter century ago, long before hundred-channel cable TV and VCRs, that

> we have never as a society acted so much or watched so many others acting. . . . [W]hat is really new . . . is that drama . . . is built into the rhythms of everyday life. In earlier periods drama was important at a festival, in a season, or as a conscious journey to a theater; from honouring Dionysus or Christ to taking in a show. What we have now is drama as habitual experience: more in a week, in many cases, than most human beings would previously have seen in a lifetime.

Around the time Vermeer painted *The Concert*, Blaise Pascal, who worried about the seductive power of distraction among the French royalty, wrote that "near the persons of kings there never fail to be a great number of people who see to it that amusement follows business, and who watch all the time of their leisure to supply them with delights and games, so that there is no blank in it." In this one respect, today almost everyone—even the poor—in the rich countries resembles a king, attended by the courtiers of the media offering a divine right of choice.

MEASURES OF MAGNITUDE

Statistics begin—but barely—to convey the sheer magnitude of this in-touchness, access, exposure, plenitude, glut, however we want to think of it.

In 1999, a television set was on in the average American household more than seven hours a day, a figure that has remained fairly steady since 1983. According to the measurements of the A. C. Nielsen Company, the standard used by advertisers and the television business itself, the average individual watched television about four hours a day, not counting the time when the set was on but the individual in question was not watching. When Americans were asked to keep diaries of how they spend their time, the time spent actually watching dropped to a still striking three hours a day—probably an undercount. In 1995, of those who watched, the percentage who watched "whatever's on," as opposed to any specific program, was 43 percent, up from 29 percent in 1979. Though cross-national comparisons are elusive because of differences in measurement systems, the numbers in other industrialized nations seem to be comparable—France, for example, averaging three and a half hours per person. One survey of forty-three nations showed the United States ranking third in viewing hours, after Japan and Mexico. None of this counts time spent discussing programs, reading about their stars, or thinking about either.

Overall, wrote one major researcher in 1990, "watching TV is the dominant leisure activity of Americans, consuming 40 percent of the average person's free time as a primary activity [when people give television their undivided attention]. Television takes up more than half of our free time if you count . . . watching TV while doing something else like eating or reading . . . [or] when you have the set on but you aren't paying attention to it." Sex, race, income, age, and marital status make surprisingly little difference in time spent. Neither, at this writing, has the Internet diminished total media use, even if you don't count the Web as part of the media. While Internet users do watch 28 percent less television, they spend more time than nonusers playing video games and listening to the radio and recorded music—obviously a younger crowd. Long-term users (four or more years) say they go on-line for more than two hours a day, and boys and girls alike spend the bulk of their Internet time entertaining themselves with games, hobbies, and the like. In other words, the

Internet redistributes the flow of unlimited media but does not dry it up. When one considers the overlapping and additional hours of exposure to radio, magazines, newspapers, compact discs, movies (available via a range of technologies as well as in theaters), and comic books, as well as the accompanying articles, books, and chats about what's on or was on or is coming up via all these means, it is clear that the media flow into the home—not to mention outside— has swelled into a torrent of immense force and constancy, an accompaniment *to* life that has become a central experience *of* life.

The place of media in the lives of children is worth special attention—not simply because children are uniquely impressionable but because their experience shapes everyone's future; if we today take a media-soaked environment for granted, surely one reason is that we grew up in it and can no longer see how remarkable it is. Here are some findings from a national survey of media conditions among American children aged two through eighteen. The average American child lives in a household with 2.9 televisions, 1.8 VCRs, 3.1 radios, 2.6 tape players, 2.1 CD players, 1.4 video game players, and 1 computer. Ninety-nine percent of these children live in homes with one or more TVs, 97 percent with a VCR, 97 percent with a radio, 94 percent with a tape player, 90 percent with a CD player, 70 percent with a video game player, 69 percent with a computer. Eighty-eight percent live in homes with two or more TVs, 60 percent in homes with three or more. Of the 99 percent with a TV, 74 percent have cable or satellite service. And so on, and on, and on.

The uniformity of this picture is no less astounding. A great deal about the lives of children depends on their race, sex, and social class, but access to major media does not. For TV, VCR, and radio ownership, rates do not vary significantly among white, black, and Hispanic children, or between girls and boys. For television and radio, rates do not vary significantly according to the income of the community.

How accessible, then, is the media cavalcade at home? Of children eight to eighteen, 65 percent have a TV in their bedrooms, 86 percent a radio, 81 percent a tape player, 75 percent a CD player. Boys and girls are not significantly different in possessing this bounty, though the relative usages do vary by medium. Researchers also asked children whether the television was "on in their homes even if no one is watching 'most of the time,' 'some of the time,' 'a little of the time,' or 'never.' " Homes in which television is on "most of the time" are termed *constant television households*. By this measure, 42 percent of all American households with children are constant television households. Blacks are more likely than whites or Hispanics to experience TV in their lives: 56 percent of black children live in constant television households (and 69 percent have a TV in their bedrooms, compared to 48 percent of whites). The lower the family education and the median income of the community, the greater the chance that a household is a constant television household.

As for time, the average child spent six hours and thirty-two minutes per day exposed to media of all kinds, of which the time spent reading books and magazines—not counting schoolwork—averaged about forty-five minutes. For ages two to seven, the average for total media was four hours and seventeen minutes; for ages eight to thirteen, eight hours and eight minutes, falling to seven hours and thirty-five minutes for ages fourteen to eighteen. Here, race and social class do count. Black children are most exposed, followed by Hispanics, than whites. At all age levels, the amount of exposure to all media varies inversely with class, from six hours and fifty-nine minutes a day for children in households where the median income for the zip code is under $25,000 to six hours and two minutes for children whose zip code median income is over $40,000. The discrepancy for TV exposure is especially pronounced, ranging from three hours and six minutes a day for children whose zip code incomes are under $25,000 to two hours and twenty-nine minutes for children whose zip code incomes are over $40,000. Still, these differences are not vast. Given everything that divides the rich from the poor, the professional from the working class—differences in physical and mental health, infant mortality, longevity, safety, vulnerability to crime, prospects for stable employment, and so on—the class differences in media access and use are surprisingly slender. So are the differences between American and western European children, the latter averaging six hours a day total, though in Europe only two and a quarter of those hours are spent with TV.

All such statistics are crude, of course. Most of them register the time that people *say* they spend. They are—thankfully—not checked by total surveillance. Moreover, the meaning of *exposure* is hard to assess, since the concept encompasses rapt attention, vague awareness, oblivious coexistence, and all possible shadings in between. As the images glide by and the voices come and go, how can we assess what goes on in people's heads? Still, the figures do convey some sense of the media saturation with which we live—and so far we have counted only what can be counted at home. These numbers don't take into account the billboards, the TVs at bars and on planes, the Muzak in restaurants and shops, the magazines in the doctor's waiting room, the digital displays at the gas pump and over the urinal, the ads, insignias, and logos whizzing by on the sides of buses and taxis, climbing the walls of buildings, making announcements from caps, bags, T-shirts, and sneakers. To vary our experience, we can pay to watch stories about individuals unfold across larger-than-life-size movie screens, or visit theme parks and troop from image to image, display to display. Whenever we like, on foot or in vehicles, we can convert ourselves into movable nodes of communication, thanks to car radios, tape, CD, and game players, cell phones, beepers, Walkmen, and the latest in "personal communication systems"—and even if we ourselves refrain, we find ourselves drawn willy-nilly into the soundscape that others broadcast around us.

Crucially, who we are is how we live our time—or *spend* it, to use the term that registers its intrinsic scarcity. What we believe, or say we believe, is less important. We vote for a way of life with our time. And increasingly, when we are not at work or asleep, we are in the media torrent. (Sometimes at work, we are also there, listening to the radio or checking out sports scores, pin-ups, or headlines on the Internet.) Steadily more inhabitants of the wealthy part of the world have the means, incentives, and opportunities to seek private electronic companionship. The more money we have to spend, the more personal space each household member gets. With personal space comes solitude, but this solitude is instantly crowded with images and soundtracks. To a degree that was unthinkable in the seventeenth century, life experience has become an experience in the presence of media.

VIRTUAL PLENITUDE

This is plenitude, but of a restricted sort. Though we may preserve them on videotape or in digital memory, ordinarily the images that come to us on screens are ephemeral traces. (The same goes for soundtracks.) Like the images that precede and succeed them in time, they belong to a perpetually vanishing present streaking by. As a rule, before they vanish, they offer only the most limited sense impressions. They transmit something of the look of things, but they cannot be smelled or tasted. They aren't palpable. They most commonly hang in two dimensions on a more or less flat translucent screen. This screen delivers light, gleams with availability, claims some portion of our attention, but is also apart from us. The screen is bright, brighter than ordinary reality (which is probably why it's so hard to look away), but often, for technical reasons, the picture may be a bit blurred, streaked with extraneous marks, interference patterns, or other reminders that the images are manufactured and transmitted from elsewhere.

Unless we click an off button or smash the screen, the images stream on, leaving traces in our minds but, despite the interactivity boom, strangely indifferent to us. They collect our attention but do not reciprocate. In the real time of our lives, we choose them and complete them by noticing, hearing, reading, or misreading them; yet they have no need of us. They are with us even if we are not with them. In the case of computer screens, we can alter the images—that is the very point—because they are our creatures. We buy and possess them. On the other hand, they compel a certain attention without reacting to us. They do not comment on our looks, raise no eyebrows at our choice of words or images (unless we have an up-to-date spell-checking program)—and so, to a certain degree, it is they who possess us.

Like flesh-and-blood people, the ones with whom we have "face-time," the virtual personages on-screen have identities and invite our emotions. They include, in the words of one of my students, "people who are sort of familiar and sort of not." At times they are part of the background noise and flow—part of the wallpaper, we say—and at times they loom up as something more. Sometimes we evaluate them as physical beings and moral agents. Often we find them desirable, or enviable, or in some other way they evoke the sentiments, the liking, irritation, or boredom, that flesh-and-blood individuals evoke. Yet an aura of some sort surrounds them. They take up ritual places as heroes, leaders, scapegoats, magical figures, to be admired, envied, loved, or hated; to *matter*. These familiar strangers exist *for us*, damn it. We root for them, yell at them. Fans commonly address letters to actors and confuse them with their characters. An actress on the soap opera *All My Children* once told me that she received fan letters that addressed her by name, complimented her on her performance, only to slide into addressing her character—why did you break up with your boyfriend?

Contact with the never-ending cornucopian flow of these faces, of popular culture itself, a torrent beyond us yet in some way (we think) under our control—this experience is at the core of a way of life. The familiar stranger is by no means unprecedented in history. People have long imagined a world populated with figures who were not physically at hand and yet seemed somehow present. What has changed, of course, is the magnitude of the flow, the range of characters that enter our world, their omnipresence, the sheer number of stories. Inevitably, today's stories are but prologues or sequels to other stories, true and less true stories, stories that are themselves intermissions, stories without end.

Most of these stories reach us through images that reside with us—though they do so in a peculiar sense we should not be too quick to think we understand. We know, most of the time, that they are not "real," although when they grip us we don't want to tear ourselves away. Real are my family, friends, coworkers. Real is the taste of coffee, or the fly buzzing around the kitchen, or the pounding of my heart after a climb uphill. Real, in other senses, is my job, or cooking, or shopping, or organizing my routines to get to work or procure food. Images, on the other hand, depict or re-present realities but are not themselves realities. We usually know the difference. If an image depicts a place we have visited or reminds us of something that once happened to us, or something we could imagine happening, we call it *realistic*. But that is still not "real." Still less is it, in Umberto Eco's term, *hyperreal*, more real than the real, the product of an "absolute fake," like Hearst's San Simeon or a wax museum. Nor is it Jean Baudrillard's *simulacrum*, a copy of something whose original does not exist, like Disneyland's Main Street. Eco is closer to the truth when he refers to "the frantic desire for the almost real" that thrives, above all, in the United States.

Almost real: we expect a certain fidelity from images, whether fictional or "reality-based." If fictional, we expect them to be plausible, in some way *lifelike*, even if they are fantastic. We recognize them as ghosts, shadows of something substantial. They are auxiliary, virtual. No wonder that, among technophiles, the idea of virtual reality—of digitally delivered sensations that we could mistake for the actual experience of "being there"—caught on before the technology was devised, for much of our experience is *already* virtual: the sort of derivative yet riveting almost-reality that television has long delivered to us but that, until recently, has been sealed behind the screen. With virtual reality, we have the illusion of stepping inside the screen, not just attending to but being attended to *by* the images inside.

Of course, the viewer is not (ordinarily) naive. She knows that fictional beings will not step out of the screen to thrill her, as in Woody Allen's *Purple Rose of Cairo*, nor will the actors recognize her in the flesh, as in Neil LaBute's *Nurse Betty;* nor is she likely to mistake the TV image of a corpse for an actual cadaver. The adult viewer is not the infant who, psychologists assure us, cannot tell the difference between image and reality—who thinks the giraffe depicted on the TV screen is "actually" a few inches tall. But child or adult, we do demand something from our images, even if they are only "almost real." We expect them to heighten life, to intensify and focus it by being better than real, more vivid, more stark, more *something*. We want a burst of feeling, a frisson of commiseration, a flash of delight, a moment of recognition—so *that's* what it's like when your boyfriend sleeps with your sister, when you lose a patient in the emergency room, when you're voted off the *Survivor* island. We depend on these images to imagine the great elsewhere: "realistic" presences that point, say, to the real ruins of the World Trade Center, or fictions that gesture toward a real world where attendants wheel patients into operating rooms and police arrest suspects, or "reality-based" shows indicating that some human beings will eat a rat to win a chance at a million dollars.

All of this is so obvious and fundamental to the way we live now that to call attention to its strangeness seems banal or superfluous. Isn't the omnipresence of media simple and straightforward? But strangely, we have no language to catch precisely the unnerving, downright bizarreness of this world of images, characters, stories, jingles, sound effects, announcements, cartoons, and logos that engulfs our lives. Even words like *auxiliary*, *virtual*, and *ghostly* are poor approximations for the peculiar stream of images and sounds that winds through everyday life, so steady as to be taken for granted, so fluid as to permit us to believe that we never quite step into the same torrent twice.

HISTORICAL ORIGINS OF THE TORRENT

How did the unlimited media come to be taken for granted? Raymond Williams posed the question this way:

> Till the eyes tire, millions of us watch the shadows of shadows and find them substance; watch scenes, situations, actions, exchanges, crises. The slice of life, once a project of naturalist drama, is now a voluntary, habitual, internal rhythm; the flow of action and acting, of representation and performance, raised to a new convention, that of a basic need. . . . What is it, we have to ask, in us and in our contemporaries, that draws us repeatedly to these hundreds and thousands of simulated actions?

A good deal about the media torrent's force, its appeal, even its inescapability, remains mysterious. Respect for that mystery is not a bad place to start. We should not be too quick to say that media omnipresence is the product of runaway technology, or the quest for profits, or a drive to "escape"; or that the hunger for sensations is built into human nature or, to the contrary, is strictly a product of "late capitalism." Pat explanations blind us to the enormity of the media flow itself.

To a child growing up immersed in the culture of images, it appears the most natural thing in the world. It appears, in fact, to *be* nature. Expecting images and sounds to appear on command (or even when uncommanded and unwanted) feels as normal as expecting the sun to rise. Because it's so easy to change channels, scan for stations, surf, graze, click, go to another source of images and sounds, you assume that if you don't like what you see or hear, you can find something better (or make your own image or soundscape). No wonder each wave of technosurprises seems somehow unsurprising—the screen hanging above an airplane seat, the car that receives e-mail and plays CDs, the watch with Internet access, the digital movie camera that switches on and off at the command of a voice. Indeed, today's inescapable hype about a brave new interconnected world has a plausible ring because a significant and growing proportion of Americans and others are already wired, or wirelessed, into numberless circuits, networks, loops of connection with images and sounds available on call. We feel about our image and sound machines as Marcel Proust once did about the telephone, "a supernatural instrument before whose miracles we used to stand amazed, and which we now employ without giving it a thought, to summon our tailor or to order an ice cream." We feel—we have no doubt—that we have the right to be addressed by our media, the right to enjoy them, the right to admit faces of our choice into our living rooms and to enter into worlds without number, to flow with them. We may not have the right to possess the beautiful faces and bodies we see there, the fortunes, celebrity, or power dangled before us, clamoring for our attention, but we have the right to want them. If we are let down, we have the right, almost the duty, to click and dip elsewhere at will.

It's easy to see how individuals grow up expecting their lives to be accompanied by image plenitude, flow, and choice. But for society as a whole, how did this blessing come to pass? Media saturation is not a gift of the gods nor of the unprovoked genius (or wickedness, or frivolity) of technological wizards. The Edisons, Marconis, Sarnoffs, De Forests, and Gateses devised and organized the media that Marshall McLuhan has called "extensions of man," but humanity came first with its hungers and competencies. Nor are our desires the unwelcome products of vast corporations, determined to stuff human time with their commodities: with products that people would be so eager to purchase, on which they would become so dependent, that they would grant their time in exchange for money to bring these commodities home. It *is* that, but it is not only that. We know that Eminem's latest CD and *The Sopranos* are human creations, but it's easy to lose sight of the fact that the media flow itself is no less human in its origins, the product of millions of people who, having been molded by a mechanical way of life, have devised a seemingly endless number of ways to relieve the strains of that way of life by mechanical means.

Unlimited media result from a fusion of economic expansion and individual desire, prepared for over centuries, and nowhere more fully realized than in the United States. The pleasures of acquisition in seventeenth-century Delft led to the pleasures of consumption in twenty-first-century New York. In both, individuals matter, and therefore so do depictions of individuals. In both, individuals clothe themselves with adornments and disguises. In both, individuals claim rights—the big difference being that once exclusive rights have been expanded, including the right to think and feel as you like, and over time, the right to love, marry, move, work, sell, buy, vote, and otherwise act as you please. One thing that ever-growing numbers have the right to buy today is access to images at all hours and in extraordinary assortments, offering, at low cost except in time, a provisional combination of pleasure and some sense of mastery. People who were already interested in images and sounds won the time to consume them. An industrial apparatus arose to produce them cheaply and in profusion. The desire for pleasing windows on the world—and windows through which to escape the world—is nothing new, but only in modern society has it become possible for majorities to cultivate and live that desire, unwilling to accept anything less. Now, the desire for play, the desire for routine, the desire for diversion, the desire for orientation, the desire for representation, the desire to feel, the desire to flee from feeling—all these human desires in their complexity and contradiction are indulged in the vast circus maximus, our cultural jamboree of jamborees.

Although the media stream is modern, it draws on ancient springs. To feel accompanied by others not physically present is hardly unprecedented. We have a profound capacity to harbor images of actual or imaginary others who are not materially at hand—to remember or speculate about what they looked like, wonder what they are doing, imagine what they might think, anticipate what they might do, take part in unspoken dialogues with them. The fashioning of replicas extends across at least thirty thousand years of human history. Throughout this time people have lived, through images and simulations, "with" gods, saints, demons, kings and queens, heroes of fleet foot and sword, absent relations, clan members, friends, and enemies. The painting of a reindeer on the wall of a cave in the south of France, or the portrait of a dead ancestor in Egypt, or a cross on the wall, or the replica of a saint in the stained glass of a chapel, each opens a portal to an imagined world, beckoning us to cross a gap between the image *here* and what is, or was, or might be *there*.

None of that is new, nor is the manufacture and wide diffusion of popular culture. Poetry and song migrated across medieval Europe hand to hand, mouth to ear to mouth. Broadsheets circulated. From the second half of the fifteenth century on, Gutenberg's movable type made possible mass-printed Bibles and a flood of instructional as well as scurrilous literature. Even where literacy was rare, books were regularly read aloud. (In a scene at an inn from Cervantes's *Don Quixote*, published in 1605, farmworkers listen attentively to a reading of books found in a trunk.) In eighteenth-century England, the uplift and piety of John Bunyan's *Pilgrim's Progress*, which went through 160 editions by 1792, was supplemented by the upstart novel, that thrilling tale of individual action, which the high-minded of the time regarded as shockingly lowbrow. From then on, reading spread, especially at home alone and silently—that is, in secret. So did the imagination of what it might be like to be, or act like, somebody else: Robinson Crusoe, Moll Flanders, Tom Jones. What sociologist David Riesman called "the stream of print" in the seventeenth, eighteenth, and nineteenth centuries opened up space for sympathy, helping to undermine theocracy and slavery. Whatever the censorious efforts of pastors and parents, Riesman wrote, "Almost always there is an underground of a more picaresque sort in which the growing boy, if not his sister, can take some refuge."

But even in Europe's most democratic outpost, America, the influx of reading matter into the household was retarded by the cost of books and the limits of literacy. The immense library of Thomas Jefferson was neither shared nor matched by his slaves or nearby tenant farmers. Still, sitting by his fire in the Kentucky wilderness, in the latter years of the eighteenth century, Daniel Boone read *Gulliver's Travels*—scarcely the popular image of the rough-tough wilderness man. The illiterate Rocky Mountain scout Jim Bridger could recite long passages from Shakespeare, which he learned by hiring someone to read the plays to him. "There is hardly a pioneer's hut that does not contain a few odd volumes of Shakespeare," Alexis de Tocqueville found on his trip through the United States in 1831–32. There were already extraordinary bursts of best-sellerdom: in a population far less literate than today's, Harriet Beecher Stowe's *Uncle Tom's Cabin* sold 300,000 copies within a year of its 1852 publication, one copy apiece for roughly 1.3 percent of the population, the equivalent of 3.6 million copies today—and then eventually ten times as many by the outbreak of the Civil War. At least in the United States, growing numbers of ordinary people had access to the "refuge" of print—and these were seldom books defending the ruling elites. As Riesman pointed out, the Bible was "the great reading-hour storehouse," and it was "not one book but many, with an inexhaustible variety of messages." Slaves reading Exodus rehearsed their own freedom. Print has long sheltered those with the urge to run away, for as contemporary housewives continue to discover even while reading romance novels, "to be alone with a book is to be alone in a new way."

In the course of the nineteenth century, long before television, stories and images entered the typical household in ever-accelerating numbers. In 1865, according to literary historian Richard Ohmann, there was probably one copy of a monthly magazine for every ten Americans; in 1905, three copies for every four Americans—an increase of more than sevenfold. As for the rest of popular culture—the carnival of theater, opera, public lectures, and other live performances—its major constraint was not literacy but cost. The declining price of commercial entertainment was crucial. Sociologist Richard Butsch has calculated that in the United States of the late 1860s, about 36 million theater tickets were sold annually (about one ticket per capita, but in a population 75 percent of which was rural, and where, as Butsch writes, "the five largest markets, New York City, Boston, Philadelphia, Chicago, and San Francisco, accounted for more than half the total national box office receipts"). Compare this with the 4 billion tickets sold per year at the peak of moviegoing in the late 1940s (about twenty-seven tickets per person, roughly one purchase every two weeks). Compare that, in turn, with the nightly TV audience at any given moment of 102.5 million people age two and up, or almost 40 percent of the U.S. population, in the year 2001.

Cost-cutting goes a long way to explain this transformation. According to Butsch's computations, the costs of the *cheapest* tickets for the most popular types of performance at various times were as follows (with an update):

	Cost for laborer *as proportion of daily wage*
18th century (theater)	More than a full day's wage
Early 19th century (theater)	1/3
1840s–50s (minstrel show)	A little less than 1/3 (25¢)
1870 (minstrel, variety shows)	1/6 (still 25¢)
1880s (melodrama, vaudeville)	1/13 (10¢)
1910 (nickelodeon)	1/40 (5¢)
1920 (movie theater)	less than 1/40 (10¢)
1960s (television)	1/360 (amortizing cost of $200 black-and-white set)
1998 (cable television)	1/100 (amortizing cost of $300 color set plus basic cable)

In other words, the cost of a day of television in the 1960s was 11 percent of the cost of a nickelodeon visit fifty years earlier, and a small fraction of 1 percent of the cost of a visit to a colonial theater. Since the 1960s, the cost of a television set alone declined further in relation to (stagnant) wages, but cable bumped up the cost of the whole package.

Obviously, more popular culture can circulate partly because costs have come down precipitously. But declining cost turns out to be a more complex affair than the crisp formula "cost declines, therefore usage increases" suggests. Declining cost, growing demand, and improved technology looped into one another. Costs came down in part because technology improved, but technology improved, in part, because demand grew, or could be anticipated to grow, something producers factored in when investing in new technologies and expanding their production lines. Demand is partly a function of price, but price is a function of desire as well as of technological possibilities and the amount of time available to potential consumers. Time unencumbered by work swelled. So did money to fill time with convenient amusements.

As a consequence of the cost-demand-technology loop, popular culture is no longer a matter of the Bible and Shakespeare at home, a play once a year, or a movie every two weeks, supplemented by a magazine and a newspaper. The scale of availability has multiplied a hundredfold. An experience once reserved for exceptional occasions has become an everyday matter as continuous as—or more continuous than—one likes. But more time and lower cost are not sufficient to explain why people today spend roughly half their waking hours around and among these manufactured presences. A hunger has become part of us. Just as we gravitate toward food even when we're full or mealtimes are still far off, we're drawn toward the screen or the speaker not only when it is right over there in the living room and we have time on our hands but when we are with children, mates, coworkers, friends, lovers, and strangers, or the screen is in another room. The culture of unlimited media takes up a place in our imagination. Its language and gestures become ours, even when smuggled into our own conversation within quotation marks ("Hel*lo*?" "Dyn-o-mite!" "Just do it!"). A bizarre event reminds us of the uncanny 1950s series *The Twilight Zone*, whereupon the *dee*-dee-*dee*-dah theme will pop into the mind. We choose among our cultural furnishings but unless ensconced in a cave deep in some remote canyon, we do not choose whether to choose any more than a young man growing up in a hunter-gatherer culture chooses to hunt, or a woman to gather. These are the ways of our tribe.

DISTRACTIONS, DRUGS, AND FETISHES

The urge to grasp the totality of the media has been with us even longer than most modern media. During the centuries when popular culture had not yet grown torrential, many critics already nonetheless argued that images and performances diverted people from more constructive pursuits. Many pointed accusing fingers at the sirens of "distraction," the better to convince people to plug their ears. Some thought popular culture a distraction from a piety that ought to have been directed toward God or Church. Some saw popular culture as a pacifying circus that offered the masses some psychic compensation for their sufferings without detracting from the authorities' power. Even defenders of today's media barrage generally agree that it amounts to distraction from the burdens of industrialized life—though, unlike the critics, they celebrate it precisely for that reason, as a valuable, even a necessary remedy. Distraction cannot by itself account for the unlimited flow of today's media. But the concept deserves some exploration.

Distraction is one of those terms—like *freedom, responsibility,* and *alienation*—that requires an object to make sense. The question is, distraction from what? Mortality? God? Pain? Subjugation? Changing the world? More than one, or all, of the above? (The German Marxist critic Siegfried Kracauer, for instance, suggested in 1930: "The flight of images is the flight from revolution and death.") Your answer to the question *Distraction from what?* reveals what you value.

Distraction from mortality and distraction from God are the historical starting points for this line of thought. The Old Testament God condemned "graven images." St. Paul and St. Augustine added their own supplementary condemnations. But Blaise Pascal, the French mathematician and Augustinian devotee, was the most pungent distraction critic of early modern times. In his *Pensées* of 1657–58, Pascal declared that gambling, hunting, and womanizing were but feeble—and ultimately futile—efforts to divert ourselves from the inescapable fact of human mortality. "The only thing which consoles us for our miseries is diversion, and yet this is the greatest of our miseries." For diversion was habit-forming. Seeking excitement, we might foolishly imagine that "the possession of the objects of [our] quest would make [us] really happy," and thereby miss the only possible path to salvation—Christian devotion.

The religious strand of suspicion continues to this day. Pentacostalists disapprove of dancing, and other fundamentalists deplore televised sex. Partisans of various creeds despise "degenerate art." But over the last century and a half, secular critique and analysis have come to the fore. During the heyday of social theory, the period between 1848 and 1918 when industry, cities, bureaucracies, commerce, nationalism, and empire were booming, the media flow was, by today's standards, only a rivulet. Nonetheless, some of the great social thinkers of Europe and the United States explored and tried to explain the nature of modern diversion. The founders of sociology elaborated concepts that help us understand the origins of our way of life and of the vast machinery society has devised to feed our equally vast appetite for wish fulfillment. Karl Marx called this way of life capitalism; Max Weber, rationalization; Georg Simmel, the least known but for our purposes the most helpful, intellectualism.

Marx died in 1883, four years before the first gramophone patent and twelve years before the first motion picture. Never having heard recorded music or gone to the movies, he still understood that capitalism required popular distraction. The great upender of the nineteenth century, Marx in 1843 turned Pascal on his head. For this militant atheist, religion was not what diversion diverted *from*; it was diversion itself. As the Bolivian peasant chewed coca leaves to overcome the exhaustion of a wretched life, so did the worker in a capitalist society turn to religion as "the sigh of the oppressed creature, the sentiment of a heartless world, the soul of soulless conditions. It is the *opium* of the people . . . the *illusory* happiness of men." Religion was mass distraction, the result of imagining man's own powers projected beyond himself into God. But according to Marx, the objects that human beings produced for the market also acquired a magical— indeed, an illusory and distracting—aspect. They became, in a sense, religious artifacts.

By 1867, in *Capital*, Marx had come to identify a new form of popular irrationality that he called "the fetishism of commodities." Commodities, he wrote, were "transcendent," "mystical," "mysterious," and "fantastic" in that they acquired a value not inherent in their physical nature. Through the mysteries of the market, people assigned value to goods that they could live without. But Marx did not anticipate that capitalism, thanks to its ongoing productive success, would serve up such an abundance of transcendent mysteries with which people could compensate themselves for their sacrifices. Marx was transfixed by production, not consumption. For him, workers were wage slaves barely able to dream of becoming distracted consumers. They were condemned to growing impoverishment, not declining hours of work and increasing amounts of disposable income. He did not anticipate that the magic loaded into commodities at the production end might rub off on people at the consumption end—so much so as to create a new, enveloping way of life brimming with satisfactions.

Obsessed by the exploitative nature of production, Marx tended to think of consumption strictly as an auxiliary process that accomplished two purposes: it circulated goods and replenished the laborer's powers. It was not a fundamental, useful human act. He missed the way in which commodities didn't just "confront" people with "alien" powers in an externalized face-off but entered into people, "spoke" to them, linked them to one another, cultivated their satisfactions, and in certain ways satisfied them. As an image or sound enters the mind, one may feel oneself, at least for a moment, going to meet it, welcoming it, even melting into it—overcoming confrontation with gratification. For Marx, such satisfaction was only a distraction from the "real conditions of life." But what are those "real conditions"?

Marx was right that markets work mysteriously, that there is magic in the way a compact disc, say, comes to be "worth" two hours of a janitor's labor or the same as a six-pack of premium beer. An act of culture produces this equation. But he underestimated the amount of magic in the world. What is going on when I walk into a music store and hold a CD in my hand? I approach not only a shiny metallic object in a plastic case whose manufacturing costs are a few cents but an aura of pleasure and a trail of resonance derived perhaps from the reputation of the band whose music it contains or from my experience of having heard a song at a party, on the radio, or downloaded onto my computer. The object of advertising is to intensify this resonance and link it with my own good feelings past and prospective. My armchair, in this sense, "produces" not only the sensation against my back and backside but a sense of comfort I may associate with my childhood. Nike sneakers produce not only a certain spongy sensation against my soles but (at least until I get into the gym) my dream of soaring like Michael Jordan.

When my friends and I shoot baskets, we aren't just compensating ourselves for what the alienation of labor has cost us; we are also forming a social relation for the purpose of play. We invest in the game some of our human powers. Why isn't our game just as real as our labor? For that matter, why isn't watching a game on TV as real and central as the labors we perform on the job?

Marx, imprisoned in the utilitarian attitude he condemned, was in this respect not radical enough. He didn't take seriously the fact that we were all children once, and all children play. They simulate and observe others simulating. Children are fascinated by mirrors and grow up impressed by games of cognition and recognition, cartoonish representations, performances in masks and disguises. Developmental psychologists point out that play has utility, increasing competencies, offering lessons in how to win and lose—but play is also gratuitous. People play "for fun," because it pleases them. Adults surrender much, but never all, of their playfulness. They do not simply put away childish things. Things promise pleasure—and not only things bought and kept for oneself. Gifts, too, are expressions of feeling, of affection, or love, or duty. Things are more than things; they are containers for love and self-love.

CALCULATION AND FEELING

In conventional usage, the media deliver an information flow. The term *information* goes with thought, cognition, knowledge. It sounds as hard (and objective and masculine) as *emotion* sounds soft (and subjective and feminine). Many commentators today think of the mind as an "information processor"; business likes to talk about IT, information technology. But what if we tease apart the notion of information? We see into our current situation more deeply if we consider information as something that happens within a human set-ting, something that people approach, seek, develop, employ, avoid, circulate, and resist. We do live in an "information society," but no less, if less famously, it is *a society of feeling and sensation*, toward the furtherance of which information is sometimes useful.

Marx starts with people required to live by their labor; the key modern social institution is the factory. In the standard sequence of sociological founding fathers, Marx's great successor is Max Weber (1864–1920), for whom people are required to live in power rela-tions, and moderns, in particular, are under severe pressure to "rationalize" their social relations—to give reasons for their conduct, to think instrumentally, to calculate means toward ends. They, we, must surrender to abstract "rational-legal" rules installed by unfor-giving bureaucracies. We may protest by seeking leaders tinged with grace, gifted with what Weber called "charisma," but charisma too becomes routinized in the end, and we are doomed to enclosure in the "iron cage" of modern rationality. It's easy enough to imagine why Weber's disenchanted moderns would turn to entertainment for relief, a sort of reenchantment, even though Weber did not take up the subject in particular.

For a deeper understanding of the wellsprings of the all-engulfing spectacle, we must turn to Weber's German-Jewish contemporary Georg Simmel (1858–1918), the first great modern analyst of what we take today as everyday experience. Simmel thought the decisive force in people's lives is "the power and the rhythm of emotions." Desire precedes rationality, chronologically in the life of the individual but also logically, in the evolution of human conduct and institutions. The human condition begins with dependencies that are emotional (the need for love and support) as well as physical (the need for nourishment and warmth). "For man, who is always striving, never satisfied, always becoming, love is the true human condition." From the moment of birth, to live is to be and feel connected. Our cognitive and intellectual faculties rest upon foundations of feeling. The emotional linkages of childhood persist and develop in ways that make all social relations finally emotional relations, compounded of desires, satisfactions, frustrations, attachments, and antagonisms.

For Simmel, the framework in which man strives for love and connection is not so much, as with Marx, capitalist production but the money economy. "Man is a 'purposive' animal," Simmel writes. He develops goals and exercises his will to attain them through making and using tools, and increasingly through money, a means that develops psychologically into an end. People treat other people, as well as things, in a utilitarian fashion, and money is "the most extreme example of a means becoming an end." People now organize their lives to make money. They think calculatingly and categorically. They abstract calculation from sentiment. They develop the mental faculties to "size up" people, things, and situations reliably and quickly. Thus (and perhaps Simmel exaggerates the point) "money is responsible for impersonal relations between people."

The metropolis, Simmel maintains, is the most concentrated locale of the money economy, and it is here, above all, that mental life becomes "essentially intellectualistic." In the epochal movement of humanity from the village to the city, emotions were sidelined. The residents of populous cities like Berlin and Strasbourg, where Simmel lived, were required to tame their passions in favor of "calculating exactness" as a style of life. What will your trade be? For whom will you work and whom will you hire? What will you buy, where will you sell, and at what prices? Of whom will you make use? All-consuming, incessant calculation, in turn, required defenses against the assault and battery of a life in which everyone was judged according to whether he or she appeared usable, and people routinely, casually treated both persons and things with formality and "an unrelenting hardness."

Moreover, money "reduces the highest as well as the lowest values equally" to a single standard, putting them "on the same level." Money, therefore, is a school for cynicism. (In our own time, the standard of monetary worth gives us expressions like "She's a dime a dozen," "He's a loser," "You get what you pay for," and "I feel like a million bucks.") Moreover, besieged by the variety of strangers and things, people frantically categorize, cultivating an "intellectualistic quality . . . a protection of the inner life against the domination of the metropolis." The modern city dweller must acquire "a relentless matter-of-factness," a "blasé outlook," a kind of "reserve with its overtone of concealed aversion." The German and French languages share a word to express this sort of cultivated indifference: in German, egal, in French, égal. They mean "equal," but with a shrug or a somewhat depressed implication not found in English: "It doesn't matter"; "I don't care"; "It's all the same to me" (in French, expressed in the all-purpose phrase "ça m'est égal").

For Simmel, "cynicism and a blasé attitude" are the direct results of "the reduction of the concrete values of life to the mediating value of money." Within the metropolis, there are special "nurseries of cynicism . . . places with huge turnovers," like stock exchanges, where money constantly changes hands. "The more money becomes the sole center of interest," Simmel writes, "the more one discovers that honor and conviction, talent and virtue, beauty and salvation of the soul, are exchanged against money, and so the more a mocking and frivolous attitude will develop in relation to these higher values that are for sale for the same kind of value as groceries, and that also command a 'market price.' " Cynicism is the subjective expression of a marketplace for values.

Cynicism can be enlivening, offering a momentary lift, a superior knowingness, but its dark side emerges in dismissals like "show me something I haven't seen," "been there, done that," and "*so* over." At an extreme, as Simmel writes, the blasé person "has completely lost the feeling for value differences. He experiences all things as being of an equally dull and grey hue, as not worth getting excited about." Simmel is writing in 1900, before the media torrent, but he anticipates our world with his startling observation that the growth of the blasé attitude produces a paradoxical result—a culture of sensation. The cynic is content with his inner state, but the blasé person is not. Hence the latter's craving "for excitement, for extreme impressions, for the greatest speed in its change." Satisfying that craving may bring relief, but only temporarily. The more excitements, the worse. "The modern preference for 'stimulation' as such in impressions, relations and information" follows, in other words, Simmel maintains, from "the increasingly blasé attitude through which natural excitement increasingly disappears. This search for stimuli originates in the money economy with the fading of all specific values into a mere mediating value. We have here one of those interesting cases in which the disease determines its own form of the cure."

So emerges the modern individual, a role player who is also a part-time adventurer and stimulus seeker, trying frenetically to find himself by abandoning himself. This paradoxical individual is primed for unlimited media.

The money economy is not the only source of impersonal social relations. Our ordinary encounters with large numbers of unfamiliar people also drive us to calculate each other's usefulness. The members of traditional or primitive economies were dependent on small numbers of people. Modern man, Simmel argues, has many more needs. "Not only is the extent of our needs considerably wider," he writes, "but even the elementary necessities that we have in common with all other human beings (food, clothing and shelter) can be satisfied only with the help of a much more complex organization and many more hands. Not only does specialization of our activities itself require an infinitely extended range of other producers with whom we exchange products," but many of our actions require increasing amounts "of preparatory work, additional help and semi-finished products." Once upon a time, we knew the people we met at the market by name and face. "In contrast, consider how many 'delivery men' alone we are dependent upon in a money economy!" As they are functionally indistinguishable, so are they interchangeable. "We grow indifferent to them in their particularity."

Simmel is writing at the dawn of the twentieth century. Already, the calculating individual has split into parts corresponding to distinct roles (worker, parent, shopper), and he experiences most other people in equally stylized roles (coworker, shopkeeper, boss). Under the sway of calculating individualism, people must mask themselves in their roles—must appear *as* their roles—in order to be recognized by others. Yet the role never seeps into all of a person's interior crevices. The mask never melts utterly into the face. Instead, we live elaborate inner lives—which, ironically, we crave all the more intensely because of the constraints under which we operate in our outer lives. We *play* roles but *are not* the roles. Some part of us is always backstage.

For Simmel, the real person, hovering behind the strutting and fretting of everyday metropolitan life, is the one who feels. Feeling is the way a person gets personal. This obvious principle, he believes, has been disguised by "rationalistic platitudes that are entirely unpsychological." Foremost among these historic misunderstandings is that of Descartes, who, starting his chain of reasoning with reasons, proceeds, reason by reason, to the famous conclusion that he exists because he thinks.

Here, then, is the grand paradox that Simmel's thinking leads to:

a society of calculation is inhabited by people who need to feel to distract themselves from precisely the rational discipline on which their practical lives rely. The calculation and reserve demanded by the money economy stimulate, by way of compensation, emotional needs and a craving for excitement and sensation. Thus does the upsurge of marketplace thinking in the eighteenth century call up its opposite, romanticism, which urges us to heed the inner voice of feeling. Real life takes place in *deep* feeling, *authentic* feeling, feeling that must be protected from social impositions, feeling that was born free and longs to go native. The idea spreads that the individual *is*, above all, his or her feelings.

Feeling too vigorously expressed, however, presents a management problem. Feeling too much, or expressing it too freely, would interfere with work and duty. (You do not want to give in to grief or, having fallen in love, go about walking on air while running a lathe or balancing the books.) Romanticism must be domesticated, made to fit into the niches of life. Emotions must be contained, reserved for convenient times when they may be expressed without risk to workaday life. Emotions must refresh, not drain or disrupt. They must be disposable and, if not free, at least low-cost. We are on our way here into the society of nonstop popular culture that induces limited-liability feelings on demand—feelings that do not bind and sensations that feel like, and pass for, feelings. A society consecrated to self-interest ends up placing a premium on finding life *interesting*.

What I am arguing, following Simmel, is not that human beings suddenly began to feel, but that, in recent centuries, they came to experience, and crave, particular kinds of feelings—disposable ones. It seems that, in much of the West in the seventeenth century and accelerating thereafter, feelings became associated ever more closely with the sense of an internal, subjective life set apart from the external world. By the end of the eighteenth century, the English language was teeming with new terms to describe feelings felt to be happening *in here*, within the person. During the seventeenth and eighteenth centuries, as philologist Owen Barfield pointed out, terms like *apathy*, *chagrin*, *diffidence*, *ennui*, and *homesickness* emerged, along with the phrase *the feelings*, while other terms for mental states, such as *agitation*, *constraint*, *disappointment*, *embarrassment*, and *excitement*, were relocated from the outer to the inner world. To these nouns for states of feeling were added adjectives that describe external phenomena "purely by the *effects* which they produce on human beings." Barfield's examples include *affecting, amusing, boring, charming, diverting, entertaining, enthralling, entrancing, exciting, fascinating, interesting*, and *pathetic* in its modern sense. As Barfield put it: "When a Roman spoke of events as *auspicious* or *sinister*, or when some natural object was said in the Middle Ages to be *baleful*, or *benign*, or *malign* . . . the activity was felt to emanate from the object itself. When we speak of an object or an event as *amusing*, on the contrary, we know that the process indicated by the word *amuse* takes place within ourselves."

So modernity, the age of calculation, produced a culture devoted to sentiment. Increasingly, the self-fashioning man or woman needed instructions in what to feel and how to express it. Philosophers wrote of "moral sentiments," sympathy foremost among them. Novels, indulging the taste for private feeling, were schools for sentiment. So were popular eighteenth-century British manuals advocating the arts of impression management. Feeling was plentiful but had to be disguised in public, lest (for example) laughing aloud damage one's ability to produce calculated impressions, or excessive enthusiasm jeopardize a woman's ability to protect herself. Middle-class strivers wished to cultivate self-control to improve their social standing and marriageability. Lord Chesterfield's volume of letters to his son on the arts of self-management, published posthumously in 1775, was a best-seller not only in England but in America. Novels conveyed not only advice about what to feel but the direct experience of feelings themselves: sympathy, surprise, recognition, satisfaction, pity, dread, and suspense; along with aesthetic pleasures in phrasing, wit, poignancy, and so on. One read, in other words, in order to feel.

By the nineteenth century, some of the main contours of present-day popular culture were evident. Entertainments like the novel filtered down from the middle class to the popular majority. It was in the United States, where the money economy and democracy developed together, that Simmel's observations about calculation and feeling prove most apropos. Usable, everyday distraction required surges of feeling and high-intensity stimuli that would be generally accessible but at the same time transitory. By the early 1830s, when Alexis de Tocqueville visited the United States—long before Times Square or Hollywood, before vaudeville or Al Jolson, Michael Jackson or Arnold Schwarzenegger, *USA Today* or the Internet—American culture was already sensational, emotional, melodramatic, and informal. Long before the remote control device, call waiting, cruise control, the car radio scan option, or the Apple mouse, before electricity, let alone the humble on-off switch, the United States was consecrated to comfort and convenience. Tocqueville accordingly wrote: "Democratic nations cultivate the arts that serve to render life easy in preference to those whose object is to adorn it." Artists in aristocratic societies perfected their craft while following established traditions, but in democracies, "What is generally sought in the productions of mind is easy pleasure and information without labor." What results, he added, are "many imperfect commodities" that "substitute the representation of motion and sensation for that of sentiment and thought.... Style will frequently be fantastic, incorrect, overburdened, and loose, almost always vehement and bold. Authors will aim at rapidity of execution more than at perfection of detail.... There will be more wit than erudition, more imagination than profundity.... The object of authors will be to astonish rather than to please, and to stir the passions more than to charm the taste."

Amusements encourage people to feel in a heightened way, to revel in familiar feelings, but also to experiment with unaccustomed ones in order to feel like somebody else without risk. The efficient production of sentiment—this has long been the essence of democratic artistry. Popular artists have the knack. Lesser ones test the waters and try to catch the wave of the moment. All of them do market research, listening for laughs and cries, looking into their audience as if into a mirror while working out their next steps. Groucho Marx wrote of his famous scoot: "I was just kidding around one day and started to walk funny. The audience liked it, so I kept it in. I would try a line and leave it in too if it got a laugh. If it didn't, I'd take it out and put in another. Pretty soon I had a character." Later, fearful that making movies insulated in a Hollywood studio had cost them their knack, the Marx brothers took a theatrical version of *A Day at the Races* out on the road. According to their publicist, Groucho's classic line "That's the most nauseating proposition I ever had" came after he had tried out *obnoxious, revolting, disgusting, offensive, repulsive, disagreeable,* and *distasteful.* "The last two of these words never got more than titters," according to the publicist. "The others elicited various degrees of ha-has. But *nauseating* drew roars. I asked Groucho why that was so. 'I don't know. I really don't care. I only know the audiences told us it was funny.' "

Tocqueville's traditional artist would have been able to say exactly why he did what he did—it was what his masters did. He belonged to a guild. His inspiration blew in from the past, not from the crowd before him. Tocqueville's democratic artist, by contrast, transmuted the popular hunger for feeling into a living manual for artwork. Cultural industries would mass-produce the results, and from a multitude of such products generate a popular culture that, given money enough and time, would come to suffuse everyday life. Thus is there a continuous upsurge from the ever-larger printings of ever more novels in the eighteenth century, to the penny press, circuses, minstrel and Wild West shows in the nineteenth, through to the Viacoms, Disneys, NBCs, and SONYs of today.

THE RISE OF THE PANOPLY

The consumption of images and sounds was an extension of the burgeoning consumption of goods. In modern society, according to Georg Simmel, a sensitive person (one senses he is describing himself) "will be overpowered and feel disorientated" by the immense spectacle of commodities. But indeed "precisely this wealth and colorfulness of over-hastened impressions is appropriate to overexcited and exhausted nerves' need for stimulation. It seems as if the modern person wishes to compensate for the one-sidedness and uniformity of what he produces within the division of labor by the increasing crowding together of heterogeneous impressions, by the increasingly hasty and colourful change in emotions."

In other words, notes Simmel's contemporary interpreter, sociologist David Frisby, "the tedium of the production process is compensated for by the artificial stimulation and amusement of consumption." One must add, since Simmel was preoccupied with the lives of men, that women at home were far less likely to be subjected to "the tedium of . . . production," but they had their own tedium to contend with.

Although present for the development of the motion picture, Simmel did not write much about images as such, except in the form of fashion, which he brilliantly understood as a declaration of both individuality and class distinction, of freedom and membership at one and the same time. Writing in 1904, he described fashion as a means "to combine . . . the tendency toward social equalization [i.e., *I look like selected others*] with the desire for individual differentiation and change [i.e., *I present to the world my unique self*]." A century ago, Simmel already grasped that fashion seized popular consciousness partly because "major, permanent, unquestioned convictions increasingly lose their force. In this way, the fleeting and changeable elements of life gain that much more free space. The break with the past . . . increasingly concentrates consciousness upon the present. This emphasis upon the present is clearly, at the same time, an emphasis upon change."

University trendhoppers have let themselves be convinced by French philosopher-historian Michel Foucault, with his brilliantly paranoid imagination, that the defining institution of the European nineteenth century was the Panopticon, a never-built prison designed by Jeremy Bentham in order to impose total surveillance on every waking and sleeping moment of a prisoner's life. But Simmel was more perceptive. The heart of modernity was not the Panopticon but the panoply of appearances that emerged in everyday life. He might have deployed this concept to look at the spectacle of images that already filled public spaces in the late nineteenth and early twentieth centuries: the posters and billboards conspicuously adorning the walls and vacant lots of great cities, the imagistic advertisements, the shop windows with their mannequins, the fabulous electrified signs and department store displays, the multiple sources of light and shades of color, the halftones and lithographs swarming through newspapers and magazines, all meant to be quickly superseded by new, often gaudier, and more elaborate versions. Not to mention the street noises of horses, wagons, cars, children playing, musicians, and hawkers all crowding into earshot with announcements of their existence, purpose, and worth.

This sensory uproar was by no means new. A century earlier, in 1805–6, William Wordsworth heard London's "thickening hubbub" and was struck, even shocked, by the sight and sound of "pleasure whirl[ing] about incessantly," by street shows and the city's display of images, which, while composed without "subtlest craft," helped overcome human "weakness":

> Here files of ballads dangle from dead walls;
> Advertisements, of giant-size, from high
> Press forward, in all colours. . . .

Wordsworth was perhaps the first modern poet to react viscerally to the posting of sign upon sign, the clamoring profusion of

> those sights that ape
> The absolute presence of reality. . . .
> . . . imitations, fondly made in plain
> Confession of man's weakness and his loves.

By Simmel's time, the clamoring confusion of posters had become a commonplace. The street shows were in decline, but the city at night had become a spectacle unto itself, for the streets were now electrified with the lamps and signs, the bright displays that promised what Theodore Dreiser called "artificial fires of merriment, the rush of profit-seeking trade, and pleasure-selling amusements," all inspiring "the soul of the toiler" to declare, " 'I shall soon be free. . . . The theatre, the halls, the parties, the ways of rest and the paths of song— these are mine in the night.' "

This vivid commotion of illuminations, images, and sounds was, in today's e-business jargon, a "push technology." The images entered into your perceptual field whether you wanted them around or not—powered, in a sense, by your own legs. Traditional signs offered useful information (repair your shoes here, buy your pork there), but the gaudier, more colossal electric displays heightened the sensational impact without adding information. To come into contact with them, you did not have to be a flâneur, Charles Baudelaire's "passionate spectator," the strolling man-about-town freed from the burdens of routine, no slave to clocks, blessed with all the time in the world to devote to the spectacle of the city. Working women and men too welcomed their strolls through the alluring streets, coming upon transitory and fragmentary surprises. The cascading images incessantly invited people to feel sensations that might not be safe or convenient in the face of flesh-and-blood human beings, who might require reciprocal relationships. Unlike palpable human beings, images offered stimuli without making demands. Strangely impersonal, displayed indifferently for everyone who might cross their path, they required nothing much—a momentary notice, a whiff of mood, a passing fancy. They stimulated sensation but required no commitment. Encountering the profusion of signs, each clamoring for attention amid the clutter of other signs, big-city dwellers learned to take for granted the gap between the present image (the cigarette with its smoke ring) and the absent, though intimated, reality (the pleasure of filled lungs).

Writers and artists were sometimes impressed, sometimes appalled by the new concentrations of dazzle, like New York's Times Square and the center of Paris, where neon lights were first put to large-scale use. The giddy illuminations of night life sometimes jarred intellectuals, who were prone to experience the panoramic spectacle, at least at times, as a loud, attention-seizing alternative to an idealized contemplative stillness. Critics of capitalist society saw the spectacle of neon, billboards, and night-lit monuments as tricky "compensations" for the burdens of exploitation—as Siegfried Kracauer put it with romantic overkill, "façades of light . . . to banish the dread of the night. . . . a flashing protest against the darkness of our existence, a protest of the thirst for life." Such critiques did not find much resonance in a bedazzled populace. The city's hearts of brightness were staggering crowd-pleasers.

The entrepreneurs who erected these thrilling displays certainly hoped to enchant those multitudes with delirious distractions. When the lights and marquees were lit, one editorial booster wrote in 1904, Broadway was "a continuous vaudeville that is worth many times the 'price of admission'—especially as no admission price is asked." O. J. Gude—an early "broker of commercial light" who first called Broadway "the Great White Way," invented the permanent signboard, and installed the first giant electric signs in Times Square—referred to his productions in 1912 as a "phantasmagoria of . . . lights and electric signs." In the same year, an advertising journal that took its name, *Signs of the Times*, with a certain ironic amusement, from millennial zealots, declared: "Electrical advertising is a *picture* medium. More-over, it is a *color* medium; still, again, electrical advertising is a medium of motion, of action, *of life, of light*, of compulsory attraction."

It was indeed in hopes of "compulsory attraction" that entrepreneurs of the public spectacle in New York City erected such imposing displays as a forty-five-foot-long electric Heinz pickle at Madison Square in 1900 and an illuminated Roman chariot race seventy-two feet high and nine hundred feet wide on top of a Broadway hotel in 1910. But the hope that any installation would become a "compulsory attraction" was routinely disappointed. Amid a clutter of signs, each beckoning in its own electric way, a particular sign might stimulate a shiver of enchantment, a tickle of pleasure, or a recoil of annoyance or bewilderment—a little burst of feeling—followed by a fleeting afterglow before fading, leaving, if the advertiser was lucky, a fitful remembrance of feeling touched by a trace of an image. Once the sensation passed, however, the passerby would resume his passage through the city in a state of readiness—or blaséness.

At times, there were purposive collective spectacles, too: demonstrations, parades, and, in revolutionary times, riots, and the placards, leaflets, effigies, torches, papier-mâché figures that accompanied them. As much as time permitted, men and women asserted the right to set their mood and stepped out—to saloon, club, dance hall, arcade, circus, amusement park, burlesque house, nickelodeon, vaudeville show, or "legitimate" theater.

And the public panoply had its private equivalents. By the late nineteenth century, family photographs reposed on shelves, mantels, and pianos, and not only in the homes of the prosperous. As the family shrank to nuclear scale, photographs extended it in time and space, ushering absent members into the intimate world of the here and now—once more, with feeling. Homes turned into private shrines of visual icons. Magic became domestic; one composed one's own personal spectacle.

Increasingly there were also images from beyond the family circle, the descendants of the paintings, maps, prints, and engravings of Vermeer's Dutch burghers, alongside crosses and flags, depictions of the Messiah, saints, heroes, and ancestors. Augmenting these were the images and texts delivered to the house at regular intervals: the newspapers, magazines, catalogs, sheet (and later recorded) music, and books, their numbers rising throughout the nineteenth and twentieth centuries. If income permitted, one "took" a periodical, a regular and familiar package of image and text that one liked because one approved of its formula, trusting the packagers to deliver approximately the right look, thoughts, and feelings, approving their taste, sharing their interests and curiosities, and through their formulas gaining low-risk access to a bountiful world. As during a walk down a familiar street, there might be surprises, too. Breaking with the imperatives of the time clock, one gambled—at low stakes. What would one find in this issue of the *Saturday Evening Post*? What adventure would beckon in this month's *National Geographic*? The novelty was finite; the material was new but not *too* new. The magazine would always be a limited liability experience. If it didn't pan out this month, one could await the next issue or subscribe to another publication with a more appealing package.

Newspapers and most magazines promised firm information, usable facts, and, at the most exalted level, knowledge, a state of comprehension. But the wonder of communications was that the carriers of information did not simply transmit facts or ideology. They occasioned a human experience—a sense of connection to the world. In a complex society, dispersed individuals had to be aware of what was going on outside their immediate milieux, in order to coordinate their activities. Thus they craved information. But this information was not pure; it arrived certified by celebrities, jostling with gossip, and, above all, accompanied by emotions. To learn what was going on elsewhere entailed some sort of mental excitement: the *wow!* of salaciousness, the *aha!* of mastery, the *click* of understanding, the *what?* of astonishment.

So not only were the factual media informative; they were diverting. The first mass newspapers, the penny press of the 1830s, as Neal Gabler has pointed out, had their origins in a working-class entertainment tradition that was already thriving.

> For a constituency being conditioned by trashy crime pamphlets, gory novels and overwrought melodramas, news was simply the most exciting, most entertaining content a paper could offer, especially when it was skewed, as it invariably was in the penny press, to the most sensational stories. In fact, one might even say that the masters of the penny press *invented* the concept of news because it was the best way to sell their papers in an entertainment environment.

Cultivating the human interest story, newspapers could be sensational yet newsy, realistic yet emotion-inspiring, vividly personal yet general in their import. They were diversions that didn't strictly divert. Or rather, they distracted readers from their immediate environs by refusing to distract them from some larger world. They cultivated curiosity, and curiosity corralled facts. Thanks to such means of delivery, the spirit of information rode high.

The money economy was accompanied by an all-embracing swirl of modernity: investments, capital flows, migrations, turnovers of taste, style, fashion, and opinion. What Simmel called "the modern soul that is so much more unstable" had a high psychic metabolism. Endlessly it regenerated boredom. "A faint sense of tension and vague longing," a "secret restlessness," a "helpless urgency" that "originates in the bustle and excitement of modern life"—all this, Simmel wrote, "impels us to search for momentary satisfaction in ever-new stimulations, sensations and external activities." Even at home, the dislodged soul needed constant replenishment, a ceaseless, streaming importation of content to play with, reflect upon, or learn from. A taste for the new ran deep, as did the economic payoff, for superficiality, replaceability, and the itch to keep up with the Joneses were good for production.

Excitements and analgesics multiplied. Modern people, led by Americans, came to expect the comfort and convenience of home access. The standard array of sensation machines grew. What could more reliably cater to the volatile spirit, delivering riffs and squirts of emotion, instructions, and pleasures? New communication technologies spurred hungers by provisionally satisfying them, but as Marx had anticipated, no sooner had old needs been satisfied than new ones opened up. Entrepreneurs continually searched for the next household delivery system to feed unappeasable hungers.

For brevity's sake, I am compressing a tangled history, downplaying national differences, and exaggerating the uniformity of a process that proceeded—is still proceeding—in fits and starts. Still, the main direction has been clear enough. After newspapers and magazines came commercial radio. As costs fell, technologies that had at first been the province of the rich drifted into the middle class and then, within surprisingly few years, crossed over to the majority. With television and its auxiliaries, what had been an exclusive right to luxuriate passed into a general right to connect—and with cable, the right to connect to a channel of your own liking, the majority be damned.

The thirst for images, for music, for reverberations from the world of public affairs could be satisfied as fast as mail could be delivered and vacuum tubes warmed up. But availability did not quench the thirst for images and sounds. To the contrary: the more technologies, the more images and sounds they could carry, the greater the thirst—and the desire to please one's private self. Boredom was a crime against plenitude. Who could say, "Stop, I have enough"? Technology came to the aid of fragmented tastes. Media conglomerates spun out multiple channels for distinct demographic niches. Why not establish your own mood, create your personalized top ten from the ever-expanding menu of entertainment and information that flows through the living room? Why stop at the living room? Why not pipe the bounty into the bedroom? Yet always there is the threat of tedium and the persistent shrug. A century after Georg Simmel wrote about "nurseries of cynicism," we find them in the household, where the bountiful screen offers access indiscriminately to an episode of fictional domestic anguish, a tennis match, a sports utility vehicle driving over a mountain, a soccer score, a salad preparation, an animal cartoon, a futurist dystopia, a murder headline, a joke, a poker-faced policeman, a nude, a hurricane victim shivering in the cold, a jewelry advertisement . . .

In George Orwell's classic *1984*, Big Brother was the ultimate coercive broadcaster, the sole controller of propaganda. But Big Brother had no chance against niche media and personal choice. In the West, at least, he was no more than a hollow bogeyman. In the widening torrent available to all-consuming humanity, you rode your own current. Why not revel in the pursuit of such happiness? Why fear engulfment?

NOMADICITY

Increasingly, you could carry your private current anywhere. The home entertainment center was, after all, a luxury for which you had to confine yourself. Images and manufactured sounds came home but you had to be home to greet them. So why not render your private amusements portable? Why not, like Pascal's well-served if pitiable monarch, have it all wherever and whenever you like?

Self-sufficiency, that most tempting and expansive of modern motifs, feels like a sort of liberation—until it becomes banal and we have need of the next liberation. People gravitate toward portability and miniaturization—each a kind of freedom—in everyday life. The mountaineer's backpack evolved into the hippie traveler's aluminum-framed pack, which in turn evolved into the contemporary frameless version, which in turn gave rise to the utilitarian but waistline-disturbing fanny pack, the bulky monster sticking out horizontally, and the trim designer variety that is, in effect, a purse that leaves the hands free. Portable nourishment is another sign of the nomadic thrust toward self-sufficiency: the Hershey bar (1894), the ice-cream cone (1904), Life Savers (1913), trail mix (1970s), the portable water bottle (1990s). The tendency has been toward performing as many functions as possible in the course of one's movements—"multitasking"—so that as we move, new accessories become mandatory. The indented tray inside the glove compartment and the cup holder next to the front seat have become standard equipment.

Not only must material provisions be available on demand; so must sustenance for the senses, not least the ears. After the portable battery-powered radio, the car radio, and the transistorized radio, the logic of individualism pointed toward that exemplary little machine for musical transport, Sony's Walkman. The theme is well enunciated in a London billboard of 2001 that does not even bother to indicate any particular product: "Give today a soundtrack."

The Walkman story shows how the convenience of a single powerful man could generate a marketing triumph. Before a transoceanic flight in 1979, Sony chairman Masaru Ibuka asked company engineers to create a stereo music player so he could hear classical favorites of his choice. Airlines already provided passengers with earphones and canned musical loops, but Ibuka did not want anyone overriding his personal taste, so Sony engineers connected headphones to an advanced tape recorder for him. Ibuka was delighted with the results, and his partner Akio Morita realized that this jury-rigged contraption might have sales potential among teenagers, who were already accustomed to carrying portable radios. The Walkman was born. What had begun as a toy for Ibuka was promptly sold to consumers less accustomed to indulging their personal whims.

Supply proceeded to trigger demand. By the end of 1998, without much advertising, Sony had sold almost 250 million Walkmen worldwide, not to mention the Discmen and all the specialized spinoff players for joggers, swimmers, and skiers.

Throughout the twentieth century, supply and demand looped together in an unceasing Möbius strip, technology always increasing the radius of contact: the pay phone, car radio, battery-powered radio, transistor radio, remote-accessible answering machine, fax machine, car phone, laptop computer, Walkman, airplane and train phone, portable CD player, beeper, mobile phone, Palm Pilot, Internet access, PCD, GPD, and so on ad acronym. Once "interactivity" by machine became feasible, the hallmark of so many communication inventions was *nomadicity*, which, according to the Internet pioneer who coined the term, "means that wherever and whenever we move around, the underlying system always knows who we are, where we are, and what services we need." Actually, not *we* so much as *I*, for more and more often the contemporary nomad travels alone, detribalized—or rather, in the company of that curious modern tribe each of whose members seeks to travel alone while being technologically connected to others. Equipped for accessibility, he may encroach upon the right of others to control their own private space: the battery-powered boom box blaring music or narrating a ball game (even the one taking place before one's eyes in the stadium itself); the cell phone trilling during the play or the concert; the caller shouting into his phone on the train, in the restaurant, at the park, or on the street.

Charles Baudelaire once lamented: "They left one right out of the Declaration of the Rights of Man and Citizen: the right to leave." Now, for hours each day, the right to leave is secure, though doubtless not in the way Baudelaire had in mind. In fact, the right to leave has merged with the right to be *somewhere else*. For a growing proportion of the population, and for a growing number of hours per day, you can, after a fashion, break the limits of space, choosing from your private menu of activities, amusements, and contacts. You are not exactly alone, because you are with others, their music, their games, their voices. Commuting or washing the floors, you are a movable node, never wholly abandoned. Even in extremis—but who could have imagined such extremity?—your voice can reach out to a loved one from the inferno of the World Trade Center about to collapse or the cabin of a hijacked plane. The horrific emergencies of September 11, 2001, put to extraordinary ends what have become the ordinary means to overcome distance.

How shall we understand the appeal of these ordinary means? Consider the humdrum experience of waiting for a bus, which Jean-Paul Sartre took as a metaphor for modern alienation. Sartre called this ordinary condition *serialization*, by which he meant losing one's individuality and being reduced to a function—waiting. The immobilized man on line cannot pursue his own ends because he has lost control of his time in favor of the bus company's schedule, the pileup of fellow travelers, the traffic that has delayed the bus. He is the creature of a routine that demands self-suppression. Now imagine this man on line equipped with a personal stereo. His ears project him, at least partially, elsewhere—or rather, elsewhere enters him, corporeal, immediate, intimate. He stands in the line but leaves it behind for a chosen communion. He blocks out unwanted contact. Now he is, paradoxically, an individual because he has company— music, familiar music at that. He feels little spurts of emotion. Music rubs up against him, gets inside him. He nods along with the beat. Against the pressures of work and environment—even against his own unpleasant obsessions—he has a compensation: he has enveloped himself in a sort of mobile bubble. He has—to quote from Walkmanned Londoners interviewed in one study—"shut everything out" and "squashed thoughts." The music, turned up loud enough to drown out ambient noise, "takes over his senses." "It's like living in a movie." Availing himself of "a life-support machine," he has taken charge of his mood.

Now imagine this man still in line or trapped in some other

serialized reality—in an elevator, on the train, or stuck in a traffic jam—and equip him with escape implements in the form of today's proliferating mobile equipment: the cellular phone, the Game Boy, the personal communication system with text messaging and Internet access, feeding him sports scores and stock quotes, eventually cartoons, jokes, slot machines, card games, and pornographic images, asking him at all hours: "Where would you like to go?" Take charge of your mood! Possessing an "arsenal of mobile technology," he comes to feel that he has the right to them. He is, to some degree, shielded from urban fear.

Some admirers of our present-day electronic efflorescence are carried away with promises of the technological sublime. One recent enthusiast heralds *techgnosis*. But nomadic access raised to the level of gods and angels rings sublimely ridiculous. Usually, the very point of dot-communion is banality. Through the most mundane act of e-mailing about the weather or instant-messaging a "buddy" about nothing at all except that you're stuck in a boring lecture, or that you exist and affirm the other's existence ("Whassup?" "Not much"), or phoning your loved one from the air to report that your plane is late or from the street to report that you are just now emerging from the subway, you have, in a sense, spun off a filament of yourself to conduct your business, secure your network, greet your friend, discharge your duty, arrange your pleasure. Intellectuals may scoff, but it is this relatively trivial mercy that most people in a consumerist culture seek much of the time.

But the freedom to be even incidentally connected is not uncomplicated. It goes with being incidentally accessible, which amounts to being on call and interruptible everywhere by your boss, your nurse, your patient, your anxious parent, your client, your stockbroker, your baby-sitter, as well as your friend whose voice, even electronically, you welcome even if you have just seen each other face-to-face. Friendship makes intrusion welcome—perhaps that is part of its definition—and nomadicity, no question, is a boon to certain kinds of friendship. In a suburb where nothing seems to happen, *something* can happen—again and again. You can send along jokes, photos, shopping recommendations, references smart and dumb. It was probably America Online's "buddy lists" for instant messaging that made that huge Internet portal so popular.

Wireless handheld devices with Internet access carry the instantaneous buddy principle out into public space. Having been launched in Japan with considerable success, they are galloping through the United States and Europe. Sony's mobile Internet device, no doubt to be called Webman, is set to go into American circulation shortly. "We believe that the mobile terminal will be a very . . . strategic product for Sony," the company's president, Kunitake Ando, told the *Asian Wall Street Journal*. "Just like we created a Walkman culture, we'll have a sort of mobile culture," he said, adding that sooner or later Sony was planning to pipe on-line music and even movies through a new generation of mobile phones. Such prognostications may be hype, but Sony's have a way of turning out accurate.

At this writing, though, the principle of instantaneous access is most firmly at work with nomad-friendly mobile phones. In the year 2000, 53 percent of Americans owned mobile phones, up from 24 percent in 1995. So did 63 percent of British adults, about as many as in Japan though not so many as in Italy, Sweden, and Finland. Their diffusion rate is tremendous, comparable to television's, exceeding that of telephones, radios, and VCRs, and more visible in public, of course, than any of those.

The mobile phone radically transforms the soundscape. Like the servant's bell, its chime or ditty is a summons, but also a claim that you have the right to conduct your business willy-nilly wherever you are, whether you're a day-trader in New York or a Hong Kong youngster chatting away in a subway car (that city has wired its tunnels). Private practices open out into public spaces. So if the Webbed-up, wired, or wirelessed nomad rarely gets to relish full-bodied freedom, there is still the pleasure of knowing one is wanted *right now.*

The new technonomadicity comes with this paradox: the fully-equipped nomad, seeking freedom of access at will, becomes freely accessible to other people's wills. The sender also receives. The potential for being intruded upon spurs technological fixes; with caller ID, for example, you can block calls from old boyfriends, or screen calls to see who wants contact, or defer contact by dumping a call into voicemail. As in a military arms race, the dialectic of offense and defense ratchets up. There is a second paradox: those who hope to control their moods when they go out in public find themselves invaded by alien noises. In theaters, concerts, conferences, parks, and churches, the trill of the cell phone is not an angelic visitation. The commons explodes with private signals. Again, the defense also improves. Theaters announce, before the curtain goes up, that ringers should be turned off—with uneven success. Devices to block mobile phones are already being marketed to restaurants and theater owners.

So communication comes at a price—not just the monetary price, which falls year after year; not just the invasion of solitude; no, the third inevitable price of nomadicity is surveillance. This is not just the risk of being overheard in a public place. After all, the mobile phoner who wishes to preserve privacy in the face of proximity can still do so, for the new devices amplify the lowered human voice with wondrous fidelity. But cellular conversations are peculiarly capable of being intercepted, not only by public agencies but by interested private parties, whether by accident or deliberately.

Still, the new nomad, intent on living out a dream of personal power, seems willing to pay the price. The omnicommunicative utopia appeals to a centuries-old passion to control one's circumstances without renouncing social bonds. This is the version of freedom that drives the civilization that American (but not only American)

enterprise and power carry to the ends of the earth. It is an omniv-
orous freedom, freedom to behold, to seek distraction, to seek distraction *from* distraction (in T. S. Eliot's words), to enjoy one's
rootlessness, to relish the evanescent. But as the Canadian songwriter
Leonard Cohen once wrote, "Where do all these highways go now
that we are free?"

SOUNDTRACKING

The new nomad may not have bargained on finding himself so frequently prey to interruption. Not only does his cell phone trill
when he may not find it so welcome, but the common world is
increasingly soundtracked. Whatever the rhetoric of networked
individualism, individuals are not the only communicators in public.
Institutions routinely use sound to orchestrate a collective mood, to
"brand" space, exploiting the fact that we can choose not to see far
more easily than we can choose not to hear. Looking away from a
screen may be psychologically difficult, but it can be done: you
crane your head or simply walk away. But the ear is less discriminating than the eye. Human beings lack earlids. Your head need not
be cocked toward a sound source for the sound to command your
attention.

Most of the soundscape is not summoned up by junior Nietzsches
just as they like. It is administered. Now, imposed sound is not necessarily noxious. When the community at large caters the sound-
surround, few people within earshot experience it as an imposition.
Performers at fairs, on street corners or subway station platforms,
festivals in public parks, brass bands in parades, street dances, even
boom boxes on beaches or stoops—these are, in varying degrees, felt
to be "expressions of the community." Living in a heavily Appala-
chian neighborhood in Chicago in the mid-1960s, I could follow the
same country-western song down the block as it wafted out of win-

dow after window, all the apartments tuned to the same radio station.

But increasingly, our desire for diversion is appropriated, packaged, and radiated back at us by an organization that has figured out how to dovetail our desire with its desire to profit from the pleasure principle. Access to the popular ear is purchased. The capacity to make oneself heard—in other words, the capacity to interrupt—becomes a dimension of social power. Mall shops and restaurants get to entertain—or exercise sonic power over—everyone within earshot. Moods have monetary value. Organizing moods is good business. And so, in Milan Kundera's words, "The acoustic image of ecstasy has become the everyday decor of our lassitude." Bathed in the "trivialized ecstasy" of public soundtracks, we are prompted to feel as the music commands us to feel.

Industry was the first institution to be soundtracked. In 1937, industrial psychologists in Great Britain proposed (in a report to the British Industrial Health Research Board titled *Fatigue and Boredom in Repetitive Work*) that music had charms to soothe the savage worker at his repetitive job when he might otherwise be absent, or going home early, or goofing off, or otherwise heeding an unorchestrated drummer. During World War II, the BBC heightened productivity in arms factories with radio programs like *Music While You Work*. Americans were not far behind, piping music into war plants and shipyards beginning in 1942. Mood management tested in war proved no less useful in peace. Convinced that the methods of sonic satisfaction had proved themselves, private industry began to avail itself of the output of the Muzak Corporation. "By 1946," according to communications scholars Simon C. Jones and Thomas G. Schumacher, "Muzak was installed in the workplaces of most major American firms, with separate programs for offices and factories." Muzak researchers went beyond the canning of comforting strains; they developed the principle of "stimulus progression," having found that a staged sequence of tunes, gradually boosting tempo, rhythm, and orchestra size on a scale from 1 ("slow and

mellow") to 5 ("bright and upbeat"), boosted productivity. Psychological lifts could be scientifically programmed. However tedious the
work, the music was smooth, for the original recordings had been
cleansed of any lurches of rhythm or melody. This was domesticated
music, laced with "a hint of nostalgia and fantasy but contained within
a rational, orderly structure," its "stylistic regularity and harmonic
simplicity" suggesting a "secure, private, domestic world that signifies
the comfort and security of home." If you could not be coaxed to
"whistle while you work," the sound system would do the whistling
for you.

If music to work by, why not music to shop by or wait by? In the
1950s, the Muzak Corporation began to orchestrate for retail estab-
lishments, aiming to induce a buying mood. Muzak filled supermar-
kets with languorous rhythms, meant to relax shoppers and coax
them into spending more time in the aisles. Other sequences built
up the rhythms, the volume inching up, producing psychic tension—
to be relieved by pulling something off the shelves. By the 1980s,
scarcely a public space lacked a soundtrack: shops, malls, airports,
airplanes, cruise ships, stadiums, hospitals, restaurants, doctors' and
dentists' offices, gyms, banks, hotel lobbies, theme parks, elevators,
bathrooms, waiting rooms of all kinds. An airliner now signaled arrival, contact with the mother-pod, by locking into its soundtrack.
Airports spawned the musical subgenre of "ambient sound," known
derisively as "elevator music," and half mocked, half indulged in the
contemporary postmodernist manner by the droll Brian Eno in a
series of records called "Music for Airports."

Meanwhile, shops catering to the young led a shift to so-called
foreground music—sounds promoting an upbeat atmosphere in an
age when electrified music is normal, and normally loud. Muzak and
other corporations now bounce signals off extraterrestrial satellites
to beam "storecasting" music to particular "consumption environ-
ments" for distinct demographic groups, even programmed for specific times of day. At clothing and restaurant chains, malls, and (of

course) music stores catering to a youthful clientele, the sound pulsates loudest, often accompanied by music video screens. Even the network news has its theme songs, broadcasting a sense of urgency along with reliability. Restaurants that "skew" older, as the marketers say, are partial to the relaxed piano tinkles of the Windham Hill label, which are to the more rarefied palettes of upscale baby boomers what Mantovani's cloying strings were to their down-market aunts and uncles. But the auditory wraparound is not always popular with customers, let alone staff. A New York Pottery Barn employee tells me he winces at the pounding of the soundtrack operating nonstop in his department. Still, it must not be an automatic irritant that at many a metropolitan restaurant or bar catering to younger-than-forty clientele the acoustics are managed so as to amplify the roar and enforce the sense that this is where things are happening. (At the same time, *buzz* has become the commonplace term for public repute.) Meanwhile, other restaurants market themselves to the middle-aged by installing acoustic baffles, turning down the ambient sound to make conversation more discernible to ears that have lost acuity, the process often speeded along by years of attending concerts in front of gigantic speakers. To every niche, a sound.

In Europe, as in the United States, wraparound sound has become a normal accompaniment to everyday life. The Beatles' "Let It Be" resounds from a Swissair flight. At a Thai restaurant in Berlin, the soundtrack features "Over the Rainbow." Evidently, many people prefer mood music, however unsubtle, to what would otherwise be their own private improvisations. At worst, they are indifferent. "Perhaps," as J. Bottum writes, "it was Hollywood that taught us to expect life to come with background music, a constant melodic commentary on the movie of our lives." The Muzak Corporation and its imitators are thoughtful enough to provide variety, so that it never seems that Big Brother or the Wizard of Noise is in charge. So, passing through the world, modern individuals hear a corporate-produced pastiche. We hear it, in Bottum's words, "in snippets, as we cross from one stereo zone to another—the radio suddenly blaring out as the car starts up, the jukebox suddenly cut off as the door to the diner closes. . . . We've all been damned to a perpetual quarter-final round of *Name That Tune.*"

Yet the private resists the public in this realm as well, fighting technology with technology. Wired, nomadic individuals play defense against institutional auditory control, drowning out the public soundtrack with their own Walkman or Discman, and while it would be silly to see them as heroes of a sonic class struggle, fighting back against the capitalist appropriation of the soundscape, the headphones surely do screen out unwelcome noise by substituting a personal soundtrack. In fact, they protect not only from Muzak and woofer-heavy hip-hop car stereos passing by but from miscellaneous motors, truck, bus, airplane, and motorcycle engines, honking horns, cracked mufflers, sirens, chain saws, and pneumatic drills—not to mention the steady drones, rumbles, whirrs, and hums emitted by fluorescent lights, refrigerators, heaters, computers, fans, air conditioners, microwave ovens, dial tones, and the rest of the apparatus of everyday electrified life. In an age of scattered urban din, the rhythmic pulsation of hip-hop may be, for its partisans, the loud intrusion that erases the minor rackets. The upbeat, tweeter-heavy, violin-drenched soundtrack may be electricity's shelter—against electricity itself.

PAYING, AND PAYING FOR, ATTENTION

A teenager in a Berkeley theater, chatting amiably with her friend during the movie, growls at a complaining patron: "What's the matter, man? It's only a movie!" At a multiplex in Greenwich Village, a woman on her cell phone during the trailer insists, "I want to see this movie just as much as you do!" No matter that theaters run "Please let us know if anything interferes with your enjoyment of this show" announcements along with the popcorn and soft drink promotions before the feature. In recent years, I've heard a baby cry at a classical concert (and the usher refuse to tell the mother to tend to her child outside). I've heard mobile phones go off in the middle of plays, though signs urge customers to turn off their phones, beepers, and other electronic equipment, and announcements to that effect are made. I've heard phones trill in seminar rooms, lecture halls, libraries and in the otherwise hushed galleries of museums. Public life is a place where private transactions go on—this is the assumption. Private life in public converges with public life in private. For growing numbers of people, the world is a multiplex, chock-full of electronics: an arcade of amusements.

It is easy to cast a rosy glow over the sacrosanctness of private space, yet even spaces that are literally sanctified are seldom places of unswerving attention. I once attended a Christmas Eve mass in Florence and, standing in the back, was startled to hear the fairly continuous rumble of Italians gossiping. During much of theatrical history, audiences have chatted, yelled, and otherwise expressed themselves as vigorously as they dared. Although Shakespeare's Elizabethan audiences were probably attentive—at least judging from the fact that the most frequent complaints about disturbing noises during performances refer to nutcracking—antebellum Americans were not. The folks in the balcony frequently made their displeasure known by pelting both the actors and the fancy people below with pennies, rotten fruit, eggs, apples, nuts, and gingerbread. In 1832, the English traveler Frances Trollope observed at a theater in Cincinnati "coatless men with their sleeves rolled up, incessantly spitting, reeking 'of onions and whiskey.'" She enjoyed the Shakespeare but abhorred the "perpetual" noises. Crowds often demanded instant encores and chimed in to recite long stretches of dialogue they had committed to memory. A New York journalist found the cheers and jeers of theater crowds a "merry and riotous chorus," adding that "compared with the performances in the audience, the ranting and bellowing and spasmodic galvanism of the actors on the stage are quite tame and commonplace." A French reporter attending a Shakespeare performance in California in 1851 noted that "the more [the spectators] like a play, the louder they whistle, and when a San Francisco audience bursts into shrill whistles and savage yells, you may be sure they are in raptures of joy." On occasion, members of the audience jumped onto the stage to examine the props. In Albany, a canal boatman screamed at Iago, "You damned lying scoundrel, I would like to get hold of you after the show and wring your infernal neck!"

Intellectuals cherish the act of attention, believing that attention is not something that happens to you but something you undertake. You contemplate, or immerse yourself and experience a sort of communion, whether with nature or a work of art. You actively *attend* to it. In this spirit, even the humble movie theater ought to be a sort of sacralized space for connection and concentration, not an amplified jukebox with up-tempo music and Hollywood trivia quizzes to fill the time before trailers.

The art historian Jonathan Crary maintains that the act of attention acquired fresh importance and virtue toward the end of the nineteenth century. It was then that what had been more or less a common culture broke in half. The great temples of culture—the opera, the symphony, the grand museums—insisted on decorum so that the act of spiritual elevation could take place uninterrupted. Elevated people wanted attention to be paid; indeed, you demonstrated your elevation *by* paying attention. The working classes moved to vaudeville, burlesque, dance halls, pool halls, and later nickelodeons. Their neighborhood movie theaters were more raucous than those of the middle class. As the high arts demanded sustained attention, psychologists began to treat inattention as a flaw. Attention was associated with willpower, craft, and love. Without attention, "the bringing of the consciousness to a focus in some special direction," warned a British psychologist in 1886, "meaningless reverie will take the place of coherent thought." A German psychologist wrote in 1893 that without the capacity for attention, "consciousness would be at the mercy of external impressions . . . thinking would be made impossible by the noisiness of our surroundings." Modern distraction, then, so frequently decried, "was *not* a disruption of stable or 'natural' kinds of sustained" perception but "an *effect*, and in many cases a constituent element, of the many attempts" to make people pay attention. People were not naturally attentive but became so. Amid the everyday buzz of what William James called "the stream of consciousness," attention was an interlude of concentration seized from an everyday life of "permanent low-level attentiveness," itself a reaction to the "relentless colonization of 'free' or leisure time."

Intellectuals, who love to cultivate attention and do it for a living, have long been indignant about intrusions upon their solitude and communion. If it wasn't the locomotive piercing the silence of the bucolic idyll, it was the menace of urban chaos: the turmoil of horse-drawn carriages, the mud, the excrement of horses, not to mention the neon, the flamboyant designs and banner headlines, the intrusive photos and garish posters of the yellow press, which in 1890 occasioned the first legal defense of the right to privacy. What the clutter of advertising did to the urban scene, billboards did to the surrounding countryside. Already more than a century ago, we were on our way to the contemporary sense of supersaturation—the overflow that seems to pour out of an overfilled atmosphere of signs and signals, generating grumpy reactions to "information overload."

But for all the refinement of their reactions, intellectuals have been paying attention, though not necessarily as the cultural industry intends. And attention is precisely the commodity that advertisers buy. "Eyeballs" and "impressions" are what the proprietors of media sell—what all the television and radio stations, billboard owners, and Internet sites market to advertisers. No space today is safe. Ads are placed on the backs of airplane seats, at eyeball height over urinals, on the backs of stall doors in women's bathrooms. In 2000, ABC installed motion-sensitive talking ads in a thousand public urinals in New York and Los Angeles to promote a new sitcom. Anyone with a screen or a surface wants to rent it out—the side of a bus or a gas pump, the top and sides of a taxi, even its hubcaps.

And today, you need not step out of doors to be poked and prodded by corporate sales bureaus, for there are the push technologies of phone solicitations, now frequently mechanized to improve the efficiency of the callers. (Answer the phone at your peril between 6 and 7 P.M., but no time is safe.) The stars of ABC's fall 2000 season called random numbers to leave messages about the new shows on answering machines. There are the banner and pop-up ads on the Internet, increasingly wiggly and obtrusive—though users have learned to ignore even these, occasioning trouble for Internet finance. There are ads on rented videos, on sports scoreboards and sports equipment, and—in the form of product placement—in movies and TV shows. My New York University identification card carries an advertisement from AT&T. This is not to mention the theme songs and jingles that aim to attach themselves to everyday consciousness like replicable viruses.

In fact, the ironic challenge for all cultural entrepreneurs, all advertisers, studios, movie and music distributors, publishing companies, newspapers, magazines, toy companies, television networks, Internet providers, and so on is to "break through the clutter." But of course the clutter is not a force of nature; it is an artifact of the frenzy of competition. The clutter consists of nothing but the sum of all prior attempts to break through the clutter. So the clutter of images and manufactured sounds is the engine that drives ads into hitherto virgin spaces.

Where is the commercial presence *not* taken for granted? Eight million students in the United States and Canada attend schools whose administrations accept free TV sets from Channel One on the condition that the students watch its daily news broadcasts, complete with youth-targeted commercials. A company called YouthStream posts advertisement boards in 7,200 high school locker rooms, reaching (according to the company's promotions) some 70 percent of American high school students. Company hype about the merits of public advertising to children is extravagant. Consider, for example, this rapturous promise from Mike Searles, former president of Kids-R-Us, a children's clothing chain: "If you own this child at an early age, you can own this child for years to come. Companies are saying, 'Hey, I want to own the kid younger and younger.' "

Branding—of companies, not of cattle—is the *cri du jour* in marketing and public relations, but it is more than that. It is integral to a way of life. Many kids want to be "owned," cheerfully trading in one set of "owners" for others as they grow up. When companies speak of branding, they mean two things: landing a symbol in front of you repeatedly and in multiple venues, hoping to attract attention, and building a ladder in the imagination from attention to belief (Prudential is rock-solid; Coke, effervescent; Apple, cool). The magic of imaginative association is nothing new; the practice of hiring celebrities to infuse goods with meaning and stoke up desire for them ballooned in the course of the twentieth century. To these testimonials have been added the symbols and logos, the typographies and labels, the long-playing theme ads and public relations campaigns that establish "corporate identity," radiating a feeling about a company's style, offering a "unique selling proposition" that links a company to a mood and a social type.

On signs, T-shirts, caps, coffee mugs, key chains, shopping bags, and posters, in shops, private and public museums, arenas, theaters, and tourist sites, branding is now normal. Companies invest grandly in state-of-the-art designers to acquire the right logos, for in a prosperous society people have so much time to pay attention and so much discretionary income with which to indulge their desires that branding rewards investment. But the most extraordinary thing is the extent to which branding is voluntary, even enthusiastic, a fashion statement of affiliation. Labels affirm membership. The United

States has reached an unprecedented degree of brand saturation, so many are the volunteers ready and eager to pay for the privilege of displaying their logos in public. In the 1930s, the down-and-out felt humiliated when compelled to wear sandwich boards to make ends meet, but children today gladly turn themselves into walking billboards. Once it was the working and farming classes who branded themselves by wearing Caterpillar Tractor and John Deere caps. But then came Lacoste's little alligators, followed by a flood of other insignia, to the point where in the 1970s it became almost impossible to buy an unbranded polo shirt. Calvin Klein, Ralph Lauren, Donna Karan, Tommy Hilfiger, and other designers branded jeans, socks, and other garments galore, each cornering a status-specific market. Marlboro did the same, selling clothing and gear from specialized shops in Europe.

But conspicuous collaboration, the desire to be branded, was not simply manufactured from on high. In an era of ever-renewed self-reinvention, when religion, region, and trade fail to provide deep identities, a brand can be a declaration, like a preprinted greeting card. The consumer has not chosen to choose, exactly, but from among the range of images on offer, has consented to choose. And why not? For the price of the artifact, you buy a statement: *I am my logo. I have this glamour, or power, or smoothness, or (fill in style) behind me.* While some stragglers proudly go without logos, the path of least resistance now is to surrender and embrace them or wear them ironically.

Those who fight profit-making corporations promote their own anticorporate logos. Greenpeace has its own, as do campaigners against capitalist globalization. Critics may try to make the media torrent swerve, but cannot imagine drying it up. In the country of the branded, even the opponents brand themselves.

2 | Speed and Sensibility

HASTE MAKES MONEY

Turn on the TV, graze around, let the tsunami of images and information wash over you. A baseball game, with stats pouring across the screen—not only batting averages, RBIs, and ERAs but the on-base percentages, the speed of the last pitch, the number of pitches and first-pitch strikes thrown, the ball and strike percentages, even a visual of the batter's "hot zone" and a cutaway to the new relief pitcher, resolute, with a "scouting report" slashing across his image. Click to a basketball game—possible now that most major sports seasons overlap, often by months. Watch a slam dunk replayed, the image rotate, the picture plane flip over and peel away into oblivion. Note the stats on the Knicks' record against the Jazz over the past five seasons, and against other Western Division teams, as well as individual players' records against their match-ups at home and away.

On MSNBC an interview is in progress. An expert is discoursing on Iraq and weapons of mass destruction. At the lower right is the network logo; to its left, the current Dow Jones industrial average, next to the current temperature and a cloud graphic. Later, three bongs will sound, signaling NBC, and the interview image will shrink, while headlines burst out below. Cut to two thirty-second commercials as images flicker by at an average of more than one edit per second.

On CNN, the secretary of state speaks as a ribbon of sports scores slithers across the bottom of the screen. On CNBC, a financial news network, a man, upper right, touts his company while a swathe of text, upper left, spells out the company's products and its strategies; at the lower right are the Dow, NASDAQ, and S&P 500 indexes, with arrows indicating whether they are headed "north" or "south." On MTV, the body of the announcer occupies screen center while, to either side of her, two small pictures of singers dangle in the ether of screen space. Cut, and a music video starts, images twinkling, blurring, jump-cutting past at breakneck speed.

On the Internet, features wiggle, ads pop up or blink and flash at the edges of the screen, words in solid color fields swell, migrate, and pop like bubbles.

Remote control devices are clicked to change channels between 36 and 107 times per hour, depending on the methodology used to study such things. Men and younger people, no surprise, click more than women and older people. According to a study conducted in 2000, three-quarters of Americans under thirty watched the news with a remote in hand, as did 54 percent of those over fifty. Imagining their audience fidgety, for good reason, the information, sports, and music networks build fitfulness directly into their displays.

Popular culture twitches.

Speed is not incidental to the modern world—speed of production, speed of innovation, speed of investment, speed in the pace of life and the movement of images—but its essence. The telegraph hastened business decisions, the telephone, military decisions, including the fateful mobilizations of August 1914. Is speed a means or an end? If a means, it is so pervasive and automatic as to *become* an end. We must run faster, fly faster, access faster, click faster. Sometimes we may exult in our speediness, like the character in Clifford Odets's play *Golden Boy* (1937), who declares: "We'll drive through the night. When you mow down the night with headlights, nobody gets you! You're on top of the world then—nobody laughs! That's it—speed! We're off the earth—unconnected! We don't have to think!! That's what speed's for, an easy way to live!" And sometimes we complain about speed (or think that we should), but without slowing down. The theme of speed-up and resistance to it streaks steadily through the literary record of the last two centuries. Here, typically, is George Eliot in *Adam Bede* (1859):

> Leisure is gone—gone where the spinning wheels are gone, and the pack-horses, and the slow waggons, and the pedlars, who brought bargains to the door on sunny afternoons. Ingenious philosophers will tell you, perhaps, that the great work of the steam-engine is to create leisure for mankind. Do not believe them: it only creates a vacuum for eager thoughts to rush in. Even idleness is eager now—eager for amusement: prone to excursion-trains, art-museums, periodical literature, and exciting novels.

Here is Nietzsche in *The Gay Science* (1882):

> One is ashamed of resting, and prolonged reflection almost gives people a bad conscience. One thinks with a watch in one's hand, even as one eats one's midday meal while reading the latest news of the stock market; one lives as if one might "miss out on something." . . . Virtue has come to consist of doing something in less time than someone else.

Paradoxically enough, the hurry-up syndrome is not new at all. It is a tradition. For centuries, the pace of production, consumption, transportation, and communication has steadily intensified. Journalists today are struck by the speed-up, casually assuming that there is something strikingly new here, something "postindustrial" or even "postmodern." But in truth, the acceleration is industrial and modern, and it is unrelenting.

The watershed was industrialization. As the historian of technology James R. Beniger puts it: "Until the Industrial Revolution, even the largest and most developed economies ran literally at a human pace, with processing speeds enhanced only slightly by draft animals and by wind and water power. . . . By far the greatest effect of industrialization, from this perspective, was to speed up a society's entire material processing system." And not only society's processing system but the onrushing pace of life, along with an awareness of that pace, of all the sensations and data that register on human psyches.

No one has caught this superflux of modernity better than popular historian James Truslow Adams, writing in 1931, long before television, the remote control clicker, or the computer mouse:

> Whether any more "events" are happening in the universe now than in earlier times would lead us into unfathomable bogs of metaphysics, but for our purpose it is enough to grant that more events are happening to each man of which he is conscious. In other words, a resident of New York to-day is getting more sensations and of a more varied sort than the Neanderthal or early man of several hundreds of thousands of years ago. Owing to this number and variety of sensations and his constantly shifting environment, modern man is also called upon to make a far greater number of adjustments to the universe than was his remote relative in the caves and forests of Germany or Java. It is the number of these sen-

sations and adjustments in a given time that makes the tempo of life. As the number of sensations increase, the time which we have for reacting to and digesting them becomes less. . . . The rhythm of our life becomes quicker, the wave lengths, to borrow a physical concept, of that kind of force which is our mental life grow shorter. . . . [S]uch a life tends to become a mere search for more and more exciting sensations, undermining yet more our power of concentration in thought. Relief from fatigue and ennui is sought in mere excitation of our nerves, as in speeding cars or emotional movies.

Nowhere has this been truer than in the United States, cradle of the assembly line, fast food, and the ATM. If restlessness is the modern condition, America is its homeland. Here, innovation is rarely retarded by ancestral lassitude, inertia, or active resistance. Not incidentally, fidgety people live in a fidgety economy. What the economy wants, most people on balance also find themselves wanting (though not always immediately and not always consistently). We fidget and upgrade if we are not who we want to be—or if our mates, careers, religions, cars, homes, garments, or sound systems are not what we want them to be. Not surprisingly, the speed of industrial innovation becomes palpable in the various speeds of life: the speed of fingers over the keyboard of a laptop computer, the speed of the electronic pulses that collect research data from cyberspace, the speed with which the new computer chips and software models supplant previous models, the speed with which they are designed and manufactured, the speed with which the materials from which they are manufactured are designed, synthesized, mined, and fabricated.

Not surprisingly either, Americans—though not only Americans—want to run fast, ride fast trains, swim fast, ski fast, rollerblade fast, charge down the sidewalk. We may want to feel the air resistance against our skin and through our hair, or save time by using machines to fly fast, drive fast, bicycle and motorcycle fast. Visually, our attention is caught by images of velocity. We want typefaces stream-lined and art photographs blurred. After fans started to abandon baseball for basketball, baseball teams went to some lengths to punch up the game with loud music, sideshows, cheerleaders, video displays featuring blooper footage and pop tunes nominated by the players, to the point where, as the sociologist Michael Schudson says, "There is not a moment between innings or when a relief pitcher is coming in when the scoreboard or sound systems are empty." On all sports broadcasts, instant replays and diagrammatic explanations (along with commercials, it goes without saying) fill up the cracks of time between actual plays. After the now comes "now this." We want to eat fast, read fast, speed-dial, send and receive e-mail, get speedy access to music or news, careen through video games, access the Internet, *click here*. We want to scratch lottery tickets, play slot machines, become instant winners. When we take new jobs or enter new partnerships, we need to be brought *up to speed*.

The payoff of a fast economy is clear. Capitalism loves speed because, as Benjamin Franklin well observed more than two centuries ago, time is money. This system of relentless turnover converts speed—of innovation, movement, and communication—into practi-cal advantage. A culture of speed is produced by driven people. A successful capitalist is not a capitalist who does things the way his father did, or at his father's speed. Goods that do not move take up shelf space. People who do not move or change are *over the hill, same old same old*. Within a capitalist society there will be those who take pleasure in a slow tempo, but they are not, as a rule, winners in the contest for wealth or power.

Today, the velocities of mobile capital, product cycles, and tech-nological upgrades are intermixed into a system that Edward Luttwak calls *turbo-capitalism*. That latest speed demon, the Internet, is itself a self-accelerating machine. Software entrepreneur Charles H. Fer-guson writes: "The phenomenon of 'Internet time,' the ultrafast development cycle that characterizes the entire Internet industry, is in large part a consequence of using the Web to distribute and receive information and technology about the Web, including software, specifications, documentation, source code, and comments from users." Whatever the type of capitalism, people must think fast, adopt innovations fast, communicate fast. It was, after all, the corporatist capitalism of Japan that devised "just-in-time" delivery to speed up distribution. Even the welfare-state societies of western Europe, when forced into competition with faster economies, feel the pressure to speed up. In the economy, technology, culture, and everyday life, what results is a state of affairs that the political scientist Zaki Laïdi calls *the tyranny of urgency*. As the pioneer French speed theorist Paul Virilio writes, with only slight exaggeration, speed was "the hope of the West."

But capitalism is rarely a simple tyranny of capitalists or merely an economic system for generating capital. Like a brain, it needs an entire body. It thrives within, and requires, a society whose people adapt—and, to a great degree, want to adapt—to its requirements for producing wealth. Capitalism, in other words, requires a way of life—sooner or later, a consumerist way of life. To take root, as in the first consumer societies, seventeenth-century Holland and eighteenth-century England, it had to dovetail its economic needs with the popular desires it was also helping to shape. Culture is never putty. At crucial junctures, ordinary people make choices—even if among a range of choices not of their own making. At various points in the development of industry, workers organizing to improve their living conditions had to decide what mattered most to them. Again and again, one crucial choice was: more money or more time of their own. Thus the first international labor demand was for an eight-hour working day—a demand carried across borders in the first International Workers' Day demonstrations of 1886. But in subsequent decades, American workers chose money. They were many things, these American workers—they might be God-fearing Christians, community builders, or radical agitators—but increasingly in the course of the nineteenth and twentieth centuries, they were consumers too, or wanted to be.

The historian Gary Cross argues persuasively that, in the early decades of the twentieth century, Americans, employers and workers alike, made a sort of bargain about what to do with the increased productivity that equipment and training permitted. They might have settled collectively for a limited working day, so that increased productivity would pay for more leisure time. This was Henry Ford's original idea, with efficient assembly lines permitting workers to accomplish their tasks in rapid order, and it was the direction of labor demands in several European countries—for example, for the thirty-hour week.

American business and labor, however, settled on a speed-up that would link production, acquisition, and obsolescence. Corporations came to understand that they needed to pump up demand in order to keep up the dynamic of production. Toward this end, they did not want people to feel satisfied with what they had already acquired. They would rather reward workers with higher wages than shorter hours. In order to excite people with thoughts of the wealth of goods that might someday be served up to those who stood and worked, advertising and marketing colonized the imagination—with the more or less enthusiastic cooperation of potential consumers. Pictures of purchasable utopias proved persuasive. Even while protesting how many hours they worked, workers came to prefer the pursuit of happiness via commodities to the pursuit of leisure.

In Cross's view, the Great Depression was a turning point, frightening workers with the burden of an impoverished free time. After World War II, pent-up consumer demand for a high-consumption way of life was boosted by government subsidies (via the low-interest mortgages and expensive highways that helped suburbanize the country). The die was cast: the public would choose money over time, preferring to seek its pleasures and comforts in the purchase of goods guaranteed to grow ever more swiftly obsolescent rather than in the search for collective leisure—or civic virtue. Through the convergence of many little decisions, this deal was complete by midcentury in the United States, with Great Britain lagging behind, and the western European continent still preferring longer vacations to higher wages.

Of course, the curious thing about consumer pleasures is that they don't last. The essence of consumerism is broken promises ever renewed. The modern consumer is a hedonist doomed to economically productive disappointment, experiencing, as sociologist Colin Campbell writes, "a state of enjoyable discomfort." You propel your daydreams forward, each time attaching them to some longed-for object, a sofa, CD player, kitchen, sports car, only to unhook the desires from the objects once they are in hand. Even high-end durable goods quickly outwear the thrill of their early arrival, leaving consumers bored—and available. After each conquest comes a sense of only limited satisfaction—and the question, what next? The engine of consumption hit an ideological speed bump in the 1960s, when countercultural impulses went up against the acquisitive lifestyle, but before long, stereo-equipped hippies found themselves zipping along an alternative version of the road their parents had traveled.

Speed may be a hope, but it's also a promise of a thrilling experience. No wonder the terms *driven* and *drives* have become conventional—usually in a complimentary sense. "We are *driven*!" in the upbeat jingle of a 1980s car commercial. "He's brilliant. He's driven," says an attorney, approvingly, about his boss, a cyberporn entrepreneur. But speed is treacherous, too. The proverbial fast lane is littered with roadkill. Fast people mutter that the cost is too high, that "someday" they will have to slow down. No matter how many "laborsaving devices" are sold—whether vacuum cleaners or Palm Pilots—we have the sense that the time we've saved is being gobbled up. Whether Americans are actually working more hours than they did a generation ago—or exaggerate the time they actually spend working—many complain about the speed-up even as they join in.

Not only do we like the sensations speed gives us when we're speeding; we like them when we experience them strictly through images. The desire for a swifter torrent is not brand-new, either. In the course of the nineteenth century, as life became faster, so did the desire swell to see images move. Eadweard Muybridge's representation of a speeding horse in 1878 was one of still photography's great achievements. And after still photography, inventors spent half a century striving for *motion* pictures. Once they had gotten pictures to move, one of the first wonders they produced was the speeding locomotive. The onrush of one shot after another, the montage intensifying the experience of speed, the movement of the camera within the shot, the movement of the spaceship, the racing car, the flashing fist, the knife, the gun within the shot—all these pictorial motions have intensified the image's promise to deliver the experience of speed without exertion. Seated, we feel speed via images more comfortably, more cheaply, and less riskily than if we had to sprint or parachute or leap from a moving car or get into a fistfight. Even physically lazy people, and those who lack strength or agility, get to be fast. Beholding the moving image, we all sense that somehow, without budging ourselves, we are living more life per second. Like a character in Edward Yang's movie *Yi Yi*, we enjoy the movies not only because they are lifelike but because they bring more life to life. If there is "two times as much life at the movies" as in our corporeal lives outside them, the result is that "we live three times!" Hyperefficient living—the triumph of life in the media torrent.

ANCIENT SLOWNESS AND MODERN SCRAMBLE

To assume that speed and the desire for speed were born yesterday would be to lapse into our obsession with the overstuffed present. Speed and the desire to speed are, in sense, built into us. On both offense and defense, agility is an advantage against enemies. Fast running, quick aiming—these are obvious benefits in the struggle against antagonists. Quick thinking often gets the better of slow thinking. Both a capacity for physical speed and an awareness of motion in the visual field are probably wired into human biology. But if evolutionary biology is the railway of human history, societies are the switches. In preindustrial societies, the advantages of speed were (and remain) largely potential. Bursts of speed were exceptional—in danger and in war. The velocity of things—spears, plows, wheels—was decidedly limited, as was the speed of the animals that human beings had to contend with. The speed that paid off was speed produced by the body, the movement of limbs and eyes.

Thinkers in ancient civilizations found reason to warn against excessive speediness. Patience was frequently held to be commendable. Plutarch cautioned, "Ease and speed in doing a thing do not give the work lasting solidity or exactness of beauty." The Greek and Roman classics recorded little pleasure in the sensation of speed as such, though speed was certainly found useful for specific purposes, as with "fleet-footed Achilles." A search of several Bible translations reveals only a handful of references to speed or its synonyms. The Koran makes little mention of speed. Nor does St. Augustine place much if any value on it. In short, among the ancients of the Middle East, speed by itself was not laudable. Aesthetic restlessness was not valued, either. In none of these societies was speed recommended as an easy or appealing way to live. Attention to movement in the environment took place within a daily routine that itself did not change much. Society, of course, was not static. Most of the history that has come down to us, perhaps tautologically, is a history of change and aspirations for change. Religious leaders and prophets, kings, and other rulers searched for new conquests, new lands, new knowledge, new experiences. Dissatisfaction was often the engine for moral, philosophical, political, and technical innovation. Intellectual restlessness was not unusual. Still, the pace of social change and innovation were, by modern standards, slow. Physical speed, demonstrably useful, did not lead to mechanical speed or speeding images.

Agrarian societies are slow-moving societies. For most of recorded history, dragging a plow across the earth was a man's agrarian work. Women mainly stayed close to home, their lives measured in increments—so many inches woven, so many garments washed, so many meals served. While invading armies sometimes swept down in a horsemen's version of blitzkrieg, many medieval battles were, by today's standards, snail paced. Even the diversions of that time were probably slower than today's.

Yet something happened to the Western pace of life in the Middle Ages—something that makes the Middle Ages middling not only in chronology but in velocity. Around the fourteenth century, the English language traces an interesting shift in the meaning of the word *speed*, which derives from *spēdan*, which had long meant "to fare" or especially "to prosper." The word that had essentially meant "go well" now came to mean "go fast." In England, prosperity and speed were felt to be linked. The German *schnell*, or "fast," seems to have stemmed from a word that previously meant "brave," "heroic," or "powerful," so here too there was an association between prowess and speed.

Interestingly, the semantic conversion of *spēdan* took place during the century when the Benedictine monks of Europe, committed to pray at precisely the same eight times in the course of each day, introduced mechanical clocks. The monasteries were then far-flung institutions, immense in their influence, as Lewis Mumford once pointed out:

> One is not straining the facts when one suggests that the monasteries—at one time there were 40,000 under the Benedictine rule—helped to give human enterprise the regular collective beat and rhythm of the machine; for the clock is not merely a means of keeping track of the hours, but of synchronising the actions of men. . . . The clock, not the steam-engine, is the key-machine of the modern industrial age. . . . For every phase of its development the clock is both the outstanding fact and the typical symbol of the machine; even today no other machine is so ubiquitous.

Activity synchronized is activity harnessed to an imposed standard, activity that can be brought under pressure to speed up, brought *up to speed*.

But for the regulation of time to produce a speed-up in the pace of life, there had to be places where rapid movement, rapid perception, and rapid communication paid off. Cities were such places. Agitation became the essence of city life, home to fast movers—or those who would be. Recent surveys of downtown walking speeds in cities in eight countries confirm that speed of physical movement consistently increases with the size of a city. What is true today was probably true in centuries past. Cities are crystallizations of energy, and the speed with which that energy circulates is intimately related to the city's prosperity. For classes linked to commerce and industry, bustle is functional. The merchant's success comes to rest, in significant part, on the pace of transactions; the artisan's, on the pace of production; and the workman's, to a lesser degree, on his efficiency. He may not like moving fast, but he'll learn that he had better, for the devil will take the hindmost.

People have traditionally been pushed into cities by rural misery and pulled there by hopes of improvement. The amalgamation of the two motives is nicely stated in Charles Dickens's phrase *desperate fascination*. Cities become—or are seen as—refuges for peasants and agricultural workers, dispossessed by the commercialization and mechanization of rural land, driven into London of the seventeenth century, or Chicago of the early twentieth, or Mexico City, São Paulo, or Bangkok today. Once in the city, they are struck by the speed-up. It is in cities that speed may translate into improvement, a prospect gilded by a chance for prosperity—and so may come to seem like a pure motive. Accordingly, for have-nots, speed feels like aspiration.

In the city, you must be alert, watchful for movement, yet unlike the hunter, you may not know what you are watching for. You live in eclectic readiness. You have errands to run, distractions to thread your way among—and cultivate. In 1939, the critic Walter Benjamin wrote that daily life in the city was a succession of shocks. He was talking about everyday sensory assault and immersion, but also about the simple kinetics of crossing the street and getting from one part of town to another. The built-in paradox of urban life is that the unexpected takes place so frequently that it comes to be expectable—not any particular unexpected event but unexpectedness categorically. You are on call . . . on edge . . . *on*. At any moment your phone may ring, your boss may call, an acquaintance may pass by, the news chimes may sound. The "future shock" popularized by Alvin Toffler—an unprecedented plunge into technological change—is but a variant of something city dwellers have known increasingly well for centuries. Urban life in turn spawned suburban life, which, however much motivated by a desire to find an oasis of calm in a churning world, in certain ways intensified the urban pace. The suburban home filled up with speedy appliances and required a car for the simplest of errands. The commute became a long, time-eating lap in the great metropolitan race. Urb and suburb blurred, or sprawled, into the megalopolis, which sprouted communication technologies, cultivated discontinuities and interruptions, invited simultaneity, demanded an omnidirectional, all-purpose alertness. More leisure hours now meant more things to do at once.

The current acceleration of tempo belongs to a two-century-long wave of speed-up, and it is foolish to assume, no matter how many times the words *new* and *revolutionary* are repeated, that today's novelties speed up everyday life more than those of a century ago. If we match the technological developments of 1895–1915—the elevators, subways, cars, trucks, buses, and airplanes that hastened our physical movement, and the motion pictures and radio that extended our vision and hearing—against today's personal computer, digitalization, mobile phone, voicemail, and Internet, we are hard put to claim that the speed-up of everyday sensation has speeded up. It was in 1909, after all, that F. T. Marinetti proclaimed in *The Futurist Manifesto*, "We declare that the splendor of the world has been enriched by a new beauty: the beauty of speed."

What, then, gives us the impression of a unique speed-up today? Part of the story is that inventions diffuse more rapidly than a century ago, affecting more people faster. My father, born the year Marinetti wrote his paean to speed, did not fly on an airplane until he was in his fifties, while I made my first flight at fifteen (not even a jet flight, at that), and my youngest stepchild when he was one year old. It took sixty-seven years for telephones to reach 75 percent of American households (in 1957); fifty-two years for automobiles (1960), forty-eight years for vacuum cleaners (1951), twenty-three years for refrigerators (1948), with only radio arriving with exceptional speed, fourteen years (1937); whereas it took twelve years for videocassette recorders to reach three-quarters of American households (1992); seven years for televisions (1955), and it is expected to take seven years for the Internet.

But the most visible, consequential speed-up today is not in bodily movement at all. The speed of a jet plane has barely increased in a half century, except for the handful who fly the Concorde. High-end trains have doubled or tripled in speed over that time, and fast cars are faster, but thrilling as these vehicles are, they are mainly for special occasions. No, it is the limitless media torrent that sharpens the sense that all of life is jetting toward—or through—some ultimate speed barrier, that each moment is thick with possibilities, that excitements and energies beyond measure ought to be ours. The most widespread, most consequential speed-up of our time is the onrush of images—the speed at which they zip throughout the world, the speed at which they give way to more of the same, the tempo at which they move. It is on screens that life seems most to accelerate, even as speeding images offer manifold reasons for our bodies to stay still. Images do not weary. They are not retarded by gravity or inertia. They do not have to be transported by heavy machines. That is why the promise of speed, the raging, luminous dream of the Futurists, is nowhere more fully realized than in the media and the culture of switching that surrounds them. Moreover, the impression of media speed-up is magnified by the media themselves, for no one's life experience has accelerated more in recent years than the fast class who produce images for everyone else—the editors, journalists, advertising copywriters, designers, engineers, news producers, and Internet entrepreneurs who are unsurprisingly impressed by all the speeding up, interconnecting, uplinking, and downloading, news of which they excitedly bring to everyone else.

In the course of the twentieth century, images speeded up in a host of ways, as did access to them. On the ever-multiplying screens that populate our lives there is endless motion within the frame where once there was stillness. There is staggeringly rapid movement from one frame to the next, one sequence to the next, one program to the next, and, if you like, one channel or station to the next. From the comfort of your seat, you press a button and watch the instant fill with images or hear it fill with sounds of your choice: your favorite serial, your customized bulletin, your Walkman selection. You can have news topics delivered by e-mail (what has been called "the daily Me") without having to rustle through a newspaper stuffed with what, from a narrow point of view, is dross. With video games, modems, remote controls, picture-in-picture (if you cannot abide the moment between the click of the remote control and the actual changing of channels), you *make things happen*. You master circumstances cheaply and without heavy lifting. Pictures and sentences march by in quick time. At your convenience, the panoply rolls before your eyes. You sit but do not feel stuck. It is hard to arrange your corporeal, marital, occupational, or spiritual life just as you want, to transform your life as rapidly as you like, but you can make images, sounds, texts flex, flow, yield as fast as you please, disconnected but seamless.

THE CULTURE OF WARP SPEED

In 1916, the Futurists heralded "cinematic simultaneity and interpenetration of different times and places," and predicted that "we shall project two or three different visual episodes at the same time, one next to the other." Their noisy utopia is now upon us, though the combination of commercials, promotions, weather and stock updates, sitcoms, "reality" shows, sports reports, and talking heads that radiate through the living room is blander than what the protofascist Futurists had in mind.

Tinsel ages spawn nostalgia for golden ages. Speed—whether of capital flows or imagery—ignites a longing for the good slow days that were presumably left behind in the dust. Intuitively, we feel that everything moves faster today. But impressions aside, how do we really know the torrent is flowing more swiftly? Where is the hard evidence?

Examining relics is useful. Watch the recycled TV shows of a quarter century ago, and you will indeed find them sluggish. A sixty-second commercial seems interminable. Children's shows before *Sesame Street* was launched in 1969 moved at what is to today's eye a tediously languid pace; the difference is so marked, some have speculated that *Sesame Street* all by itself must be responsible for today's reputedly shrinking attention spans. Certainly, it seems unlikely that teaching the alphabet through modules patterned on advertising slogans has made anyone more patient.

Look through any video archive. Pre-MTV rock concert footage seems to sleepwalk. Jump cuts were the preserve of avant-garde cinema, not de rigueur in commercials for spectators younger than thirty. Look back fifty years, and it is hard to resist the impression that the movies were slower, newspaper and magazine articles longer, sentences longer and more complex, advertising text drawn out. TV images appeared one at a time, without hyperspace peel-aways. Series episodes of an earlier era ended with the slow roll of the credits, where today the credits speed by, sharing screen space with a tease, a follow-up joke, an outtake, a promo—the screen split two or three ways—to stall that finger poised on the remote control device. The evening news showed a single picture, if any at all, to the side of an immobile anchorman, where today's anchor, light of foot, glides through a set swirling with clips and graphics.

Many measurements will bear out the sense that the pace of image and text alike have picked up. Compare the qualities and quantities of pictures and words in the movies. To the contemporary eye, commercial films of the 1930s, 1940s, 1950s, and even the careening 1960s are strikingly slow. In many scenes, two characters simply talk while the camera watches, unbudging. Such stationary two-shots are punctuated only by an occasional cutaway for a reaction, a slight pan to follow one character walking away, or, on special occasions, a slow pan toward a close-up. In *Mrs. Miniver*, which won the Academy Award for best picture in 1942, the lead actors, Greer Garson and Walter Pidgeon, play a scene in an English bunker during a German bombardment that goes on with barely a cutaway or camera movement for more than eight minutes—an eternity by today's standards. Mainstream audiences were moved by such scenes.

Today's camera, by contrast, cruises, glides, swoops, circles, inches, zooms, hovers, cranes, and jiggles past and around the fugitive objects of its attention. The foreground—trees, buses, pillars—goes sliding by, heightening the impression of unceasing movement. No matter how static or far-fetched the story, how leaden or cobbled-up the characters, the movie *moves*. During the three-and-one-quarter rusty hours of *Titanic* (1997), the camera is rarely steady for more than a few seconds. If the movie ship takes longer to go under than the actual *Titanic* did, this is because time has to slow to permit Leonardo DiCaprio and Kate Winslet to careen from starboard to stern and back again—and again—and again. The point, as in video games, is to prolong the sweet agony, complicate it with "eye candy," and stave off the inevitable reckoning.

Speed on top of speed: there is the swirling dynamic within a shot, and then the edit between one shot and the next. Montage is as relentless as the camera is restless. Just as silent film spectators learned to interpret montage as simultaneous action, today's spectators have learned to fill in the gaps, so that if, in the 1940s, it was necessary to show a character hailing a taxi at the train station, sitting in its backseat, getting out, beholding the front of an apartment building, getting into the elevator, ringing the doorbell of the apartment, and getting admitted, editors now cut directly from the train station to the interior of the apartment, safely assuming that the spectator will follow the narrative. In the late 1960s, directors of action scenes began to experiment with intensifying montage. In *Bonnie and Clyde* (1967), Arthur Penn deployed several cameras shooting the same murderous scene at different speeds and angles, combining quick cuts with slow motion to pump up a mingled sense of horror and excitement. Freed of censorship, Penn blasted apart the integrity of the body to make a point—what he called "the shock and at the same time the ballet of death."

A movie car-chase sequence of the 1940s, 1950s, or 1960s, as George W. S. Trow has observed, "looks wonderfully realistic and old-fashioned. . . . The car speeds up, and you see a cop car, and he puts on his siren, and you have a little bit of a chase"; whereas Peter Yates's *Bullitt* (1968) featured "the first car-chase, car-ride sequence that went into hyperspace":

> The car rocketed through the streets of San Francisco, up and down hills and past trolley cars. The screenwriters who wanted to be successful in Hollywood, watching *Bullitt*, saw that *Bullitt* was successful because of that car chase. So what if we had three car chases, what if we had four car chases, what if we had ten car chases? It's not that difficult a concept to master. Most people have a will to power that is imitative, and when they see something that works, their imitative mind says, "Well, we'll do that, but we'll do it three times better, or bigger."

This, in turn, led to "an increasing level of hyperactivity in car chases, down to *Speed* (1997)," where (perhaps half jokingly) even so lumbering a vehicle as a bus is prevented from slowing down.

Trow grasps the self-feeding dynamic of the media frenzy, the combination of competition, challenge, thrill, and pride in craft that drives hyperactivity forward in the movies, on television, in video games, and in virtual-reality simulators: "a sort of hyperactive quality, a kind of unreal, speeded-up violence, which has to do as much with the aesthetic of the people making the product as it has to do with the specific action." As Trow points out, "one wants this kind of hyperactive quality of click, click, click, click, click to hold . . . [the audience's] shallow attention, and the easiest way to do that is violence and the car chase." (Attention-getting dialogue requires a rare talent.) Welcome to *Star Wars* (1977), with its spaceship chases and vertiginous plunges. Welcome to digital editing, images shrinking into hyperspatial planes that peel up and away, the financial screen with its streaming tickers and multiple sectors, the animated Internet ad, the moving galactic Netscape logo, signaling that *something is happening* while we wait. Whoosh!

In a world where video games outgross movies, on-screen speed makes entertainment careers. Commercials and video games are now career training grounds for movie directors. No wonder movie edits frequently work not to speed up linear consciousness but to assail it. Narrative is nothing but pretext. In action movies, chase follows chase, one vehicle after another: cars, sports utility vehicles, trucks, buses, trains, planes, helicopters, hovercrafts, ski lifts, tanks, you name it. The point is to shake, rattle, and roll us, to keep us breathless, to delight, dragoon, and rollercoaster us into an eager suspension of disbelief. To say that the resulting plot "makes no sense" misses the point, since the goal is usually to make only enough sense to permit the senses to take over.

I do not wish to exalt the static or stately as such. Slowness can produce excellence or mediocrity. So can speed. Superior action movies—*Speed, The Matrix*—reach toward the kinetic sublime. Some of the Hong Kong action pictures directed by John Woo and Wong Kar-Wai are thrilling. Swooping around the action, the camera plunges the willing viewer into a sort of rapture. The chase exhilarates as freedom tempts fate and tests limits. The speed aesthetic can cut the spirit loose from the gravity of ordinary preoccupations. The violence that punctuates these movies, despite all the worried critics, is least important as a spur to copycat crimes; it matters far more as a drug. The rat-a-tat-tat of the editing rhymes with the violence of the action—these are two ways to rage against stasis. As cigarettes are instruments to deliver nicotine, action movies are instruments to deliver adrenaline—whiffs of the ineffable. No wonder they are rated and reviewed for their kinetic efficacy, as if they were pharmaceuticals.

Explosions, crashes, and conflagrations ignite more than one kind of pleasure. There is potency. Man uses machine to destroy machine—here lies an anarchic mastery. There is the joy of beholding the destruction of things in an overstuffed age. Conspicuous violence against property amounts to a demolition derby for material plenty. Most of all, violence pumps up the viewers. Censorious moralists who muster more energy for crusading against violent images than against guns themselves are missing the point. Violence in the movies offers a magical way out of the inertia and perplexity of everyday life—even if one that leads nowhere except the theater lobby.

In a calculating society, people want *safe* thrills, which is why most of the young go to the movies in the first place, desiring the unexpected satisfactions that will, for a while, satisfy their predictable expectations. An audience inured to speed awaits ever more and different thrusts and collisions. Once a technique is inexpensive, it becomes common enough to be expected. Whip-pans, rapid zooms, helicopter and crane shots, vertiginous camera swoops, once unusual, are now normal. The Steadicam, invented by a cameraman and first used in a feature film in 1976, made perpetual motion cheap. A moving camera could now follow the action for several minutes, through narrow corridors, without jitters, and without the expense of laying track—a technique that has slipped from movies to commercials and then to TV shows, becoming part of everyday experience.

In the days when the camera mainly stood still and the scene stayed put, velocity was confined to one aspect at a time: horses or dialogue. In Westerns, the action movies of their time, drama hinged on horseback chases and gunfights. A lumbering style of speech reigned, muscular, terse, and functional, expressing plot and character. Strong silent men spoke with their six-shooters. But in drama and comedy—Easterns, we might say—actors snapped out their lines like New Yorkers while no one went anywhere to speak of and, dance numbers aside, nothing much moved. Standard speech was in the "smart" style, knowing and nervous, inflected in mid-Atlantic tones familiar from New York theater and radio.

In Frank Capra's slaphappy *It Happened One Night* (1934), the first film to sweep the Academy Awards, Claudette Colbert and Clark Gable delivered their lines at the rate of roughly two words per second. Torrents of language poured out of the screen in the screwball comedies that followed, pleasing reviewers, audiences, and members of the Academy of Motion Picture Arts and Sciences alike. For Capra, this was a deliberate choice. He put it this way:

> I like to speed up the pace of my films. The pace of my films is much faster than normal, because I think things slow down on a large screen. I don't know if stimuli affect people more quickly because a thousand pairs of eyes and ears are perceiving something simultaneously, or if those thousand pairs of eyes and ears simply accept stimuli faster than we think. But I do know that a person in a crowd reacts faster to images than a single person would. I know that you have to speed film up to make it look natural to a thousand people.

Visual speed in Capra's day was, by present standards, unhurried, but the dialogue ripped along.

In the old talky movies, impressive characters showed a command of wit, and wit often required more than stand-alone wisecracks. It required extended cascades of talk delivered at high speed. In *The Thin Man* (1934), *The Philadelphia Story* (1940), *His Girl Friday* (1940), and the like, the unit of repartee was an entire dialogue spoken right up to the edge of audience comprehension. In the 1930s, even the otherwise laconic James Stewart and the laid-back Ronald Reagan spoke at a motorized pace. If one line was a dud, never mind; the dialogue's momentum carried the audience along. Rarely did a single line wag an entire scene. By contrast, contemporary comedy has been so deeply affected by sitcom and stand-up that the one-liners are freestanding. Slice any gag out of the whole and splice it elsewhere into the sequence, and it will work as well.

Today's sensibility ranks images far above words—but even the nature of the pictures can be misunderstood. Advertising images, streaming screen savers, music videos, and video games are made up of pictures that "work" insofar as they are instantly recognizable, but whose overall effect comes from the fact that they rub against one another pell-mell in a simulation of motion. Toward that end, each image is prestereotyped—designed as a tableau, a cartoon, so that without much effort the ensemble can be taken in at a glance and arouse the prescribed sensation. A sequence of images bursts like so many firecrackers, but the bits, taken one at a time, have little to offer. Pictorially, they often lack interest. In other words, the pleasure of beholding these freestanding images speeding by is not strictly visual but amounts to a different sort of pleasure, the kind Mark Crispin Miller calls "subvisual"—visceral pleasure at the disorientation that results from a sequence of bursts, pleasure at immersion in a wild procession of fragments, the sort of pleasure that, extrapolated from moving pictures to the other arts, has come to be called "postmodern." The montage is the message, and the message is that the torrent *feels good*.

In action movies, words have been downgraded, of course. They erupt from collages of action, as if they were emanations of physical movements. As the astronomical successes of Steven Spielberg, George Lucas, and James Cameron productions demonstrate, box-office success requires no facility with dialogue. The opposite is assumed: accomplished language is, if anything, an impediment. The less distracting the language, the more exportable the product. Non-English-speaking audiences, now expected to deliver a large chunk of box-office revenues, will not be troubled by clichés or grunts—or so it is believed. Given the high offshore returns even from action movies like *Waterworld* (1995) that bomb in the United States, the least-common-vocabulary position is plausible. Commercial directors who refuse to sacrifice speech to sight do not generally make blockbusters. Even directors who know the difference between clichés and quality dialogue play a zero-sum game, thinking they have to choose between visuals and language. The eyes get dazzling special effects. What the ears get is not remarkable language but elaborate sound-mixing, Dolby and THX systems, the better to relay the thud of fist against flesh, the crash of waves, the roar of tyrannosaurus around the auditorium.

Indeed, movies and video games have melted together. In today's multiplex arcades, they may even pound at you under the same roof, so that you can fill time waiting for the movie to start by racing down a freeway, through space, or over white water, or by blasting the skin off the faces of aliens, all the while rumbling to the percussion of bass notes. Video game connoisseur J. C. Herz writes:

> Arcade games may be increasingly cinematic, but it's the cinema of Hong Kong. In a kung fu flick, it's not important why two characters are poised on a particular roof ledge or who's supposed to be avenged. You just want to see them fly through the air. They could recite the Hong Kong phone book and it would hardly detract from the martial arts movie experience. . . . In fact, if the ever-shrinking script of a modern action movie shriveled to its logical extreme (a one-page memo outlining pyrotechnics and facial tics) it would be a pretty decent videogame. No flashbacks. No zippered story lines. Just explosions and fight scenes episodically arrayed like firecrackers on the Fourth of July.

Or consider typography, where the aesthetic of the blur has come into fashion. Following trends in photography and video (stop-framing, stutter-motion, and out-of-focus shots), many younger magazine and logo designers forswear legibility and linearity in behalf of fuzz and foam, a visual representation of the torrent. The visual style introduced by the French Impressionists in the 1870s, to convey the instant of motion, the instant *in* motion, recorded as if the artist's hand were in motion, has now reached typography, the

representation of language itself. Sleekness, simplicity, and recogniz-
ability, the hallmarks of influential logo designer Paul Rand (IBM,
Westinghouse, United Parcel Service, from the mid-1950s through
the mid-1960s), are no longer universally admired. A clutter of
simultaneity burst onto the magazine scene in the 1980s and 1990s,
as commentaries trickled down the margins of the pages in London's
The Face and San Francisco's *Wired*. Soon Michael Bloomberg was
splitting his financial news screen into multiple moving tapes, charts,
statistics, and talking heads. Here, at least, each visual unit was meant
to be decipherable. Not so in the work of trendy designer David
Carson, who began his career producing a surfer magazine, *Raygun*,
that prided itself on illegibility, but soon found his style of blur,
superimposition, and clutter in demand by mainstream companies.
At the 1997 convention of the American Institute of Graphic Artists,
Carson's afternoon workshop, titled "The End of Print," attracted
more than a thousand aspiring designers. They had seen the future
and couldn't read it, but knew they liked it.

The breathless, torrential style seized television news and comment, too. The term *sound bite* made the transition from backstage
professional jargon to the public lexicon because sound bites became
standard practice—most consequentially in the filmic quotations performed by Ronald Reagan ("I paid for this microphone," "Make my
day") and the Clint Eastwood adaptation of his weak understudy,
George H. W. Bush ("Read my lips: No new taxes"). According to
a widely cited 1989 study by Kiku Adatto, the average weekday
network news sound bite from a presidential candidate shrank from
42.3 seconds in 1968 to 9.8 seconds in 1988 (with only 1 percent
of the bites lasting as long as 40 seconds that year). By 2000, the
average was 7.8 seconds. Almost 75 percent of news talk time was
now taken up by journalists, compared to 11 percent for the candidates. Journalists today tuck sound bites by public officials into
their own sentences, preceding and following the snippet quotes
with voice-overs.

The style of commercials and sound bites infected all kinds of TV and radio talk. In 1981, in a sort of digitization of discourse, the *McLaughlin Group* sped up the pace of pundit gabfests, making glibness, quickness, loudness, and rudeness routes to pundit fortunes. Talk was now to be percussion. Whenever the pace slowed, the blowhard host John McLaughlin would shout, "Let's get out of it"— this according to Group alumnus and imitator Chris Matthews, whose *Hardball* on CNBC pushed the form to virtuoso pugnacity. "To his credit," Matthews has said, "John knew that speed was the missing element in public affairs television." Speed and aggression, actually—a combination mobilized on radio by the aptly named Rush Limbaugh.

As always, there are brisk precedents for this rhetorical speed-up. Interestingly, the high-minded have not always deplored rhetorical condensation, realizing that slow exchanges of extended sentences, replete with subordinate clauses, are not necessarily the soul of either wit or sense. In 1824, Thomas Jefferson declared, "Amplification is the vice of modern oratory. It is an insult to an assembly of reasonable men, disgusting and revolting instead of persuading." Abraham Lincoln's Gettysburg Address numbers a mere 266 words. In 1924, the *Milwaukee Journal* editorialized: "In the long run the country is governed by the people who pay attention to what candidates say; whatever makes them speak less and more to the point will improve government." "The only thing we have to fear is fear itself" is not the most elaborate of sentences—though, like the luminous compressions of the King James Bible ("The race is not to the swift"), it has rhetorical virtues lacking in Ronald Reagan's "Government is not the solution, government is the problem" and Bill Clinton's "The era of big government is over." So a speed-up is not an automatic defeat for good prose or vivid rhetoric. Nor are simple, brief declarations inimical to democratic debate, at least as long as they come supplemented with arguments that engage contrary arguments. These supplements today are in short supply, pundits being more likely to comment on the manner of the sound bite (is it too inside-the-Beltway?) than its matter (is it true?).

In the land of article and book condensations, speed reading, easy listening, and CliffsNotes (the official name, for branding today abhors the space between words), where plot summary is a standard feature of fiction reviews, where magazines feature pull quotes and "executive summaries" head up reports, it will come as little surprise that popular fiction has also accelerated. To see what has changed in prose style in the course of the twentieth century, it will not do to declare with a flourish that Stephen King is no Edith Wharton. But what might be learned if we compare popular reading taste in the present with popular reading taste in the past—and not by seat-of-the-pants assessment but by counting?

A look at the top ten best-selling novels according to *New York Times* lists from the first week of October (chosen arbitrarily) in 1936, 1956, 1976, 1996, and 2001 reveals some significant shifts in what it takes to be popular. (Since four of the ten from 1936 were impossible to locate—such is the perishability of the popular—the total sample consisted of forty-six books.) It is, on the face of it, extraordinary that in 1956, Simone de Beauvoir's lengthy, sophisticated *The Mandarins* was ranked at number 4 (for the fourth week in a row) and Yukio Mishima's *The Sound of Waves* showed up at number 13. But this could well be accidental; there have been weeks in recent years when books by Saul Bellow and Philip Roth were simultaneously on the best-seller list. More systematic measures, however, tell a similar story. Taking four sentences from each book, the first ones that begin on pages 1, 50, 100, and 150 (or 120 in the case of the two books that don't reach page 150), my research assistant Marco Calavita; my wife, Laurel Cook; and I counted the number of words per sentence. We also counted the number of punctuation marks excluding the periods, with a set of ellipses or pair of parentheses counted as a single punctuation mark. (This we took as a crude measure of the complexity of sentence structure.)

Finally, we looked to see whether the sentence was dialogue, wondering whether popular novels today more closely approximate screenplays.

The findings:

	Sentence length (average number of words)	Punctuation marks (average number per sentence)	Dialogue (as percentage of all sentences)
1936	22.8	2.2	25%
1956	17.8	1.5	28
1976	13.6	0.9	33
1996	16.6	1.0	35
2001	13.1	1.5	25

Between 1936 and 2001, sentence length declined by 43 percent, and the number of punctuation marks by 32 percent. Were it not for one intricate sentence in Garrison Keillor's *Lake Wobegon: Summer 1956*, the 2001 average for punctuation marks would have fallen to 1.2 and the decline from 1936 would have been 45 percent. With respect to all three variables, dramatic changes took place between 1936 and 1976, followed by some bounceback. The use of dialogue grew steadily until 1996 before falling back in 2001.

The sentence brevity record is held by Tom Clancy for *Executive Orders* (1996), with a total of 23 words spread out over four sentences. ("It had to be the shock of the moment, Ryan thought." "Its symbolism was clear." "Mark Curling was whimpering now." "Not everyone did.") In 2001, Sandra Brown's *Envy*, with a total of 26 words, was a close runner-up. The longest opening line, 50 words, comes from Francis Brett Young's *Far Forest* (1936), which begins: "Jenny Hadley was born and reared—or dragged up, as they say in those parts—at Mawne Heath on the Staffordshire side of the River Stour which at this point divides it from Worcestershire: a heath only by courtesy, and a blasted heath at that if ever there was one." The first sentence beginning on page 100, which I shall spare the reader, numbers 103 words. In 1936, it was possible for a book to be a best-seller while including a sentence of 103 words.

One doesn't want to make too much of such results. The sample is small. It's possible that these five weeks were aberrational; or that the four missing books of 1936 would make a substantial difference in the averages for that year; or that 1946, 1966, and 1986, or a comprehensive rundown of every year as far back as records go, would produce different results. Possible but also unlikely. The changes between 1956 and 2001, where we have access to all thirty books, run toward shorter and simpler. Given the numbers we have, the striking thing is the unidirectional shift between 1936 and 1976. To put it in streamlined fashion, best-seller sentences have gotten briefer, simpler, and (until 2001) closer to screenplays.

As with political rhetoric, skeptics may object that shorter and simpler are not necessarily shallower. Streamlining, as Italian designers know, can make for elegance. "In the beginning God created the heavens and the earth" clocks in at a mere ten words, fewer than the bottom-scraping average for our best-sellers of 1976, and a more rounded and sonorous ten words are hard to imagine. Still, the sentences in our sample lack the compensating virtue of poetry. Anyone who knew the author of Genesis would have to concede that Tom Clancy is not Him, or Her.

The span between 1936 and 1976 is, of course, the span that includes the arrival of television as the center of national culture. It should come as no surprise that popular novels now read more like scripts. This period includes the ascendancy of Ernest Hemingway, himself influenced by the punchy, direct style of popular newspapers in his youth—though the trend has outlasted him, replenished by the influential fiction of Raymond Carver. There is likely both a supply- and a demand-side to sentence compression. Writers aspiring to write popular fiction are writing more simply; while hurried, harried, or lazy readers looking for accessible work are reading more simply. The upshot is that popular fiction has gotten stripped down and now looks more like television. It goes down easier and makes fewer demands. As for the modest bounceback in number of punctuation marks between 1976 and 2001, possibly some law of literary compensation is at work, with oversimplification generating a countertrend, the way fat-free pasta, say, might produce a taste for zabaglione at the end of the meal.

But what good are such numbers? Hard numbers have a pleasing firmness, but they are easier counted than interpreted. Serious methodological objections to these modest exercises in hard social science might well be registered. Book sales, contrary to common lore, have actually grown per capita since 1936. In 1936, a best-seller cost $2 to $3, comparable to today's prices in constant dollars. Sales figures are notoriously hard to unearth—and publishers are known to inflate them—but it stands to reason that the population interested in purchasing hardcover books (as opposed to borrowing them from the library) was far more restricted in 1936 than in 1976 or 2001. We can't know the average reading level of best-seller readers, but we can reasonably guess that today's best-sellers, being much cheaper (in relation to average income), attract many readers far less educated than in 1936, in which case the simplification of sentences might be a function of the changing readership base, not of the shrinking attention of readers at the same educational level.

Is there any way to address such objections? Suppose we look at equivalent trends in other venues of writing. Is the trend in best-selling novels unique? Inspecting popular magazines, we do indeed find a similar trend. My research assistant Jennifer Kelley looked at two magazines published continuously over the last century, the *New York Times Magazine* and *National Geographic*. Articles printed in the former's first Sunday of October issue and the latter's October issue yield the following average word lengths and punctuation counts:

	Times Magazine		*National Geographic*	
	Sentence length	Punctuation marks	Sentence length	Punctuation marks
1896	26.5	1.3	NA	NA
1906	26.9	2.4	30.3	3.4
1916	25.3	2.0	26.0	2.7
1926	32.1	2.2	31.6	2.8
1936	18.4	1.7	25.1	1.3
1946	28.3	1.3	28.9	2.2
1956	29.9	2.4	18.8	1.3
1966	23.0	1.4	27.3	2.4
1976	21.4	1.3	23.1	2.3
1986	22.6	2.0	17.8	1.1
1996	20.0	1.2	18.4	1.4

In these two middle-class magazines, then, a rough downtrend in sentence length and complexity is detectable starting in 1956 and 1966, respectively.

Linguist Geoffrey Nunberg has wondered whether sentence length might have decreased across other genres. He and his colleague Brett Kessler took it upon themselves to look at two publications published continuously since the nineteenth century: the *New York Times* (since 1856) and *Science* magazine (since 1896). Their findings: In the *New York Times*, sentence length "hovered around the historical mean [32.2 words] in 1856, 1876, 1896; then rose by 1916; after 1936 fell to a profound low by 1956; then rose again by 1976." By 1996, it was back over the mean, at 34.7 words. *Times* readers were, or were assumed by the editors to be, growing more patient and attentive during the forty years after 1956—precisely the years when television was diffusing through American life. Yet in *Science*, whose readers must overlap with the *Times*'s, sentence length was at a high in 1896 and 1916; fell by 1936; then fell again between

1956 and 1976. If we assume that the educational level of readers of *Science* remained relatively steady—an assumption more plausible than the assumption that the educational level of best-seller readers remained relatively steady—the tendency for *Science* matches that for best-sellers. "I wouldn't describe this as a dumbdown," Nunberg writes, "or at least *Science* hasn't become an easier read over the past century." Fair enough.

In the *Times*, at any rate, there is a countercurrent to the speed-up in novels and magazines. Not everything streamlines.

HASTE MAKES FUN

The onrush of the media torrent—the speed of its images on the screen, its sentences on the page, and its talk over the air, as well as the quickness with which images move through space and the velocity of its product cycles—all these speeds depend on an overall social speed-up and are but its most visible features. A fast society produces fast people who, in all these senses, produce a fast culture. The question is, what drives the machine?

Isn't speed rational? It is natural to assume so. We are accustomed to a more or less Darwinian explanation of its economic advantages. Capitalist organizations are in the business of changeover because the environment changes and they must adapt, and because they scramble with rivals. Peasants compete for markets. Nation-states compete for wealth. Corporations compete for customers. Universities compete for students. All follow trends, trends consisting of evidently successful strategies pursued by competitors. Permanence is a drag, toast, so over—or, to use a term that is derogatory only in the United States, *history*. When novelty pays, institutions have rational grounds to search for faster techniques, to access information faster than their competitors, to devise fresh products. Aren't the fast more than the slow likely to win the great games to which we apply ourselves? From this point of view, we have a speedy society because it's rational to be speedy—to develop novelties and get them to market first. To offer a better mousetrap is perhaps not so important as to offer the *first* mousetrap, assuming that you can offer it all around town and at a sensible price.

But speed is not always rational. Speed can, in fact, backfire. If Company A is too quick to market with a new technology, it may lose out to Company B, which took its time developing a rival method—or appropriating the best of its rival's method, as Microsoft's Windows did vis-à-vis Apple. Sony was the first to develop and market a home videocassette recorder, and many aficionados believe that its Betamax technology produced clearer pictures than the rival VHS system. But VHS, with its longer playback capacity, prevailed, and Betamax remains a technology for specialists. The earliest manufacturers of home computers, Altair, Osborne, Morrow, and others, were outdone by those that were slower to market with more advanced systems. For a business, as for a nation, there is such a thing as the *dis*advantage of going first. The culture of speed is before all else a market culture—a culture in which the prime reason to manufacture things is that they will (or so the producers believe) sell. But *will* they sell? Much of what is produced, no matter how speedily, flops. So it is more accurate to say that in a market culture, people do things because they *believe* that they will sell.

Can't it be said, then, that *on average*, speed can be counted upon to deliver practical, material, calculable advantages? Surely the search for productivity motivated massive corporate investment in computerization in the 1980s. Still, for years, economists debated whether computerization actually made for productivity gains. The Nobel economics laureate Robert M. Solow quipped in 1987, "You can see the computer age everywhere but in the productivity statistics." Today, even many economists who were previously skeptical accept the claim that computerization brought productivity gains. Solow himself in 2000 amended his previous doubt: "You can now see computers in the productivity statistics." The interesting thing, however, is that the argument for productivity increases was put forward for many years before the boom time of 1995–99, when the payoff wasn't measurable. In other words, when corporations made their massive investments, they had no assurances they would pay off. They acted on conventional wisdom or ideology—in short, on faith.

But there is another reason to doubt that utilitarianism explains all or even most of our culture's disposition toward speed. When we perform an action, we do not necessarily know what the results will be. In the world of the fast class (whom I am calling "we"), we speed even when it's not rational. On the road, we court danger. We invest in speedy improvements even when we were content with the previous models (at least until the new models were launched). Clearly, speed has more than dollar value. The dirty little secret is that ours is a civilization that revels in the pure experience of speed. We share a yearning for the kinetic sublime. Excepting the phobic among us, we revel in sensations of bodily speed: the sound of engines revving, the feeling of forward movement, the look of the earth passing beneath the wheels, the sensations of the wind through our hair, the blast of air—or at least air-conditioning—against our skin. Upscale people jog, and working-class people throng to NASCAR races. This is—hush!—fun.

The joy of speed drives the interactivity sector of the media torrent, too. Of course, there are competitive, utilitarian motives for the Internet mania—moving capital into and out of markets, buying and selling goods and services, making deals, collecting usable information, and so on. Efficiency may turn out to be a result of all the clicking of keys and punching of numbers. Surely companies boost their efficiency when their data are entered by overstressed offshore assembly-line workers. Speed is the workers' enemy. In the poor countries, where electronic data entry has been relocating since American Airlines moved a ticket processing center to Barbados in 1981, the work is especially grueling. The proprietors of Internet servers can count their employees' keystrokes per minute. These low-end workers lack the luxury of interactive distraction. But higher-end employees often enjoy a daily electronic experience that transcends—may even substitute for—calculation. What is incalculable is the emotion attached to the experience of a certain instantaneous efficiency, the fun of connection via Internet, cell phones, and the rest, the joy of making things happen *now*, the tiny, disposable, real thrill of getting a rise out of the world with your fingertips. Whatever the eventual economic outcome, you have your reward. You are wired, plugged in; you click, you transmit, you retrieve, you download—therefore you are.

Moreover, the Internet offers speed and distraction galore in addition to (or at times instead of) any promise of institutional efficiency. Chat with your buddies. Check sports scores. Gamble. See women and men cavort in interesting postures. Circulate jokes. Sign petitions. Otherwise divert yourself from the rigors of business life. At the upper end of the workforce, in the world of freelance professionals, outsourcers, ubiquitous consultants, all others who tickle their keyboards on contract, easy distraction is as close as the keyboard. According to one study, 43 million American workers access the Internet at work—many to shop. Of course, in the end, distraction may be just what they need to work more keenly—and longer hours.

But whatever the eventual efficiency costs (or benefits) of playful distraction, corporations certainly believe their employees to be making unseemly use of the new gadgetry—whence surveillance and the threat of it. Managers can easily count employee minutes spent rummaging among sites where employment would not spur one to rummage. Surveillance programs can count obscene words, risqué pictures, trade secrets, whatever. The office computer is legally fair game for on-site inspection, too, as the dean of Harvard Divinity

School discovered in 1999. Once pornographic images were found on his university-owned computer, he resigned in disgrace.

No doubt, when managers invest in speed via computerization and electronic networks, they think they are acting rationally. In fact, they are acting culturally. Reason has its limits. They gamble. They *like* speed. Who would want to go before a board of directors and defend a decision—*any* decision—to slow down? Their technical people *love* speed. It is, for them, a devotional exercise. In their own lives, they adore being *on*. They are *pumped*. Speed's visceral aspect is crucial. You want to cut loose from onerous calculation, to rip away from the sticky stuff of reason. Speed gives speeders a rush. It cannot be accidental that *rush* is vernacular for the burst of acceleration you experience on drugs, not least on methamphetamines, commonly known as *speed*. Surely it is no accident that as drugs spread into the middle class, the fast lane came to be prized, while activities that were not enjoyable, or speedy, came to be called a *drag*—in other words, a resistance to speed, a brake.

If speed is an easy way to live, then pixels and digital data are the easiest ways to speed. Though chemical boosters are still very much in use, today's fast lane is largely licit, the torrent-soaked way of life available instantly to the professional, metropolitan, commercial classes, via laptop computers, cell phones, handheld organizers, Walkmen, pocket TVs, and the rest of our portable instruments. Educated fast-laners carry their—our—connections on their laps, clipped to belts, clutched in hands, to mountain and shore, on train and plane, detached from any fixed place, or rather, converting every fixed place, each automobile, sidewalk, theater, church, into *our* place, usable for our convenience and that of our networks; that is, into nowhere-in-particular, a noplace where we are equally accessible and in that sense equally detached. Rushing from node to node of the media torrent, in a strange town, a motel room, on the road, we are never *away*. Or rather, here *is* away. Strange as it is, the torrent becomes our home.

If time is God's way of keeping everything from happening at once, then multitasking is the antidote. Simultaneity is the goal, multitasking the means, and a *segue*—another commonplace term—the next best thing. Open envelopes while on the phone, read e-mail while on hold for "customer service," play a video game while watching a soap opera—the reader is familiar with these attempts to stretch time, to turn sequence into near-simultaneity. Bored with channel 46, switch to channel 47. We multitask because we are busy, and we are busy because we cannot multitask fast enough. No matter how many calendars we keep, how many task lists we make, how fast we clear our literal or figurative desktops, how upgraded our central processing units and modems, how many channels we get, how many Napster downloads we perform—or perhaps precisely because we have all these calendars, lists, desktops, channels, and downloads—we cannot, cannot possibly keep up.

THE DIALECTIC OF SPEED AND SLOWNESS

But the United States is not all of a piece, everyone equally speedy, equally frantic. The fast and the slow coexist. The static picture of uniform speed is painted by a class of speed freaks—journalists who rush the news, pundits who frame its significance, and marketers who wrap goods in it, almost all of whom live in the fast lane themselves, socialize with others who live (or wish to live) in the fast lane, report on and read about those who live (or wish to live) in the fast lane, and write about those whose business is to cater to and nudge still others into that same fast lane. Many of these speed freaks are driven by the fear that they may end up the roadkill of a hyperkinetic society.

　　With wind-tunnel vision, our chroniclers of the rush of everyday life commonly lose sight of one essential thing about the culture of speed. Harnessed to the love of speed is its contrary: resistance to speed. Speed is relational—relative to speed in the past and others' speed in the present. If, as stock market folklore has it, "The market climbs a wall of worry," then speed climbs a wall of slowness. Within a capitalist economy, the desire for speed is powered by a market imperative to overcome resistance to speed. For consumer demand to grow, increasing numbers of slow people must be brought up to speed, else they will not process the data the information machine requires, else telephones, answering machines, computers, Internet access will not be bought. What drives modern civilization is not speed by itself but the dialectic of speed and slowness.

To put it another way: a culture of speed rubs up against a culture of slowness and conquers what it can. The subsociety of the fast is the engine that pulls the whole. One of the pleasures of speed is to leave the slow behind—*eat my dust*. In the last half century, an era of vast disposable income and voluminous marketing, the consumer goods industry has recruited generation after generation of allies among each wave of children by pitting them against the style and pace of sluggish adults.

Yet no society can long thrive on the breakneck extension of a single principle and the suppression of all others. Sooner or later, rectifications spring up. Speed brings relative sluggishness in its wake. It is also counterbalanced by routine, a slowing and channeling of human initiative. So the assembly-line production of culture has the surprising consequence of accentuating at once American restlessness and formulaic predictability. In streamlining and typecasting, speed and stasis meet.

Like many facts of popular culture, this one is best observed from outside. Having watched Armed Forces Network Television as a boy in postwar Germany, Professor Berndt Ostendorf of the University of Munich has observed how its commercial origins, its formulaic storytelling, and its stereotypical characters all fit together. To make spaces for commercial breaks, and keep viewers' attention, production companies divided programs into short units—*acts*, producers still call them, hanging on to the theatrical precedent, even if they are but a few minutes long. Viewers, disposed to be fidgety, came to expect these breaks. Now, Ostendorf writes, the plot, with its traditional unities of time, place, and action, "is chopped up into short sequential bursts, each with their own simulacrum of a micro-plot. . . . The goal is to create an unending series of reversals, moments of ecstasy and anticipation, which then may be usurped by the commercial." Interruption was thus built into the program. Not surprisingly, in the era of television, the term *attention span* began to be heard—and worried about. Shortening attention spans led to an emphasis on formula.

To keep a fidgety audience in place, characters had to be rapidly recognizable. Since a mass audience is diverse, there had to be a variety of predictable types. In Ostendorf's words:

> This serialization of micro-plots favors roles and characters with direct audience appeal. Hence there is at least one character in each sit-com with whom any section of the audience may identify. Therefore a noticeable typecasting prevails in series such as *Bonanza*, the *Bill Cosby Show* or *General Hospital*. . . . Instant dramatic effects that will entertain are more important than dramaturgical considerations of sentiment or character development. The chain of motivation is often interrupted by the logic of sensation. The overall consequence leads to a dramatization of effect and the foregrounding of character types.

A fast society grumbles about speed, and selectively cultivates some deliberate slowness. From the speediest society under the sun, the United States, came one of the slowest sports, baseball. For go-getters, the slowness industry includes golf, sailing, and hiking; for women mainly, cooking and gardening. In the age of MTV, soap operas still move at the pace of drying paint. (Observing my seventeen-year-old stepson clicking from his basketball video game to MTV to a soap opera, where he landed only now and then, I asked him how it felt. "Perfect," he said, "no danger of missing anything.") Next to the fast lane runs the slow lane, and next to the slow lane the breakdown lane. While our professional and managerial classes are commuting, multitasking, ad-scanning, channel-grazing, Web-surfing, call-waiting, cell-phoning, chat-grouping, desktop-organizing, remote-controlling, picture-in-picturing, gambling, and day-trading, they are also complaining about their hectic lives and plotting their retreats to the country. Secretly proud of their velocity, many of them also think there is something demented about their pace. They boast of a week in the country without e-mail or the bold weekend when they leave the answering machine unplugged. They made Juliet Schor's *Overworked American* a best-seller. The men often say they would like to spend more time at home with their kids. (Some working women, beset by conflict at home, actually prefer working longer hours. The corporate environment may now offer some satisfactions more reliably than home.) They practice tai chi as well as the treadmill—a sort of biathlon of modern pacing. They seek time out for golf, fishing, and yoga. Travelers to Italy are pleased to discover restaurants that proudly advertise "slow food." Storefronts offering ten-minute back rubs flourish in frantic city centers, malls, and airports. Tape and CD players and new car radios come with a pause button. Some people use a Walkman to slow themselves down, to repossess their sense of time. Enough people enjoy "easy listening" and New Age music to sustain those market niches amid the more raucous alternatives.

Overall, men seem to want speed more than women do. Men are more partial to action movies, women to soap operas, prizing them partly because they creep along so viscously, they seem to slow down the world. (The fact that "nothing happens" is part of what makes them attractive—they do not demand rapt attention, and leave the viewer free to attend to household tasks.) Men, more likely to graze, have itchier fingers on the remote control clicker, though the differences seem smaller among the young. Men tend to surf—or hunt—the Internet; women, to stick to a small number of sites, gathering useful information.

Contrary tendencies are even built into the visual culture of warp speed. Televised sports undergo their own forms of slow-down, compensating for the speed-up of the action and its entourage of surrounding commercials. The twenty-four-second clock in professional basketball sped up the game, but multiple time-outs (many imposed by networks to squeeze in more commercials) now turn the closing seconds of basketball games into endless events. In baseball, it is normal now for half a dozen pitchers or more to come into a game, each requiring time for a trot from the bullpen and then for a warm-up, each stepping off the mound after each pitch as each batter steps out of the batter's box, looks for signs, and performs mysterious rituals. Baseball's longueurs are so drawn out that the double-headers of the past are almost inconceivable. The sports seasons themselves are so drawn out that they overlap, and the playoffs seem to last almost as long as the regulation seasons themselves.

In movies, the era of the almost-subliminal cut and the hyperkinetic rush is also the era of the pause (the stop-frame) and the prolongation (slow motion). Slo-mo has become a standard feature of action sequences, stretching the moment, allowing you to admire the details—in sports, the elegance of the block that takes out the linebackers; in the movies, the bullet entering the skull, the car hurtling through the plate-glass window, the helicopter exploding in flames—all of which natural speed would otherwise force you to miss. Slo-mo prolongs suffering, permitting that ur-slo-mo film *Bonnie and Clyde*, as Pauline Kael beautifully wrote, to "put the sting back in death." It makes action look simultaneously more fateful and less inevitable—perhaps the tailback will elude the interception! Jack

Ruby will miss Lee Harvey Oswald! Critic Mark Kingwell nicely observes another strange juxtaposition of slowness and speed:

> Action movies get faster, and more kinetic, all the time—a sharp acceleration of retinal-nerve stimulation from the wide-screen scenes of old epics like *Spartacus*. But some movies are now, Titanically, longer than ever; and John Woo, perhaps the best action-film director alive, has a fondness for extended slow-motion sequences, protracted exercises in the instant mythologization of anti-speed, that rival, in sheer unreality, the massed, from-every-angle replays of a televised professional football game.

With a productivity boost from the computer, popular books like Tom Clancy's thrillers bulk up, as if telling the reader: *On this long flight or this week's vacation, you are permitted to slow down.*

Fast people, in other words, are aware that they pay a price for speed, that after a certain point they sacrifice not only the very efficiency that was its purpose but also the physical gratification that is its by-product. Few live by speed alone. Some slowdowns of recent years descend from the counterculture of the 1960s and 1970s. "Slow down, you move too fast/You got to make the morning last," as Simon and Garfunkel sang in those years. Panicky moralists lost sight of the fact that marijuana—unlike alcohol—generally had the effect of *slowing things down*. Even suburbanites wanted to be *laid-back*. Aging boomers nap, and businesses look into the merits of furnishing employees with cots. Fast-laners need *downtime*. Slowness keeps up its fitful resistance in surprising forms. One must wonder whether it is purely coincidental that even as the rampant diagnosis of attention deficit disorder hits children, the psychiatric label du jour among young (and older) adults is *depression*, and that depression is the negation of speed, a state of mind in which the world seems to have ground to a halt.

Against the onslaught of hectic modernity, many a literary figure throughout the centuries has counseled the contemplative life and hoped to find for it a safe harbor in the gathering speed of the world. The partisans of slowness are always sure that the world is going to the fastest dogs, and feel called upon to denounce the impoverished quality of overhasty writing and reading. The specter of the death of reading is a hardy perennial. Samuel Taylor Coleridge in 1810 feared that " 'reading made easy' . . . would give men an aversion to words of more than two syllables, instead of drawing them through those words into the power of reading books in general." Eighty years later, the London *Publishers' Circular* clucked: "The impatience of the age will not tolerate expansiveness in books. There is no leisurely browsing and chewing of the literary cud such as Charles Lamb describes with the gusto of an epicure. As a people we have lost the art of taking our ease in an inn, or anywhere else; assuredly we do not take it in the library or in a corner under the bookshelf. The world presses, and reading has to be done in snatches." In the words of literary historian Richard Altick: "The doom of the reading habit has been falsely prophesied ever since the invention of the pneumatic tire, which spelled the end of the fireside reading circle by putting the whole family on bicycles."

Now, writers who deplore speed are biased. They are invested in slowness, and good at it. As sentences get shorter, reading faster, visual competition more intense and itself speedier, how can established writers not feel the onrush of obsolescence? How can journalists fail to note the speed-up in popular periodicals—*Time* with its weekly news snippets, the *New York Times Magazine* with its cheeky front-of-the-book interview fragments, Internet magazines with their punchy, semicolonless sentences. Partisans of earlier film cultures likewise deplore today's jump-cutting pace. But for all their vested interest in relative slowness, the critics are not insincere when they deplore the pace of the plunging torrent or bemoan the spectacular funfest that competes with their work for public attention. Neither are they misguided in what they notice. For centuries, speed has dragged slowness along in its wake, hastening it. None of the naysayers has been crying wolf. While the slow protest, the fast drag them along, kicking and screaming.

In recent decades, the media torrent is where speed-up is most unmistakable. The images steadily thicken, the soundscape grows noisier, montage more frenetic. This process transcends the conventional polarities of politics. It is a curiosity of our present civilization that many of those who call themselves conservatives embrace the revolutionary daemon of capitalism, the most reckless, hard-driving force in the history of the world, and celebrate Joseph Schumpeter's "gales of creative destruction" that blow through production, marketing, taste, and everyday life. But among radicals, too, who will organize Students for a Slow Society? Not the rocking and rolling, post-MTV, music-downloading, raging-against-the-machine cultural left. Who is against upgrades, jump cuts, more channels, better speakers, the Sensurround pleasure dome of everyday life?

The real answer to the rhetorical question is: hardly anyone. Yet the prospect of unending, out-of-control acceleration is unnerving. Can all this clutter and haste really be good for us? Some who accept the inevitability of ever-increasing speed wonder whether the acceleration will someday—perhaps soon—crash against barriers of nature or psyche. How fast can montage go without leaving perception behind? How much shorter than seven seconds can a sound bite shrink? How much quicker can Internet access get? How much multitasking, how many advances in Palm Pilotry, can customers bear? How many channels can we surf more or less simultaneously without going mad? In the pilot of the inventive 1980s TV series *Max Headroom*, a network covered up the fact that some of its commercials were so compressed they caused viewers to explode. Perhaps, in the end, the ever-quickening torrent approaches some asymptotic limit that it will never quite reach, faster than which the brain cannot go. Yet in the face of such small comfort, bewilderment and dread do not disappear.

Finally, the raging torrent of images and sounds brings with it a paradox that ought to challenge any casual presumption that more is better, that the superflux of media is synonymous with progress. While our eyes and ears are taking in images and sounds in all their abundance, we are usually sitting down to receive them. The torrent speeds by, but we ourselves—despite the treadmills, the Walkmen, the sports radios—are mainly immobilized. The novelties pour forth, but the couch potato remains inert. About the human consequences of the sedentary life, some hesitancy might be called for, but it does seem improbable that fast food is the only reason why the people of the remote control clicker, cable television, and the Internet have turned out to be stunningly obese. No doubt medical researchers will be heard from on this subject in growing numbers over the years to come as reporters pound on their doors for confirmations of the intuition that inertia adds fat to the flesh, and new chemical remedies for obesity are promoted—on television, where else? In the age of the unceasing image flow, there is no social anxiety that cannot be addressed with a commodity, a craze, and a news exposé—none of which quite dispels the anxiety.

One of the worthiest remnants of Karl Marx's nineteenth-century thought is the passage in the *Communist Manifesto* where he and Friedrich Engels write that capitalism means "constant revolutionizing of production, uninterrupted disturbance of all social conditions, everlasting uncertainty and agitation. . . . All fixed, fast frozen relations, with their train of ancient and venerable prejudices and opinions, are swept away, all new-formed ones become antiquated before they can ossify. All that is solid melts into air." Marx and Engels thought this swirl would culminate with man "compelled to face with sober senses his real condition of life and his relations with his kind." Instead, when all that was solid melted away, what it melted into was an unceasing stream of images and sounds, an infinite promise of sensations and disposable feelings, an endless cacophony of energies and noise, the "uncertainty and agitation" of the greatest and most spectacular show on earth.

3 | Styles of Navigation and Political Sideshows

I have been arguing that nonstop mass-produced images and sounds are central elements of our civilization; that any item may look and feel like a trifle—indeed, that may be its point—but the onrushing torrent is an enormity. It may seem at times like a cornucopia of delights, or a grotesque wilderness of mirrors, or the humdrum furniture of life, or a waste of time, but one way or the other it requires attention and response—coping, in short. How do we manage this strange normality, so strange as not to be recognized as strange? How do we go about living so much of our lives with, around, and despite it? For hardly anyone in the cosmopolitan, wired, image-choked, soundtracked, speed-driven world has the luxury of living as if the unlimited media were not rushing by. There is no choice but to navigate. Sink or swim.

This takes some doing—more than we recognize. It takes not only principles of selection but stratagems of inattention. To begin with, because there are so many clamoring signals, and because they interfere with one another, everyone must learn one particular cognitive skill. An unavoidable consequence of all the flashes and shouts for attention, all the message casters casting their messages simultaneously more or less in the same direction, is clutter and cacophony. As a result, when we pay attention to any particular signal, we must pay inattention elsewhere. Coping, in other words, demands a willed myopia. Everyone learns not only to see but not to see—to tune out and turn away.

But tactics of inattention are hardly enough. We need navigational strategies as well. A great many elements of contemporary culture (Western but not only Western) have evolved, in part, in response to the torrent, to its enormity, its omnipresence and speed. We are aware of it piecemeal but oblivious of its huge place in our day-to-day lives. It is everywhere, too much to take in. It is, in a sense, like nature—that overwhelming presence human beings once found so threatening yet auspicious that they conjured gods and demons to imagine their way through its ungraspable allness. Today, we want to reduce its enormity to human scale. To live comfortably with it, we gravitate to our favorites, classify the parts, get our minds around segments while doing our best to ignore the rest. We try to get clear, climb out to survey the scene. To manage the unmanageable, we cultivate navigational strategies, which, when they firm up and become habitual, deserve to be called styles.

By definition, a torrent is indivisible. What washes over us cannot be tidily named. Nonetheless, perhaps to manage the flood myself, I've given names to our navigational styles. I've come to think of us as fans, critics, paranoids, exhibitionists, ironists, and jammers, all churning within the currents of image and sound, trying to keep our heads up; and sometimes, also, as secessionists or abolitionists, conscientious objectors trying to clamber to dry land. These labels hardly encompass all the ways we approach the media onrush, or the complexity and subtlety with which we try to live with its plenitude, respond to its temptations and risks, variously enjoying it, steering through it, trying to redirect it, and protecting ourselves against it. But they are a start.

None of these types exists in unadulterated form. Each is what Max Weber called an "ideal type"—a tool, "good to think with." Nor is there a single reason why people become fans, critics, exhibitionists, ironists, and so on. Moreover, few of us are strictly enthusiasts, show-offs, or mockers. I may be a fan at midnight on Saturday, an ironist Monday morning, and an exhibitionist at dinnertime. I may be mainly a fan as a teenager, a paranoid as a young adult, and so on. However we mix them, all these styles, meant to help us navigate, themselves succumb, in the end, to the same torrent.

To anticipate a reasonable concern: Who cares whether we are bathed in images and sounds galore? Where's the harm? Perhaps fun is just fun. But in the face of avoidable violence, disease, inequality, oppression, poisoning, and other global afflictions, it makes sense to worry about the public cost of media bounty, to fear that it distracts from civic obligations, induces complacency and anesthesia, and works to the advantage of oligarchs. Related questions crop up: Are the media self-correcting? Do they, in the interstices between entertainments, stir up constructive sentiments, useful sympathies and impulses toward remedies, or only fugitive publics and new styles in disposable feeling? Is it sensible to hope that new media can be harnessed for popular mobilizations, fueling social movements and currents of feeling that might help create a global civil society?

I want to introduce the subjects of navigational style and political consequences with an embarrassingly cautionary tale—not because it's personal but because on a small scale it addresses the immense force of the media. It concerns news, not entertainment, but the pressures on navigational style are similar. It's a story about how, while attempting to be critic, exhibitionist, and jammer all at once, I learned in the end—for the thousandth time, but vividly—where the powers of the torrent lie, and how hard it is to steer a true course.

ON BEING SOUND-BITTEN

Start with the obvious: those who produce for the media want their audiences, more than anything else, to stay tuned. They have a flow to manage. Even non- or semicommercial players like the British and Canadian Broadcasting Corporations increasingly seek to justify their shares of government revenue with sensational and punchy pieces. Professional attention-getters produce the shows, supply the story lines, cast the parts, write the scripts, and insert the sound bites accordingly. So when "news" happens in your vicinity and you as a nonprofessional agree to appear on camera, you also agree, like it or not, to play whatever part the producers are casting. "Preinterviews" enable them to ensure that you will be counterposed to your opposite number. You are not to play against type. If you tell the reporter what the reporter doesn't want to hear, or try to carry the conversation in unexpected directions, you are apt to be left on the cutting-room floor. This is rarely strictly because of political bias, whatever watchdog groups may think. It has as much to do with the imperatives of simplification. A complicator disrupts control, threatening to break the narrative flow. Unusually outspoken but not unusual in his opinion is Neal Shapiro, former executive producer of NBC's *Dateline*, who told producers pitching their stories, "My sixth grader won't understand" or "It's gotta be high school."

In January 1991, with the onset of the Gulf War, I received a call from an NBC correspondent named Bob Dotson. Based in Atlanta, he said he was interested in doing a piece about "veterans of the 1960s" and their opinions about the current war, and asked if I would help him find some of these types in the San Francisco Bay Area, where I then lived. I told him I thought the real story was that, while many people I knew felt mixed emotions and saw arguments cutting both ways, still, in the end, the overwhelming majority of the " '60s veterans" opposed the war passionately. I gave him the names and numbers of several such people.

A day later he called back, said he was flying out, and asked if I would be available for an interview. I was horrified by the war and by the enthusiasm with which the media had enlisted to promote what Tom Engelhardt has called the Pentagon-media coproduction. In previous months, I had written articles and given talks denouncing both the war and prowar propaganda. Judgments as to whether to cooperate with network news are always seat-of-the-pants, intuitive as much as calculated, but if the pros and cons had lined up in my mind methodically, they would have gone like this:

For a war opponent, any access to major media is rare enough. In the days following the launch of Operation Desert Storm, antiwar statements were conspicuously absent from national television, although during the run-up to the war American public opinion had been deeply divided. Virtually all members of Congress, clergy, and former administration officials who had argued for continuing the economic sanctions against Iraq but not going to war had fallen silent, and the news media, infatuated with the ways and means of war, were avoiding debate on the rights and wrongs. Since my name and phone number were on reporters' Rolodexes as a 1960s expert, and I had published articles and been quoted widely on current antiwar sentiment, I was one of the few antiwar people with access to major media during those dreadful days. Moreover, I was convinced that the organized peace movement was squandering its opportunities. Of the two national antiwar coalitions, one said little and the other nothing at all against the Iraqi takeover of Kuwait; neither supported sanctions; both categorically opposed the presence of any U.S. troops in the Middle East, and neither supported their replacement by United Nations soldiers. I hated to leave the field to these knee-jerk views and wanted to make a case that one could have complicated feelings—as most Americans certainly did in the weeks up to January 15, 1991—and still oppose the war. Wasn't I obliged to take advantage of my relative visibility to make the attempt? Then, too, I am no stranger to exhibitionist vanity, performance pleasure, and the allure of the camera.

On the other hand, I knew full well that those who stick their faces too close to the floodlight get scorched; that to speak sound bites is not to control the use of them. I had years of political experience and reflection to prove it. I had written a book on this very subject, *The Whole World Is Watching*, showing how the antiwar movement of the 1960s was disparaged (though sometimes also promoted) by media coverage that focused disproportionately on violence, extravagant rhetoric, and cartoonish gestures. While the movement was not innocent in the process, its most flamboyant leadership and the media had entered into a symbiotic relationship that helped undermine the movement itself. On this topic I was, in fact, expert.

In crisis, one takes risks. I told Dotson I would talk to him. As it happened, on January 23, 1991, the day the NBC crew was to be in Berkeley, I was to speak at an antiwar rally in Sproul Plaza on the University of California campus. I arranged to meet Dotson directly thereafter.

That morning, just as I was leaving my office to speak at the rally, CNN reported that another Scud missile had hit Tel Aviv. I saw TV pictures of wrecked buildings. When I got to Sproul Plaza, the rally was in progress. A speaker was screeching into a microphone so tinny it left the impression that he was attacking his listeners, which in a sense he was. The crowd was sparse. Two large banners stood next to the speaker. One depicted the face of Malcolm X, joined to a quotation: "We are not Americans, we are the prisoners of Americanism." The other showed a Palestinian wearing a bandanna, with the banner: "Down with Israel, long live the Intifada." I told the rally organizers that in the light of the Scud attacks on Israeli civilians, I would not participate in this rally.

Meanwhile, NBC's Dotson showed up with his crew and shot me

arguing with some students about antiwar tactics—there had been two days of disruptive civil disobedience, including a sit-down on the Bay Bridge, which I thought counterproductive. I accompanied the crew to a nearby café, where I made my antiwar arguments to the camera at some length and discussed tendencies in the movement. Making the point that it was difficult to know exactly what to propose at this juncture, I said that I thought it justified, as long as Scuds were attacking civilians, to attack Scuds. I also said that we who opposed the war needed to establish that we were not hostile to the American troops in the field, and that I was in favor of donating blood for them. Dotson asked if I would do that on camera. I said certainly.

I called the blood bank and made an appointment for the next morning. There, I told Dotson I wanted to make it absolutely clear that while opposing the war, I distinguished between the war and the warriors. Lying in bed at the blood bank with a syringe in my arm, I made the point on camera—a little performance piece, an act of symbolic jujitsu (or so I imagined) meant to jam the synapse that equated concern for the GIs with support for the war.

Dotson's piece aired on the *NBC Nightly News* of January 28, 1991. It began with a shot of a photo of myself talking with the radical journalist I. F. Stone during an anti-arms-race demonstration in Washington that I had helped organize in 1962. Dotson's voice-over said, "He manned the barricades at Berkeley during Vietnam. . . ." There was a shot of me on Sproul Plaza in that argument with the militants about the right way to oppose the present war. The only on-camera sound bite from me about the Gulf War, however, was the line in which I said it was justified to attack Scud missiles. Over a shot of me giving blood, Dotson spoke these words: "The old activists never thought there would ever be a conflict they could support, yet Todd Gitlin passed up a campus protest to send blood to the troops. He is still fervently antiwar, but he sees both sides now."

That night, a couple of friends called to say they were surprised to hear that I supported the war. Seeing how they could have gotten that impression, I called Dotson the next morning. His piece, he told me, had originally been three minutes long—an eternity on network news—but at the last minute he had been ordered to cut forty-five seconds. It was then, he said, that the shot of me denouncing the war had been cut and he had substituted his voice-over. I told him that by omission the result had badly distorted my position. Not at all, Dotson replied, no one in *his* office had any trouble discerning from the piece that I was opposed to the war. It wasn't necessary to show me saying so in my own words. The fact that I was antiwar was a "gimme"—something so obvious it went without saying.

But reverberations kept coming in. Three months later, a renowned antiwar writer with whom I had been on friendly terms greeted me with, "I'm not talking to you." She had seen the NBC piece. She hadn't taken in Dotson's voice-over about my opposition to the war. Neither had anyone else I knew. I had argued against the war in the *Village Voice, Dissent,* and *Tikkun,* and on local radio and national public radio, at teach-ins and rallies, on *The MacNeil/Lehrer NewsHour* and CNN—total circulation a fraction of the *NBC Nightly News.* Nine months later, people who took it for granted that television had distorted the facts of Desert Storm still assumed that I had supported the war.

Now, I had been naive to the point of stupidity to expose myself to a film interview under those circumstances and think I could bend the outcome my way. I should have guarded my every word. In a live interview, at least you stand a fighting chance to make your own points in your own sequence while clarifying, modifying, cautioning, and dancing around distractions. The game of wits can be demanding, but it can be reasonably fair. When you donate film clips, however, you donate control. The script chops off the heads who talk out of turn. In the struggle for control, the advantage is to the producers. Refusing to stay "on message," I had offered up a great deal of what I actually thought, including my horror at Iraq's attacks on civilians. The NBC crew had shot, I would guess, four hours of film with me, from which Dotson had extracted a few seconds. He had made the piece that he had set out to make before we ever met. I had walked into his script. It's a mistake I haven't made since.

But leave my foolish miscalculation aside for the moment. This episode also told me something about the eerie life of a television image. People who disdain television as well as people who credit it, people I never would have imagined to be (and would never have imagined themselves to be) impressed by Tom Brokaw's version of the world, people who know full well that film is edited and discourse is partial—all took my words on camera as my entire statement about the wrongs and rights of the war. None of them took in Dotson's voice-over. They saw me donating blood to American soldiers, snapped up the stereotype, and drew the wrong conclusion. People who have devoted years to attacking, dissecting, deconstructing, and otherwise looking askance at media images, people who wouldn't be caught dead saying out loud that the news (to use the media's own favorite metaphor) "mirrors" reality, who know full well that networks form and foster ideas about the world, saw a media image and assumed it to be not a construction, not a version, but *the truth*.

Critics and teachers strive to convince us to suspect images. Teachers of film try to implant the rigors of a frame-by-frame analysis in which every element (framing, movement, color, music, mise-en-scène) gets its due. But in everyday life, despite these efforts, few of us devote ourselves to the study of images. Immersed in the torrent of clips, blurbs, news "bumpers," trailers, "now this," "we'll be right back," "we have to take a break," fifteen-second commercials, seven-second sound bites, headlines, pull quotes, logos, where each image is not only itself but a prologue and a sequel, where *now* is always about to recede into *then*, we don't care to make images stand still. We don't fix them like fully developed photographs or inspect them for their multiple meanings. We dwell in them, not on them. We let them rub off on us in real time. Even to ward off the overflow of images requires discipline. And one way to navigate through the flux and overflow is to preserve certain images on the hard disk of near-consciousness while regularly dumping the rest. Flooded with vastly more versions of reality than we could ever begin to grasp, verify, or think through, we learn how to tune in and tune out with ease—the electronic metaphor is apt—how to disbelieve and suspend disbelief a hundred times a day. And yet we also want to think that we know—well enough—how things are. If we think that we can penetrate to the truth, "get to the bottom of things," haven't we found solid ground beneath the media flux?

In politics, as in other forms of salesmanship, the road to success is paved with good impressions. This is why legions of image managers go to the trouble of arranging their photo ops—why Ronald Reagan's handlers organized what one of them called "our little playlets" featuring the president smiling upon the Special Olympics, say, never mind that back at the White House he was slashing funds for the disabled. The power of images to impress is the reason why the Pentagon went to the trouble of arranging the Gulf War as a photospectacle, shooing reporters away from B-52 bases and plying them with whiz-bang smart-bomb videos so that after endless reruns even a skeptical viewer could not begin to grasp that, *according to Pentagon sources*, as many as 95 percent of all the bombs dropped on Iraq were of the old-fashioned dumb, indiscriminate variety.

Generations have now been saturated with television and its spin-offs. Postmodernists claim that the profusion of images induces a state of vertigo, a sort of rapture of indeterminacy, in which people no longer care whether images correspond to the world in which they think they live—or, in fact, that they relish the discrepancies between images and realities, between signifiers and signifieds. Yet this is plainly not so, partly because of inattention and doubt, but partly because, amid the profusion, and for all the irony and bemusement with which we manage the flow, people still search for solid ground—a search that, perversely, leads us astray, as the cultural and political industries exploit our old-fashioned, unhip longings. "Nothing up my sleeve," proclaims the magician as he proceeds to produce an astonishing live bird from his garment. As P. T. Barnum well understood, the audience not only clamors for more but, later on, loves to be ushered backstage to see how the trick was performed.

Most navigational styles take for granted that the media flow is full of tricks. We *expect* tricks, in fact, because mainly what we expect from the onrush of images, sounds, and stories is diversion. For the most part, these are not supposed to help us discern reality; they are supposed to deliver feelings and sensations, however fragmentary and evanescent, even if we fear, in the end, being engulfed. I turn now to the main navigational styles to which we have recourse as the torrent washes over us.

THE FAN

> I can't promise you life everlasting but
> I can promise you life *right now*.
> —Bruce Springsteen,
> New Jersey Meadowlands, July 1999

Life right now: this is the high promise of modern media. A wonderful paradox—that media, which are by definition connections, between-things, should promise immediacy, the condition of not being mediated. Yet the experience of immediacy is what media immersion is largely for: to swell up the present, to give us a sense of connection to others through an experience we share. We will not have to ask, with the bumper sticker, "Are we having fun yet?" Our feelings will furnish the answer.

When Bruce Springsteen shouted out to his sellout crowds (largely white, largely middle-aged) in a set piece halfway through each concert during his 1999 tour that he was bringing them tidings from "the ministry of rock 'n' roll," he meant it playfully but not mockingly. He was borrowing from the millennial spirit of Christian ministry, identifying himself with the screaming preachers in the African-American call-and-response tradition, and the vigor of his fans' cheers in response showed that they—we—reciprocated in the same spirit. We were a congregation, if a fugitive one. We had paid for our tickets precisely in order to congregate. We *believed*, though obviously not in any doctrinal sense. At the least, we believed in being there, *alive right now*. We were what the French media scholar Daniel Dayan has called "a vast festive diaspora."

The fan's link to the star—or the team, the favorite composer, the game, the genre, the style—is emotional, visceral. Despite academic efforts to parse this connection, to interpret and explain it, it is finally a not-quite-decipherable occasion for feeling. Fandom is a form of love, which is finally incomprehensible: though unlike romantic love, which is exclusive, it must be shared, experienced in at least an imagined crowd. To dismiss fans for displaying an excess of feeling by calling them *teenyboppers* or *wannabes*, or to declare, in the words of one snob, that "soap operas are for fat old housewives who have nothing better to do . . . than sit around in curlers, eating bonbons, and getting fatter," is to miss the point while indulging in a feeling of one's own: a twinge of superiority.

But fandom is not only feeling; it is also focus. No one is, or can be, indiscriminate about the unending media bounty. People may tell interviewers that they like "watching whatever's on" or "surfing around," but we all learn to play favorites (and least favorites). What choice do we have?

The most discriminating fan is the connoisseur, seeking the high ground. He too hunts for a feeling, a pleasure of recognition that he expects to find with an object worth appreciating. As Emily Dickinson put it, "If I read a book and it makes my whole body so cold no fire can ever warm me, I know that is poetry. If I feel physically as if the top of my head were taken off, I know that is poetry." The connoisseur takes this experience, as it were, to a higher power. But Proust, synonymous with the highest of literary standards, had the connoisseur's number back in 1922:

> The art-lovers are as touching to contemplate as those early machines which tried to leave the ground and could not, but which yet held within them, if not the secret, the still to be discovered means, at least the desire of flight. "You know, old boy," goes on the music-lover, as he takes you by the elbow, "this is the eighth time I've heard it, and I promise you it won't be the last." And indeed, since they fail to assimilate what is truly nourishing in art, they need artistic pleasures all the time, they are victims of a morbid hunger which is never satisfied.

Whether in high, low, or middling culture, or culture that refuses these categories, high-magnitude stars serve to screen out low-magnitude stars, not to mention legions of asteroids, shooting stars, and, from the fans' point of view, space junk as well. In a world where consumer sovereignty is taken for granted, the fan or connoisseur is the most discriminating of sovereigns. But it is hard to find anyone in the modern world who is not a fan of some star, team, program, band, artist, writer. Fandom exists in strong and weak forms and at most ages. There are more or less loyal fans (of soap operas and sports teams) and fickle fans (of musical groups in recent years). But fandom is especially for the young.

Americans know American fandom, so to show the breadth of the phenomenon, let us consider French teenagers, who, since 1990, have gravitated to weekly (and then, with the arrival of *Beverly Hills 90210*, daily) broadcasts, first of American TV series, later of their French counterparts. Actress Hélène Rolles, star of the French series

Hélène et les garçons (Helen and the boys), received at least one thousand letters a day during 1993–94, most of them from girls aged eight to twelve living in rural areas and working-class suburbs. Fans frequently watched in groups and gathered to replay taped episodes. On the basis of extensive questionnaires, interviews, and an analysis of fan letters, French sociologist Dominique Pasquier concluded that the series offered the young a "soft" initiation into romantic relationships—an intimation of their future. But it also delivered membership in a here-and-now community of fans. Viewers of *Hélène et les garçons* knew that the episodes were unrealistic, artificial, wooden, and excessively happy in their endings. But to leave it at this, Pasquier argued, was to miss the point:

> Teen series do not supply information about society, *they supply the emotions* around the two main areas a child worries about on becoming an adolescent: friendship and love. Young people don't watch teen series to learn, they watch them to experiment with new feelings. . . . They want to experience how one feels in these romantic scenarios. At that age, role play is very important. Friends gather in the playground at school and reenact the previous day's episode. The roles might be fixed . . . or they might change. . . . *But the goal is clear: it is to experience emotions.*

And, she might have added, to experience them with one another, safely, via the screen. And what is true for teenagers remains true, after a fashion, later in life: Whether we watch or listen, individually or in groups, we know we are not alone. We are always in touch with an invisible crowd. We are fans linked to other fans. Each of us may feel like "the only one in the audience," but we also know we are each being addressed as one of *us*. At more glorious moments, we feel like and unlike ourselves at the same time—ecstatic (out of the self) and integrated (made one).

So fandom is one way of feeling our way out of the churn of the torrent and joining something more definite—a "community" where fans follow the lives of their particular celebrities, debate the merits of their latest work, their characters and values, express appreciation and scorn. Fans use stars as markers of distinction: the Aimee Mann fan not only can't stand Britney Spears but can't understand how anyone else could be caught dead loving her. Fans proselytize. Generously, they do not think there is less of the star if others share in the aura. What they find in the star—Marilyn Monroe's sexy vulnerability, John Lennon's insouciance, Public Enemy's or Eminem's transgressive anger—they wish to share, for the more people who come on board, the sturdier the raft appears. The fan communities who attend oldie fairs and spectacles (*Star Trek*), buy memorabilia or wannabe costumes (*Rocky Horror Picture Show*, underwear to be worn on the outside à la Madonna), take part in caravans (the Grateful Dead), also take heart from one another. Personal want ads identify potential dates as Mozart, Sinatra, Springsteen, or Seinfeld fans with knowledge that through this shorthand they are not only including some candidates but excluding others. Some committed fans devote themselves so zealously to a team as to take on a sort of identity from the attachment—for example, Cleveland's Dawg Pound Dawgs and Green Bay's Cheeseheads. For lesser attachments, *identity* is too strong a term. But connective tissue does form.

The fan aspires to cut through the torrential foam—to replace thoroughly disposable feeling with something more powerful. The star, the show, the set are what Robert Frost said a poem was: "a momentary stay against confusion." Reminiscing about favorite episodes of *Dawson's Creek*, great Mets games, or Machiavellian moments in *Survivor*, attending the nostalgia fair, shopping for Springsteen tour T-shirts or basketball jerseys with your favorite player's number on the back, bidding for Beatles artifacts on-line, buying movie memorabilia at the Warner Brothers outlet, a fan is conservative amid the flux of new faces that flow by each week—a flux promoted unceasingly by the culture industry, for each week new CDs must be marketed, new covers found for *People*. The high-velocity turnover of commodities engenders attachments to things, signs, auras, almost-sacred objects whose distinguishing character-istic is that they do not—or not yet, anyway—require replacement. This conserving temper of fans can be the bane of artists. At one extreme, there are the notorious Bob Dylan folk music fans scream-ing at him for going electric ("Judas!" sounds one harsh voice in the bootleg of Dylan's 1966 concert at the Royal Albert Hall). Dylan's pre-electric fans, possessed by him, thought they possessed him.

The same goes for commodities. Consider the 1985 consumer revolt against New Coke, when spontaneously—though not without a boost from national news media—many consumers rejected the makeover that was being marketed for Coca-Cola's one hundredth anniversary. Granted, the conversion of this consumer preference into a media frenzy could only have happened during a summer month when hard news was scarce. Granted too that Old Coke, soon relabeled Classic Coke, was more effervescent, less cloying than the New relaunch. But why did so many people seem to care so pas-sionately? In a young country, where obsolescence is a way of life, a brand that lasts a century is a fixture. Nostalgia, literally the pain of a lost home, launches a thousand starships in a homeless world.

In a democratic culture ruled by the market, the star—even the star-licensed product—ennobles and steadies me. In her presence, because she is more than me, my life is more than it was. "I shook hands with X. I'm not going to wash my hand!" "I can't believe I'm sitting on Furillo's desk!" my girlfriend told me on the set of *Hill Street Blues* (referring to the police captain character), where I was doing research for a book about the television business. I knew exactly what she meant, having felt the aura rub off on me before, which is why I had brought her there in the first place.

Now, the importance of fandom can be exaggerated—indeed, fre-quently is so by academics quoted in the press speaking about the

Cultural Significance of the popularity of one star, character, hit or another, and so finding their own momentary place in the media parade. A shared cultural interest is not the same as deep commitment. A fan is not a servant, an employee, or a follower. Stars are not jealous leaders. You can be a fan of more than one star at once, or serially. You can be a mild fan or a fickle one. You can get slightly excited from sighting a star on the street, but quickly move on. Even strong fans will stop themselves from going "too far." They may scream over Elvis or U2, dream, write letters, long for a one-night stand, but do not, in general, sign over their possessions, build formal shrines, or pursue the stars' causes: John Travolta's Scientology, Arnold Schwarzenegger's Republicanism. Despite the word's English-language derivation, a fan is not a fanatic. Even after the rise of Ronald Reagan, stars on the whole remain what Italian sociologist Francesco Alberoni called them: a "powerless élite."

Yet not altogether. They have the power to draw attention, and in the process, to catalyze the formation of groups. Even low-magnitude stars today launch Web sites, connect to fans through computer-linked bulletin boards, offer samples, sell products, come to the aid of causes—and so stand out. Standing out, however, in an egalitarian culture, can also incite envy and resentment toward those whom we love because they bring us the bright gifts of themselves. Normally daydreams drown out resentments, but when the ratio is reversed, the benign mood breaks. When fans fail to respect limits and make private claims on the star, we judge them insane or criminal. Stalkers are people who cross the line. John Hinckley, notoriously, thought he would get Jodie Foster to love him if he succeeded in assassinating Ronald Reagan.

The lust and rage of the rare demented fan can exact a high price. The sane fan is content with a low-cost benefit: the promise of ballast in navigating the flux. Never mind that stardom is evanescent and fandom fickle, and stars and fans ordinarily know it. Never mind that the torrent throws up an ever-swelling number of wannabe stars, midrange celebrities, has-beens, and burnouts. Perhaps the next frisson will last. The feeling of feelings is hope.

THE CONTENT CRITIC

The critic, like the fan, steers with preferences, but where the fan works by affirmation, the critic works by aversion. Etymologically (from the Greek), a critic is a chooser. Choosing good against bad work, the critic steers away from reefs toward safe harbors. In the current metaphor, an aesthetic is a search engine. Style refines the search.

Everyone must be not only a fan but a critic. To each his own distaste. Everyone makes aesthetic judgments, sorting the good from the bad, distinguishing oneself from others through such judgments. Technology has made it ever easier to cross the line from private judgments to public declarations, for anyone can put up a Web site offering idiosyncratic rankings of movies and books, and anyone can (and thousands do) affix a paragraph or two, and one to five stars, to any book offered by Amazon.com, referring the reader to his or her other reviews, even getting to be one of Amazon's "top ten reviewers." (The winner at this writing has posted 2,164 reviews. Number 2 offers his own "Review Don Mitchell's Reviews Contest," offering "modest prizes" for essays on, and suggested improvements to, his own 1,464.) This wild proliferation of criticism has an affirmative consequence. In the colossal bazaar of a successful consumer society, critics get rewarded not only with status and membership but also, eventually, with niches—with goods tailored to their particular eyes and ears. The consumer cornucopia has offerings for the most ruthless (or bland) critic—whether highbrow, lowbrow, or furrow-browed.

The same goes for political criticism. Critics of all ideological stripes cruise in and around the torrent. On the standard view, what is wrong with images, particularly those on television, but also in movies and video games, is that they are the wrong images, inducing people to act, feel, and think as they ought not to act, feel, and think. In the spirit of rectification, African- , Arab- , Jewish- , Italian- , and other ethnic Americans, Christians, right-wingers, left-wingers, feminists, gays, lesbians, transsexuals, businessmen, fat people, religious people, and Americans of many other descriptions have campaigned in recent years against negative stereotypes and for positive ones.

I am calling these campaigners content critics, and asking to be indulged for the double entendre. At their most inventive and active, such content critics of character and narrative stereotypes may actually turn the tables on the images they hate, embracing them mockingly—as when the militant Yippies Abbie Hoffman and Jerry Rubin in the 1960s dressed up in flags, Uncle Sam suits, war paint, and bandoliers, or even more effectively, when the body-pierced ACT-UP insurgents and self-proclaimed "queers" in the 1980s and 1990s carved out media space with their garish looks and disruptive slogans, and succeeded in reforming AIDS research. But mainly content critics are content to criticize. They adopt a spectatorial stance. Beholding the media flux, the content critic tries to keep a certain distance from the foam to avoid a soaking. But in such a stance there is also the implication that if the content were only improved, so would the world be.

In what is still a realist age, images are assumed to refer to realities. Thus the alarm about *infotainment*—the blurring of lines between news and amusement, with the news using reenactments, trailers, and music while entertainment opts for docudrama. When signaled that he is getting the news, nonfiction, the critic wants it straight. Fun and emotion are not enough. When media purport to open a window on the world, the window ought not to be either rose-colored or fish-eyed. The critic wants transparency. Verisimilitude is still central to the news's claim to special privileges—its intrusiveness, its right not to reveal sources—and for all our savviness about contrivance, we want to believe that there remains an inner sanctum of truth, a domain of the unretouchable. No one holds to a firm belief in truth like a person surrounded by liars.

So the media keep stumbling into misrepresentation scandals, mostly about photos, whose special authority must be kept sacrosanct, for they record emanations of light from a world that we persist, whatever postmodernists may say, in calling real. In a news photograph, the reference is transparent: these Palestinians actually existed; the father tried to shield the son, but he was shot and killed. So scandals erupt when digital technology is used to move objects closer simply to fit them on the page, or to distort a face (in 1994, *Time* apologized for darkening a police mug shot of O. J. Simpson), or to create the appearance of a face-to-face relationship (in 1994, *Newsweek* spliced together two separate pictures, purporting to show the skaters Tonya Harding and Nancy Kerrigan sharing the same ice, and in 2000, the *New York Daily News* front-paged a composite of Bill Clinton shaking hands with Fidel Castro at the United Nations, labeling it "Daily News Photo Illustration"). Docudramas are regularly spiced with controversies about composite characters, mangled chronology, imagined dialogue, and imaginary conspirators, as in Oliver Stone's movie *JFK*.

Such scandals produce reliability panics, rounds of ethical agonizing among the media's professional content critics that are so extensive as to constitute news in themselves. A misrepresentation scandal is the tribute that transparency pays to show business. The truth is supposed to be tamper-proof. Reporters are not supposed to make up quotes. Impostors on "reality" shows will be expelled. Never mind that pictorial news is full of contrivances, the fancier ones so common as to have their own label: photo ops. The president and the ambassador chat, the "character" walks into her office building, the professor processes words on cue, the victim's mother poses next to his photo—all because the correspondent, the photographer, or the professional spin doctor has asked them to. Still, facticity remains sacrosanct. The pose actually took place. The assumption of credibility underwrites the manufacture of illusion. Even in our entertainments, we believe that things ought to look roughly like what they are. The set of *ER* might be remarkably clean, the patients disproportionately young, the actors unusually attractive, but the set shouldn't feature medical equipment that doesn't exist, and the illnesses mentioned shouldn't be fabricated. Even the fictions we call ads often display episodes in what purport to be real lives. Ads usually depict ideals—icons of how people ought to be—but they manifest a form of realism too, because the image of a model shot from a flattering angle is meant to depict an intermediate state of being in which a real person is being represented in such a way as to make her approximate an ideal.

Content critics commonly take the media to task for defining how things are or ought to be in ways that they believe unduly influence, if not their independent-minded selves then all those credulous others. The media declare what it is like to be female, young, old, working-class, black, Hispanic, and so on. If these definitions are skewed, content critics maintain, we will lack a true sense of how things are. We will dislike our bodies and so become anorexic or bulimic. We will treat others as lessers and make them ornaments for our exploitation and selfish pleasure or objects of our abuse. We will be misled by systematic bias, belittling women and minorities, or devout Christians, Muslims, or Jews, or members of any other underrepresented group. Among political activists, media representation is a common explanation for the fact that we are not more like whatever the critic wants us to be. Why are we homophobic, amoral, violent, sexist, secular, insufficiently civic-minded, revolutionary, Christian, fundamentalist? The answer is the brainwash—not the compressed, nightmarish, high-intensity reprogramming made popular in movies like *Invasion of the Body Snatchers* (1956), *The Manchurian Candidate* (1962), and, more recently, *The Matrix* (1999), but a prolonged marinating that is unobtrusive moment-to-moment yet cumulative, from which the brain emerges irretrievably stained. The more intensely the critic feels a tension between how the world should be and how it is, the more blameworthy are those central carriers of imagery, the media.

But just as Amazon.com can absorb the content critic into the selling process itself, and the movie studio can carve a rave adjective for advertising purposes out of the most innocuous review or obscure magazine, so the media can absorb the endless critiques of itself into its flow. The image of nightmarishly influential popular culture is itself a staple of popular culture. In the movie *Pleasantville* (1998), for example, the black-and-white fantasy world of 1950s TV stands for stultifying, antisexual inauthenticity (no one has desires), provincialism (there is no world beyond white-bread Pleasantville), and social lies (everyone is white, all men like their jobs, all women are thrilled to be housewives). The characters discover that life is better when desires flourish, individual longing overcomes dull routine, and a Technicolor existence erases the old black-and-white one. What bland, flattened America needed, in other words, was more and better media, wider access to consumer goods, and more explicit sex. The antidote to old, dumb Hollywood is new, bright Hollywood.

Scratch an advocate of any social position, and you're likely to find a content critic making not only semiotic claims about media bias but sociological claims about causes and effects. Such arguments are by no means new. There were already precedents for the radical feminist view that "pornography is the theory, rape is the practice," or the charge by Vice President Dan Quayle in 1992 that the television series *Murphy Brown* bore responsibility for out-of-wedlock births, or the effort to blame violent video games for the 1999 Columbine High School killing spree of Dylan Klebold and Eric Harris, in earlier claims that movies romanticized crime, offered training in criminal technique, and caused juvenile delinquency, or that comic books did likewise, or that rock 'n' roll, "jungle music" as it was called by some adult opponents, turned the young into salacious beasts. Whether the issue is racism, gun violence, sex education, drugs, or you-name-it, advocates point out that since advertisers devote billions of dollars to persuading people to view their products or positions or candidates in a favorable light, it does not stand to reason that they would waste their money.

Some of these criticisms are more convincing than others. Indeed, there are ample demonstrations of systematic skews in media representation. Among the more rigorous, focused findings on the skews of television in particular:

• In local television news, African-American prisoners are more likely to be shown full-face than white prisoners charged with the same crimes.

• Gulf War coverage systematically relayed extravagant claims about Iraqi crimes in Kuwait, while vastly exaggerating the prevalence of "smart" bombs and the accuracy of Patriot missiles (94 percent *ineffective*, not 94 percent effective, as the military and the contractor claimed).

• Political campaign coverage emphasizes horse-race questions (who's ahead, who's behind, who's gaining) and handicapping coverage (who is adept at spinning the media, how candidate X "won the week") over coverage of issues and positions.

Effects are a separate question, but there is compelling evidence for strong effects, at least in the short run, including these:

• Television violence makes young people who are already disposed to aggressiveness more aggressive, makes people disposed to fearfulness more fearful, and tends to weaken their sympathy with victims.

• News framing "sets an agenda" for the issues that will be considered important by public opinion.

• Television news significantly influences the criteria that people will use to judge the real world—for example, that it matters whether a candidate in a debate performed "better than expected."

• Television news convinces viewers that individuals are more important than social forces in explaining why people are poor, on welfare, et cetera.

Although the assumption that media imprints are uniformly potent is discredited by most research on the detectable effects of media on actual audiences, variants keep cropping up like horror-movie monsters who refuse to die. The occupational hazard of the content critic is to collapse the whole of life into a shadow projected by the garish light of the media, a dumb show played out on the walls of Plato's cave. (Thus Neal Gabler writes that "life has become a show staged for the media.") Denouncing media hype, often for good reason, the critic easily enough slips from disgust with the corruptions of media into a belief that the media are responsible for well-nigh everything undesirable, corrupt, or deceptive. In particular, political critics, convinced that the media are rigged against them, are often blind to other substantial reasons why their causes are unpersuasive. Is there not the unspoken correlate that if only we, the righteous and smart, could man the gates, then it would be *our* version of true facts and correct ideas that would flood the popular mind, and we would prevail? The critics rarely address the popular passion for illusion, the will *not to know*. They do not acknowledge the pleasures of the white-water trip down the torrent.

Now, it is far from my intention to dismiss particular claims about media influence. Media surely influence ideas, conduct, the tone of our civilization—though not all by themselves, and not always irresistibly, or reliably, or permanently, or necessarily in obvious and predictable ways. Since we are all immersed in media, where solid perspective is hard to come by, and since many factors come together to influence us and our world, we're unlikely to know just what the torrent as a whole is doing to us. So it's neither surprising nor reprehensible that many of us attribute both biases and powers to the media *regardless of whether or not we have reason enough to do so.* When the evidence for any particular charge is selective at best or largely anecdotal, when we ignore awkward counterevidence and leap too easily from a belief about bias to a belief about its effects, we are awkwardly trying (and failing) to come to grips with the media as a whole, and to register protests.

THE PARANOID

Criticism easily shades into paranoia. There is a continuum. Somewhere at the far edge of the commonplace that images matter is the folk mystique that They are programming Us—that television (the usual culprit) is an addiction, a hypnotic agent, a cause of hyperactivity, or worse. There is also the notion that television in particular—the *idiot box*, the *boob tube*—is an all-around agent of stupefaction, a pacifier that turns us into infants, paralyzing analytical faculties, dumbing us down, reducing us to couch-potatohood, pathetically basking in our weakened condition. In the brave new world of amusements projected by Aldous Huxley in 1932, a dystopia renewed by Ray Bradbury in *Fahrenheit 451* (1953) and frequently since then, television is *soma*, the perfect drug—one that, like heroin, as William Burroughs once wrote, makes the consumer come to it. From this point of view, the fact that *idiot box* and *boob tube* have fallen away as terms of abuse, and *couch potato* and *vegging out* have grown into terms of ironic affection, measures television's success.

Versions of the so-called hypodermic hypothesis cropped up around World War I, when many people came to believe that a wave of anti-German propaganda in the press had driven the United States to intervene in that war and that Lenin's mastery of propaganda explained the Bolshevik Revolution. Propaganda was also the target of Marxists, who thought bourgeois media were designed to spread and reinforce values conducive to the health of capitalism and inimical to its enemies. Varieties of hypodermic theory were the starting point of modern media research, further elaborated by refugee intellectuals—most influentially T. W. Adorno and Max Horkheimer, of the Frankfurt School, in their 1944 essay "The Culture Industry: Enlightenment as Mass Deception," later recycled in Herbert Marcuse's influential 1964 book, *One-Dimensional Man*. In the early days of television, a variant of this view entered the mainstream of American sociology, with Paul F. Lazarsfeld and Robert K. Merton pointing fingers at television's "narcotizing dysfunction." Of course, these dystopian hypotheses would not have flourished without a history of monstrous propagandists in power, as witness Hitler and Stalin, vindicating the view of the power of propaganda popularized in George Orwell's *1984*.

The paranoia of the Frankfurt School was brilliant and elaborate, motivated as it was by a plausible (though exaggerated) sense of political catastrophe in Europe and the intellectual disgrace of American culture. It became corrupted and caricatured in later, more simpleminded versions—in effect, propagandistic assaults on propaganda. Consider the vogue for Wilson Bryan Key, an itinerant journalism professor who, in two books published in the 1970s, *Subliminal Seduction* and *Media Sexploitation*, maintained that media images were loaded with subliminal messages. The mass-market paperback cover of *Media Sexploitation* left nothing to the imagination: "YOU ARE BEING SEXUALLY MANIPULATED AT THIS VERY MOMENT. DO YOU KNOW HOW? . . . THE HIDDEN IMPLANTS IN AMERICA'S MASS MEDIA—AND HOW THEY PROGRAM AND CONDITION YOUR SUBCONSCIOUS MIND." Key purported to find the letters *S, E, X* engraved on jars in Vaseline ads, superimposed on ice cubes in liquor ads, embedded in campaign literature ("If you relax under a good light, the very lightly etched letters are easily apparent"), even inscribed in newspaper photos of American helicopters in Vietnam. To Key, Simon and Garfunkel's "Bridge over Troubled Water" was a song about a drug trip, complete with hypodermic syringe ("Sail on, silver girl"). Everywhere, popular culture had jammed poisoned needles under delicate American skin.

The paranoid belief that We are being drugged, mesmerized, or programmed by Them is one of the abiding fears of our time. Key's hypersensitive cryptography was a sort of crackpot successor to Vance Packard's best-selling *The Hidden Persuaders* (1957), which attributed considerable powers to a "motivational researcher" named Ernest Dichter who specialized in telling automobile and other consumer-goods companies how to appeal to crass (usually sexual) fantasies. Key anticipated such reveries as the 1968 fantasy that if you played the Beatles' "I'm So Tired" backward you would hear the words *Paul is dead*, and a Christian fundamentalist belief that Procter & Gamble's star-and-moon logo was the sign of the devil.

The paranoid is a negative monotheist. With the gift of paranoia, the mind spies out the agents of darkness, seeing through the big lie to the big truth that bamboozled creatures are blind to. Paranoia mobilizes not only shared ideology but emotions—terror along with smugness, pity for the naive. When the primary sources of insecurity are natural, the most prevalent forms of paranoia concern inhuman forces. Astrology blames the stars; Manichaean religion, the devil. In contemporary society, on the other hand, individualism is supposed to guarantee autonomy. If we are still at a loss, drifting or suffering, it must be because They—the Government, the Liberal Media, the Media Monopoly, the Zionist Occupation Government (ZOG)—are pushing the buttons. Paranoia is alienated magic. No wonder the torrent itself loves paranoia—a plot device that requires no special introduction, invoking audience sentiments as familiar as any. Post-Vietnam, there is scarcely an action film where the government does not harbor a sinister conspiracy to cover up the truth, where the hero is not subject to surveillance, where ostensibly good guys do not turn out to be bad. In *The X-Files*, government agencies not only are riddled with spies, soldiers of fortune, and good cops gone bad but are literally at the service of aliens.

In its extremity, paranoia is a warped version of legitimate fear. It can be argued, for example, that the indiscriminate fear of television in particular displaces justifiable fears of actual dangers—dangers of which television, in its most realistic mode, for all its shortfalls, provides some disturbing glimpses. The philosopher Stanley Cavell has proposed that "the fear of television . . . is the fear that what it monitors is the growing inhabitability of the world, the irreversible pollution of the earth, a fear displaced from the world onto its monitor." In other words, we fear and loathe television the way people who feel ugly fear and loathe mirrors. In a reformist spirit, Cavell proposes that better television could be an instrument of collective enlightenment: "if the monitor picked up on better talk, and probed for intelligible connections and for beauty among its events, it might alleviate our paralysis . . . sufficiently to help us allow ourselves to do something intelligent about its cause."

Yet fright in the face of the media Medusa with a million glassy tentacles misses something essential about contemporary experience. Raised in the media torrent, most of us have come to expect—demand—nothing less than its bounty. This plenitude compensates for something we would otherwise lack. Most people, most of the time, experience media as signs of society's generosity. The profusion of images offers fun, stimulus, feeling, or a sense of connection, however fugitive. We feel flattered to have the access.

While others welcome the nonstop gift of images, the paranoid refuses to feel flattered. This refusal is admirable. But the soft dystopia of the torrent rolls on nevertheless.

THE EXHIBITIONIST

The exhibitionist is a positive paranoid—through sheer force of presence, she will stand out and thus be outstanding. She will not pretend to relax while the torrent rolls over her. She is not drowning but waving.

There is no way to judge whether present-day societies contain more of the sort of characters who enjoy exhibiting themselves, but what is certain is that appearances are convertible to the currency of public esteem. When television was new, it already demonstrated a "status-conferring effect." When you are a guest on TV or radio, people will tell you gleefully, "I saw/heard you on the such-and-such show!" Rarely will they remember anything you've said, and this should not be taken as a judgment on the special forgettability of your little contributions. What rubs off is mainly *the fact of having appeared*. "As seen on television," as the ads say.

There are surely more occasions for self-exhibition than ever before. The camera is no longer so exotic, and neither is the desire to be enshrined by it. Couples about to exchange their vows first turn to face the video cameras. Children stick their heads into the frame, make faces, yell "Hi, Mom!" when a camera—any camera—rears its lens. People like to be walk-ons, call-ins. Should a revered personage die, fans and admirers bring personal objects, homemade signs, letters, converting the sidewalk near a home or burial site into an improvised shrine. Fans bring punning, self-referential, and network-flattering signs to the stadium, the sidewalk outside the NBC studio during the early morning broadcast of the *Today* show. They mug for the camera on cue. Once it was the trademark privilege of the director Alfred Hitchcock to play a cameo role in a movie; today, it may be the true-life figure (the real Erin Brockovich, who appears on-screen as a waitress while Julia Roberts plays the actual her), the director's friends, parents, or children.

In his 1962 book *The Image*, historian Daniel Boorstin famously described celebrities as "well-known for their well-known-ness." Today, there are vast possibilities for microcelebrity: the talk show guest, the studio spectator, the Web site proprietor, the volunteer during the public television fund drive, the amateur performer selling downloads or CDs over the Internet. There is the celebrity du jour, a phenomenon noted memorably in Andy Warhol's famous and long-lived observation (despite his own far more enduring fame) that "in the future, everyone will be famous for fifteen minutes": the lottery winner, the eyewitness to the shooting or the airplane crash, the neighbor on camera after the kidnapping next door, the character wedging into the margins of "real life," saying, "Look at me, I'm here too!" Commercial radio broadcasting began with amateur performances, and over decades of professionalization, places in the broadcast circus were still reserved for "real people" in shows like the *Original Amateur Hour* and *Candid Camera*, and later in home video displays of embarrassing moments. Having *been* fans, spectators wanted to *have* fans.

Even everyday existence could plunge you bracingly into the torrent, turn you into a character in your own on-screen psychodrama. In 1973, the Loud family of Santa Barbara, California, hurled themselves into the torrent in a cinema verité show called *An American Family*, where during the course of ten weeks on public TV, businessman Bill revealed his extramarital affairs, housewife Pat threw him out, and son Lance came out of the homosexual closet. Talk shows began to cast folks as "themselves," seeking revenge, sympathy, reconciliation, or just plain attention, enacting personal rituals for the distraction, bemusement, outrage, or superiority of onlookers. Jenny Jones, Sally Jesse Raphael, Montel Williams, and Ricki Lake specialized in sexually deviant types, many of whom could plausibly view their appearances as campaigns for inclusion among the common run of men and women. In 1991, MTV launched *The Real World*, casting young personables representing various target

demographic niches in a show meant to simulate unsimulatable actu-
ality and promise *relatibility*. At the turn of the twenty-first century,
Dutch and British producers delivered *Survivor*, *Big Brother*, and
their various knockoffs, in which (if any reader does not yet know)
recruits are hurled into concocted situations (a remote island, a house
filled with surveillance cameras and microphones) to play elimination
games.

New technologies multiply points of entry. Anyone with a mod-
icum of computer skill can put up a Web site. Since tens of millions
have grown up around video cameras, it is hardly surprising to see
the Internet flooded with amateur porn and music. The Web camera
proliferates. A Web page designer named Jennifer Ringley launched
jennicam.com on-line, offering free glimpses of her room from a
static videocamera every fifteen minutes while charging admission to
those who prefer their scrutiny constant. A "new media artist and
entrepreneur" named Josh Harris offered WeLiveinPublic.com,
exposing the loft where he lived with his girlfriend, Tanya Corrin,
to thirty-two cameras and motion sensors. (Within three months,
Corrin called it quits—in an amply illustrated newspaper article, of
course—calling the experience "hellish.")

Jennicam posts links to others, mainly female, including a self-
described "singer/songwriter/performance artist . . . visual artist"
named Ana Voog at anacam.com who claims to offer "the internet's
first 24/7 art/lifecam," as well as hundreds of photographs of herself,
a chance to "receive strange emails from me:)," and links to affiliated
sites that include, variously, "pre-surgery photographs" and "a
strange song someone wrote about me!" Voog explains herself thus:
"i'm an artist to my core. it was such an intense idea, and I like
intense, and I like to push boundaries of what people think a woman
is and isn't. . . . but mostly, all analyzing aside, i'm just doing this for
the pure surreal fun of it." Voog lists her measurements (including
shoe size), the length of her index pointer finger from the knuckle

down, her favorite colors, scents, foods, movies, books, comic books, and music, her worst fear, pet peeves, biggest flaw and asset, sexual preference, spiritual and political beliefs ("I hate politics"), turn-ons, and collectibles, and adds that fans can download MP3s from her site.

Voog raves about her site as "totally spontaneous . . . immediate . . . no middleman! no marketing strategy! no political showbiz bullshit! yay!" The life performance offers the lure of the real thing. Jennifer Ringley of jennicam.com also declares herself an avatar of authenticity, an alternative to the phony acting of teen fictions like *Beverly Hills 90210*. Yet the exhibitionist's open secret is that she will perform for the camera acts she would not perform for voyeurs in the flesh. Screened away from touch, she creates impressions whose artifice is part of their seductiveness. To convey a reality beyond poses, she poses—and comments upon her pose ("don't I look cute?"). So the exhibitionist is a bit of an ironist. Yet something unposed slips out from between her quotation marks.

Call it generosity. This is how she will rise above the torrent. Gratis, she offers a second life to her spectators, who see enacted in her performance the drama of their own doubleness. For everyone is both a subject (of one's own perceptions) and an object (of others' perceptions). In an individualist society, where people believe (with some reason) they can affect their destinies, everyone cultivates impressions and is interested in how others manage to cultivate impressions. Because we are at least somewhat aware of the gap between our presentations of self and our inner lives—because we are all social performers with a repertory suited to different situations—we are fascinated by the masks and concealed faces of others, and the discrepancies between them. We are especially interested in the backstage lives of the Big Names, but not only them. We have not given up the aspiration for truth. We want candor or the reputation for it—frankly, candidly, in all honesty. We want to get real, to the real skinny, the bottom of things. *That* might get us to dry land.

The screen flatters the exhibitionist that she has something to offer, and flatters the spectator that he deserves a gift. But the screen not only reveals; it also repels. It ensures physical distance—see, don't touch. It screens *away*, arranges for contact without the risks of tactility. For the spectator, screen sex, like phone sex, is safe sex. There is but a limited emotional cost. No reciprocal gift of the self is required. Commanding the attention of spectators, the exhibitionist achieves some exemption from the anonymity of the torrent, some power apparently without risk. But because this power is riskless, it is trivial.

THE IRONIST

Even the flattered require defenses. One of the best is irony.

The ironist tries to relax and float downstream. Her knowingness permits her a good conscience, for she's confident that the spectacle is nothing but weightless contrivances. This trend is hot, that star is so over—such judgments come with a bodyguard of air quotes. She surfs with ease and without commitment, amused, and amused to be amused. She can enjoy the spectacle on two levels at once, or alternate between them—as a faux-naive fan (who always liked the smile of that faded star) and as a knowing insider (who knows that the faded star started touring again because she was broke). She follows the Nielsen ratings, the movie box-office figures (what opened big, what collapsed after its first promising weekend)—indeed, it is for readers like her that these numbers started to appear on *Entertainment Tonight* and in newspapers from *USA Today* to the *New York Times*. She likes to know how things work backstage, how the production package is assembled and the publicity campaign mounted. Her knowingness makes for a certain feeling of superiority, which insulates her, yet she can drop it to have a plain good time. She can take the latest stuff or leave it (or so she flatters herself).

The ironist descends from Georg Simmel's "blasé" type of a century ago, but she is less jaded—both more knowing and better-humored. She is a close cousin of David Riesman's "inside-dopester" of half a century ago, whose goal was "never to be taken in by any person, cause or event," but she is more playful and less suspicious. She reads *People* or *Vanity Fair*, follows the gossip columns, wants to know what Julia Roberts, George W. Bush, or Dan Rather is *really* like, but makes a point of knowing that their images are fabricated, that celebrities and politicians tailor their appearances to make impressions. She delights in bemused commentaries defending or trashing popular culture icons-of-the-week—Kato Kaelin, Darva Conger, this or that survivor of *Survivor.* She may be ideological: *check out what liberal Hollywood/consumer capitalism's come up with this week!* She knows that models are airbrushed and colla-gened, that commercials do not depict slices of life accidentally stumbled upon, that studios manufacture programs and campaign teams candidates, that actors are not characters, that they perform more than one take, that film footage is edited, that docudrama characters are frequently composites, that when a major character dies on a TV series, it's because the actor is leaving the show. She may acquire irony as a fashion—a proof to her peers that she is one of the girls: no dope, though no snob either. She may revel in the postmodern blankness of David Letterman or shows like *Talk Soup,* compilations of silly or pathetic moments culled from the week's talk shows. (In a higher artistic register, Andy Warhol performs the same function.) This highbrow has her lowbrow and lifts it.

The ironist's style itself pours into the media, in the form of postmodernist knowingness. The omnipresent bashings, chain-saw slashes, blood spatters, and cartoon pulverizations on our movie and video screens capitalize on her ironic turn—and promote it. Consider the meteoric rise of director Quentin Tarantino, who within a few years in the mid-1990s artfully spilled jazzy dialogue and over-the-top violence all over well-built scenes based on interesting shaggy-dog scripts. In *Pulp Fiction*, for example, one character blows out another character's brains by accident, and this becomes the occasion for an extended joke. In such hipness tests, *Saturday Night Live* meets the Saturday Night Special, wink wink, nod nod.

Tarantinian irony—having your gore and eating it, too—is both a result and a cause of the surfeit of brutal images in the torrent. Violence becomes an arty twitch—and is taken as such. Tarantino has said: "Saying you don't like violence in movies is like saying you don't like slapstick comedy or . . . dance sequences. I think it's gratuitous if it screws up the movie, if it's badly done. . . . That's how I look at it—completely aesthetically." The ironist follows along, muttering, "Cool!" Only a geek would shudder. The ironist rolls her eyes if anyone objects to the cartoon aggressiveness that has become a code of American adolescence, with victims being offed, terminated, wasted, taken out, blown away, thus to become history, dead meat, toast—an exaggerated version of the language of everyday life: she has a drop-dead body, he would kill for that job, magazines pay kill fees, computer companies look for killer aps, candidates crash and burn, performances bomb, quarterbacks throw bombs, and the celebrity of the month *is* the bomb (a good thing). The ironist feels, or affects, or thinks she ought to feel, a distant bemusement.

On television, irony has a history. On the *NBC Nightly News* from 1956 on, David Brinkley was an astringent observer of the passing parade of political goings-on, twinkly and knowing in contrast to his earnest collaborator, Chet Huntley, and the other sober-sided commentators of that time, while in 1966 TV's *Batman*, with its speech balloons of *pow!*s, *wham!*s, and *bang!*s, turned its live actors not so much into comic-book figures as camp spectacles, yucking up the conventions of media violence and bringing the drollery of *MAD* magazine to the small screen.

In the wake of the Vietnam War and Watergate, bemusement darkened. On *Saturday Night Live*, starting in 1975, every public figure, every politician and bigwig, was a fool, a knave, and/or a liar. David Brinkley's arch dismissiveness morphed into ABC reporter Sam Donaldson's jeers. Irony soon flowed late into the night, as David Letterman threw paper planes at the camera lens and hosted "stupid pet tricks." Letterman calibrated his eyebrow-raising with microscopic care. The cavalier hipness of *Saturday Night Live* became a generational marker. Now, not only comedians but politicians review their own performances (Al Gore acknowledging that he was not "exciting," George W. Bush making a joke of the way he turned the word *subliminal* into *subliminable*). Starting with the Isuzu commercials in which subtitles deflated the claims made by Isuzu's own blowhard salesman, ads regularly winked at the absurdity of their assertions. ABC even launched an advertising campaign for an upcoming TV season with slogans like, "If television is bad for you, why do they have it in hospital rooms?"

Thus is knowingness, which began as a defense against the clutter that is the sum of all the image makers' attempts to break through the clutter composed of all the other attempts, itself a style that clutters the media stream.

THE JAMMER

The culture jammer, like the content critic, believes that images are power, but goes farther. He thinks that he can change them and thus, in some small way, redistribute power.

The jammer defaces—and refaces—images in order to upend omnipresent clichés. He exploits their omnipresence by turning them against their producers. Offense is the jammer's defense. The early refacements were on the earnest side: death's-head labels stuck onto cigarette posters, "This ad oppresses women" on underwear ads. In recent years, however, jammers have become more playful. Where an offending image promises fun through consumption, the defacement delivers fun on the spot.

There is a lineage. In the 1930s, left-wing German photomontagists stood Nazi propaganda on its head. In 1932, for instance, John Heartfield showed Hitler saluting while behind him a fat capitalist deposited banknotes into the führer's hand. Heartfield captioned his poster with a Nazi slogan: "Millions stand behind me." In the late 1960s, jammers similarly performed visual jujitsu with ads: Cuban artists inserted photos of Vietnamese War victims and starving Third World children into advertising scenes of consumable plenitude, and a surrealist calling himself Violet Ray published brilliant color versions of similar juxtapositions under the title *Advertising the Contradictions*. Subsequent refacers, performing what Naomi Klein calls "semiotic Robin Hoodism," went after cigarette billboards, among others. In 1998, Hocus Focus, an "underground art action group" based in the San Francisco Bay area, was appalled by the Apple "Think Different" marketing campaign, which likened Apple users to Gandhi, Einstein, and other heroes. The group set out in the dead of night to "reanimate the archetypes whose images have been rendered lifeless," by pasting onto Apple billboards their own revisions, like "corporate colonization of the unconscious" (over Gandhi's image), "marketing is censorship" (the Dalai Lama), and "imagine lovers are not hucksters" (John and Yoko Ono Lennon).

Jammers usually work alone or in small groups, but the more ambitious efforts to insert unorthodox images into the torrent require crowds. To interrupt "business as usual," jammers plant a political image within a conventional ritual—a banner unfurled at a graduation ceremony or the Cambridge-Oxford boat race ("Oxbridge Paddles Whilst Vietnam Burns") or the Rose Bowl (a plane flying overhead in 2001 with a sign proclaiming "Hail to the Thief"—namely, George W. Bush). Recognizing that power sanctifies itself with spectacular displays, the demonstrator heads for the floodlit proscenium: Washington's Mall, Mexico City's Zócalo, Beijing's Tiananmen Square. So does the demonstrator within the demonstration, jamming its dominant imagery, seizing attention by burning a flag or carrying the enemy flag into a sea of friendly flags, relying on media to relay the discordant image. The demonstrator may then rush home and turn on the evening news to see if his people appeared, how prominently, and how framed. The powerful make their points by holding press conferences; demonstrators make theirs in the streets. Since the command of images is an element of power, it makes perfect sense to rush home to see how one's crowd plays on the evening news.

At the far edge of the spectrum of jammers is the terrorist. Unlike the assassin, the terrorist targets ordinary civilians and produces, in effect, a snuff movie. Images of the event, endlessly rebroadcast, inflict wounds that do not heal. Or refusing to rely on media controlled by his enemies, he distributes his own videotape—a Hezbollah tactic in southern Lebanon, for example. He may also seize the means of communication directly: the revolutionaries seize the television station, the putschists demand an hour's access, or, more modestly, Theodore Kaczynski combined threats and promises to convince the *New York Times* and *Washington Post* to print his antitechnology screed as an insert. The more he killed in the name of antitechnology, the more the torrent welcomed him with profiles, punditry, family background pieces, instant books, and sage analysis of his POV.

The hacker, on the other hand, doesn't threaten but intrudes, mounting counterpropaganda, disrupting operations, or dismantling sites of power. If information is power, impersonate power. Unlike the exhibitionist, the hacker may be anonymous or take on a cute moniker. Hacking into Pentagon or Microsoft networks, he interrupts. His electronic sit-in aims to clog information facilities—say, the Mexican government's, in support of the Zapatistas. One hacked

Mexican government site declared: "Telmex [the state phone company] sucks!!!" A hacked site of the government of Colombia featured a devilish logo of Immoral Daemon Killers with this message: "We demand 25 kiloz of dank chronic herb and a big old pile of coca leaves."

The hacker's disruption may interfere with corporate workings for a while but then joins the foam of ephemera rushing down the torrent of the day's news. It may boost his side's morale, though whether he contributes to lasting change is another question. As for the distributor of viruses or worms, whose disruptions of normal computer use and Internet traffic have become ordinary, his vandalism does have a concrete effect: it creates jobs, not least for ex-hackers, in the antivirus security industry.

Consumer-friendly hacking is, thus far, more potent than jamming. Jamming breaks into a sealed room, while consumer-friendly hacking copies the key and passes it out. Consider the inventors of MP3 and Napster, distributing free access to music and backing the music industry into years of litigation. Or consider Jon Johansen, a sixteen-year-old Norwegian who allegedly helped develop a technology called DeCSS that enables users to decrypt encoded DVD disks, and Eric Corley (a.k.a. "Emmanuel Goldstein"), who posted a hyperlink to it on a widely used hacker Web site. Young Johansen and his father, Per, were arrested by Norwegian police, and the movie studios, with a lot of money riding on DVD sales, sued Corley for "traffic[king] in a circumvention device." On the day Jon Johansen testified in federal court in Corley's defense, his father told a *New York Times* reporter that "Jon's grandfather fought the Nazis in World War II," adding that he himself had supported anticommunist Solidarity in the 1980s by carrying money into Poland and smuggling out documents. " 'Jon is in an historical line,' Per Johansen said proudly. 'He is fighting for freedom.' "

There are legions of such self-styled freedom fighters. A hackers' convention for which Johansen and his father came to New York, called h2k, for Hope 2000, claimed 2,300 attendees. Johansen's hacker version of the "fight for freedom" is a fight for the right to consume the movie of choice. "I think everyone should have their own billboard," in the populist view of the Billboard Liberation Front. Like the inventor of the remote control device, or the utopians of the World Wide Web, these liberators think *everyone* belongs in the swim.

THE SECESSIONIST

For some, however, the torrent is simply intolerable. It not only steals their time, and therefore their lives, but squanders human capacities. That absorption in media appears voluntary only shows how gravely the public will has been paralyzed. The media are beyond reforming, not least because the economic interests that profit from the collective attention of humanity will not lightly suffer any loss of control.

The secessionist takes direct, personal action: she turns her back, or at least her head, and seals her ears. She does not care to interfere with, blur, displace, jam, supplement, or otherwise reform the media. In darkened living rooms, she has seen how automatically people's eyes dart or drift toward the bright light. Her own eyes have darted and drifted, too. She knows seduction when she sees it. She rations her television watching, decides not to fix the set when it breaks down, eventually gets rid of it. She abstains from mobile phones and declines to learn e-mail no matter how many friends tell her what she's missing. At the very least, she refuses to take her communications equipment on vacation, refuses to buy clothing bearing designer logos. She takes self-discipline as a character test because self-discipline is precisely what the media conspire to undermine. The secessionist refuses to be addressed by idiots, boors, and knaves, with their gross designs on her senses, their disrespect for her solitude, her unaided imagination, and her deepest emotions. She tests her will against the barrage and comes out (partly) triumphant. She has no illusions about the glut in which she lives, but resolves to win herself an exemption.

The roots of this sort of revolt are ancient. Plato warned that poetry is flabby imitation and images are mere cave projections, poor flickering substitutes for the reality that is humanity's proper pursuit. Romantics proposed unplugging from the "perpetual whirl/Of trivial objects" in order to "look/In steadiness" (William Wordsworth), to "loafe and invite my soul" (Walt Whitman). The philosopher Martin Heidegger proclaimed in 1936 that modern man, deprived of "the cinema, the radio, the newspaper, the theater, concerts, boxing bouts, travel"—all the means of distraction then in existence—would (in his biographer Rüdiger Safranski's paraphrase) "die of emptiness," having lost the capacity to live simply. Contemplation, he thought, could redeem this loss, converting emptiness into an opportunity for "remembering Being." But even Heidegger, in his eighties, watched European Cup matches on television at a neighbor's house in the Black Forest. Once, a theater director who met him on the train tried to engage him in conversation about literature and the stage, but Heidegger, fresh from watching a match, preferred to exult over the great German player Franz Beckenbauer, demonstrating some of his moves.

Modern secessionists are often convinced that by applying the proper discipline they can find their way to absolute presence, the non- or postphysical mystery at the bottom of all things, to God, Nirvana, Being. Some leave elaborate accounts of their reasons for seceding. But philosophical secessionists are outnumbered by ordinary ones: people who do not regard themselves as mystics but despise the coarsening, mind-stealing, image-soaked, sound-degraded media, and not only abstain from them but try to arrange for their children to do the same. The "Kill your television" bumper sticker is popular at least on the coasts. The promoters of "National

TV-Turnoff Week" (the last week of April) claim a total of more than 18 million participants in their first five years—a mass movement of a sort, though how many pursue the group's suggested course of reading and recreation on top of simple abstention is unknown.

The mystic gives meaning to his secession because there is a way of life he prefers waiting for him once he climbs out of the torrent—perhaps Nietzsche's joyous and sociable recommendation of "excursions with thoughts and friends." The ordinary secessionist's turn away is a thin alternative and a rearguard action. Ask people to give up their television sets for a month, even pay them to do so—such experiments have been done in the United States and France—and you are asking for restlessness and family fights. Some of those deprived may feel relief, but for most, media deprivation feels like a form of banishment. Condemn a teenager to the backseat without the protection of his Walkman, and you have sentenced him to solitary confinement.

In educated circles, despite decades of pop-cultural studies, television remains lowbrow, and it is still common to meet Americans (and others) who say they never watch television—except, perhaps, for the occasional news special or quality tidbit. How many such people actually exist and how many only claim to exist while watching like the rest of us is unknowable. According to official 1997 figures, 1.6 percent of American households (a total of roughly 1,616,300) were without television. This figure has been stable for many years. People unexposed to billboards, newspapers and magazines, televisions in bars and public spaces, and so on, are scarcer still.

History has made it impossible to live in a world that is not saturated by mass-produced images and sounds. But perhaps, after all, secession is a matter of degree. You can tune out—if you are reconciled to feeling out-of-it. You can fight for autonomy by taking what you like and leaving the rest. Faced with trivia quizzes, you may pride yourself on your ignorance. Refusing attention—not keeping up with the celebrities of the hour, not knowing who does what on *Buffy the Vampire Slayer* or *Ally McBeal*—is a discipline. It must be frequently renewed.

The population of partial secessionists is surely huge, and so is the market for gadgets that say, *Secede as you please.* The ordinary spectator is an eager consumer of tune-out equipment: remotes, mute buttons, car radio preset, scan and search buttons, headphones that double as earplugs, answering machines, Internet voicemail that collects calls you would otherwise miss while on-line, boxes to check on junk-mail lists in order to prevent your name from being sold to other junk-mail lists. The cable box and the on-line musical download service are devices for saying, selectively, no as well as yes.

We come full circle. The would-be secessionist shades into the fitful secessionist, who in turn shades into the discerning consumer, the ironist, the content critic. It is not too much to say that consumer markets today are peopled by fitful secessionists, pickers-and-choosers all, for whom market fragmentation is a boon. Availing themselves of computers from the late 1960s on, media companies have served up to marketers increasingly precise demographic slices of the mass audience, successfully inviting advertisers to spend their money attracting only the eyeballs most useful to them. "The more attractive a population segment was to marketers," writes media researcher Joseph Turow, "the more they segmented it." Women, for example, at first were divided between working and nonworking, the former being the bigger spenders, whereupon, according to a J. Walter Thompson researcher, working women could be distinguished between the "just-a-job working woman and the career-oriented working woman," and so on to still finer gradations. In the magazine world, this meant *Working Woman, Working Mother, Self, Vital,* and *Savvy.* Gen Xers were broken down in like fashion. So were teenagers, gays, blacks, and Hispanics. In 1981, the president of the Ford Motor Company called cable television the beginning of the end of the "shotgun" approach to network viewers. Even in auto sales, the future belonged to precise "rifles." All the giant corporations today narrowcast, spinning off demographically segmented products tailored to specific age, "lifestyle," ethnic, and regional "niche markets."

Torrential culture, in other words, produces the means to profit from occasional, incomplete, but nonetheless widespread secession. No major nation has entered into this spirit more than the United States, imperfectly nationalized from the start. Its motive force, a compound of individualist ideology, entrepreneurial energy, and the pressure to reduce all value to money value, disposed it to organize, respond to, and partially satisfy its legion of partial secessionists— those who, through group identity or individual pursuit, recognize their commonality by affirming their differences from others who are themselves declaring their own differences from *them*. Thus the paradox: secession is an American ritual. The freestanding suburban house with its standard package of consumer goods spins off the children's room with its own standard package.

Herbert Marcuse celebrated the Great Refusal, but what we have for the most part is a stream of Little Refusals.

THE ABOLITIONIST

If diversion distracts from virtue, and criticism merely confirms that the torrent is hospitable to criticism, and private abstinence turns out to be little different from consumer choice, then what? The revolutionary answer is: dry it up! Society as a whole must be forced, in Rousseau's classic phrase, to be free. The abolitionist chooses virtue (for everyone) and thereby joins a tradition that runs from Plato to Mao. Yet one need not be a full-blooded revolutionary to suspect, at least in idle moments, that surrounding oneself with amusements— "amusing ourselves to death," in media critic Neil Postman's phrase—

tranquilizes us, wrecking not only democracy and spirit but even deep pleasure itself. In a society so much of whose treasure and time are taken up with diversion, isn't it self-evident that character is damaged and the public good fatally wounded? Confronting a child who refuses to turn off the TV, log off from the Internet, shut down the video game, take off the headphone, is there an exhausted parent who does not flirt with the abolitionist impulse?

Finding the media politically pacifying, life throttling, mind sapping, even physically damaging, the abolitionist refuses to accept their existence as a good argument for why they should continue to exist. The inertia of precedent, the fact that history disgorged an all-around entertainment civilization, does not convince him. Even as he frees his mind from dependency, he has the courage to ask, what is to be done? But this question immediately demands completion. *What is to be done in the face of all the history that brought us to this pass?* Today's best-known abolitionist, Jerry Mander, author of *Four Arguments for the Elimination of Television*, once admitted to me in conversation that it was naive simply to argue against television as if television could be surgically "eliminated," like an isolated tumor. If television is "structural," the ineluctable product of a destructive society, as Mander argues, then it is unimaginable that television could be stripped away while leaving the rest of society unchanged. Appropriately, Mander's second book advocated an essentially different society, spiritualized and antitechnology. Just as Marx maintained that a serious argument against religion had to be an argument against a condition that required religion, the abolitionist must argue against a social order that requires unlimited media.

If the argument of my book is even approximately valid, unlimited media are exactly what an urban-based, industrial society with a money economy and a division of labor requires. The whole panoply and soundscape of everyday life are compensation, recreation, tranquilizer, partial transcendence—a realm of felt freedom and pleasure.

So consistent abolitionists have little choice but to be root-and-branch, scorch-and-burn primitivists, scornful of the rewards of a consumer society, committed to cutting the links in the indivisible chain connecting modern production, consumption, and the technologies implicated in both. Only unabashed primitivism can create postindustrial wholeness.

Today's committed abolitionists are mainly found among the young anarchist bands who roam the United States and Europe, disdainful of authority, angry entrepreneurs of action. In the eyes of one writer said to be influential in their ranks, John Zerzan, of Eugene, Oregon, technology is "the power behind our misery," our "ever-greater levels of sadness." We live in "a speeded-up Information Age emptiness drained by computerization and poisoned by the dead, domesticating imperialism of high-tech method. . . . [A]s the earth rapidly approaches its extinction due to technology, our souls are shrunk and flattened by its pervasive rule. Any sense of wholeness and freedom can only return by the undoing of the massive division of labor at the heart of technological progress."

Recognizing that the information age has deep roots, the abolitionist resolves to uproot it. "Can we justify our lives," Zerzan asks, "by anything less than . . . a politics of rage and dreams?" Hence black-masked marauders in Seattle (and subsequent sites of globalization meetings) smashed Starbucks windows, manifesting their rage and perhaps their dreams. Another channel for rage was taken by Theodore Kaczynski, whose murderous designs (complete with bombs that were themselves models of technological wizardry) did not inhibit sympathizers from printing up bumper stickers after his arrest saying, "The Unabomber was right."

These are gestures, nothing more. Abolitionism is wishfulness. Short of catastrophic war, global depression, or a marauding asteroid, what could roll back the consumer cornucopia and unlimited media, centuries in the making? For about this the abolitionists are right:

our present civilization did not arrive with television or the Internet. The media bounty of everyday life is not the brand-new product of an unprecedented "information society" or the sum of the inventions of university X, research park Y, and start-up Z.com. The culture of saturation and speed is the future of the past—a future long prepared for.

In fact, the media torrent is so broad and sinuous as to have made a place for virtually everyone. There is no navigational strategy that cannot be enfolded there. There is no navigational style that cannot provide subjects for sitcoms, talk shows, cop shows, exposés, docudramas, or *People* profiles. There is room among hot topics for those who believe that ZOG controls the airways, or that murdering John Lennon makes sense, or that stalking David Letterman enlarges their lives. The pure embodiments of the navigational strategies just outlined would obviously be gravely damaged people, but not extraterrestrials. They are rather extreme exemplars of styles that, in moderation, are common, often appealing, and at the least comprehensible. True, each style wears out. Diminishing returns set in— which is one reason why we tend to shift among styles in the course of our days, not to say lives. But it is not a sign of psychological damage to have recourse to these strategies or adopt them as personal styles. It is, rather, a way of trying to cope, a sign of a certain alertness to limitless media.

FUGITIVE PUBLICS AND 24/7 SOAP OPERAS

So most of the time we manage, as individuals, for better or worse, to navigate. We make our own ways, but what of the common good? If the media flow is central to our civilization, where is democracy? The answer is: largely reduced to a sideshow.

This is partly because of the media's political skew toward the hypervaluation of private life and the devaluation of public life. It is true, and far from negligible, that the media, by flooding people with generally inoffensive images of others unlike themselves, have invited tolerance and, even more, egalitarian and antiauthoritarian sentiments. But surely giant corporations are not in the business of supplying opponents with images likely to arouse opposition to giant corporations or to American geopolitical power (or, in other nations, their own governments). As Jeffrey Scheuer has powerfully argued, American broadcasting is systematically biased because it gains our attention by virtue of being kinetic, episodic, personalized, and conflictual, because it systematically breaks large subjects into small chunks. Automatically, then, it leads to simplification. Since conservatives tend to be more Manichaean than liberals, and more zealous about their politics, conservatives play better on the air, and so, for commercial reasons, television and radio talk will be disproportionately right-wing.

But skew, much castigated by critics, is the least of the media's political impacts. The bigger story is demobilization. The ceaseless quest for disposable feeling and pleasure hollows out public life altogether. If most people find processed images and sounds more diverting, more absorbing, than civic life and self-government, what becomes of the everyday life of parties, interest groups, and movements, the debates, demands, and alliances that make democracy happen? On any given day, at any given hour, if pressed to choose between watching television, say, and going to a political meeting, writing a letter to a public official, or organizing a demonstration, most of us know what we would sacrifice. We expect some usable curiosity, some jolt of feeling, to await us on TV, at the movies, on the radio, on-line, or in stereo. Can we say the same of public life?

In his famously titled *Bowling Alone*, the political scientist Robert D. Putnam argues compellingly that obsessive media use makes civil life and self-government wither. After scrutinizing many statistics, Putnam concludes that, although watching TV *news* and reading newspapers are associated with higher voting rates in the United

States, the opposite is the case for *total* TV viewing. In the 1970s, "those who said they were spending more time watching TV than in the past were significantly less likely to attend public meetings, to serve in local organizations, to sign petitions, and the like than demographically matched people who said they were spending less time on TV." According to surveys from 1994 and 1995, the more television people said they watched, the less likely they were to be registered to vote. Those who "definitely agreed" that TV was their primary form of entertainment were twice as likely to be unregistered as those who "definitely disagreed." Habitual viewers, those who turned on the TV regardless of what was on, and left it on in the background, were especially disengaged from civic life. Overall, Putnam reaches the stark conclusion that, among all the factors that might predict civic disengagement, "dependence on television for entertainment" was *"the single most consistent predictor."* The additional hour a day Americans on average spent in front of the TV in 1995 as compared to 1965 might account, by itself, for "perhaps one-quarter of the entire drop in civil engagement." Though a correlation is not automatically a cause, logic and evidence suggest that television is the cause and disengagement the effect.

Moreover, if Putnam is right, it would follow not only that television weakens civil society but also that national politics will tilt to the conservative side. Governing interests thrive when there is no popular mobilization to contend with. Those who wish to conserve their economic power have less need to mobilize voters. On the other hand, those who want to shift the balance of power toward the left—the poor, minorities, and labor—need to stir up action. This media saturation certainly retards.

Overall, I have been arguing, the torrent cultivates disposable feeling and an ongoing sense of Feeling Lite, which is the ideal state for political retreat. Yet in a peculiar paradox, the media carnival itself also offers the occasional and inadvertent promise of reprieve. It offers a stop button. Punctuating the flux, there come ritual moments of total saturation and relative motionlessness when vast numbers of people attend to the same "breaking story." Along with coronations, state funerals, and natural disasters are events of overt political import: President John F. Kennedy is assassinated, Congress investigates Watergate, the Iranians seize American hostages, the pope visits Poland, Anwar Sadat visits Jerusalem, Nelson Mandela is released, Chinese students occupy Tiananmen Square. In an era of all-news channels with hours to fill, we are treated to ever more frequent rounds of 24/7 saturation: the month of the Nintendo Gulf War, the year of O. J. Simpson, the month of the death and trans-figuration of Princess Diana, the year of Bill Clinton and Monica Lewinsky, the week of John F. Kennedy, Jr.'s death, the months of the Elian Gonzalez standoff, the weeks of the Florida election debacle, the Chinese capture of an American spy plane, the Gary Condit–Chandra Levy affair, and the World Trade Center massa-cre—my juxtaposition of the latter two glaringly demonstrating that broadcast saturation does not discriminate well between the trivial and the momentous—not to mention the hurricanes, earthquakes, floods, wars, school shootings, air crashes, hijackings, hostage tak-ings, rescues, the many minor crimes and scandals that erupt in the interim, each good for at least a day or two before melting away into nourishment for talking heads staving off withdrawal pangs.

In such a nonstop jamboree, the media produce a Cubist hodge-podge of recognizable characters and spotlit scenes, logo-festooned and orchestrated to theme music. All-over coverage—the right word, for once—absorbs the lion's share of network news, newspaper front pages and newsmagazine covers, local TV news and specials, morn-ing shows and late-night comedy. Cable channels supply instant grat-ification, and their ratings spike up, while for viewers without cable or the time to attend to it, the network news follows suit. During the year of the Lewinsky scandal, the three major networks among them devoted a total of more than thirty-two hours of weeknight network news to the Clinton-Lewinsky story—almost 12 percent of their total news hole. During the first six days after young John Kennedy's plane crashed, the ABC, CBS, and NBC evening newscasts ran 131 pieces—27 more than during the first week after Princess Diana died—and the network newsmagazine shows devoted seven hours and fifty-one minutes to the subject. This is the proverbial "feeding frenzy"—"avalanche journalism," the British call it. A slow-motion avalanche would be more like it.

The wall-to-wall soap opera is a tempting target for the content critic who sees it—rightly, in most respects—as degraded news, a trivial pursuit presided over by breathless, pompous opinionators. In the era of All Monica, All the Time, if political life is going to compete with entertainment for scarce attention, it will have to produce continuing narrative, melodrama, and emotional jolts—ideally, gigantic scandals. Old-fashioned journalists murmur that these obsessional exercises embarrass them. After nine months of Lewinsky saturation, John Seigenthaler, Jr., an MSNBC anchor, spoke the obvious on one private occasion: "Whether [Clinton-Lewinsky] is interesting enough to warrant all the attention we gave it, I doubt." Gesturing helplessly at the spanking-new MSNBC headquarters, with its automated cameras, multiple satellite feeds, and elaborate Internet connections, he added: "If you're trying to make back the $70 million it cost to build this place . . ." And his voice trailed off.

But might it be, nevertheless, that the United States is confronting its major social and cultural conflicts through these celebrity or catastrophe or celebrity-as-catastrophe orgies of talk and imagery? Keeping a straight face, one might argue that the Simpson saga, for example, was not a frivolous waste of time but virtually our only way today to conduct a national conversation on race and justice—and very much secondarily, spousal abuse—while *l'affaire* Lewinsky was a fight over where the boundary between public and private conduct belongs. Whether such "conversations" are illuminating is another matter; they generally have the intellectual content of food fights. But the slow-motion spectacle does get the population to pay a kind of attention to a version, at least, of public events. Half the Americans in a 2000 audience survey said that they followed national news only "when something important or interesting is happening." Even when many people tell pollsters that they are appalled by the media frenzy, they tune in—even if the all-news network ratings remain *relatively* low, and even if much of the public distinguishes between the delectation they feel as consumers of spectacle and the gravitas they think proper to bring to bear on matters of state.

If, on the whole, wraparound spectacles are no gifts to democracy, they have a peculiar aspect that might help explain their appeal and their consequences. During these episodes, people may feel not only enthralled but relieved. For the wraparound saga has the virtue of sluggishness. The everyday onrush of lightweight fluff . . . grinds . . . into . . . slow . . . motion. The anchor declares breathlessly, "This just in," the commentator expostulates, epiphanies arrive—moments of revelation and showdown, partial resolutions, true and false leads— but in the main, padded by "backstory," the story moves glacially. Like the soap opera, it does not require rapt attention. The "real" news, the "latest," will recycle at the top of the hour, if not sooner. Meanwhile, during the search for young Kennedy's plane, the screen read "Breaking News" while boats crisscrossed a placid Nantucket Sound looking for debris and the camera showed only open water. During the state funeral, the wedding, the hijacking, longueurs take over. The impounded plane sits on a runway. The reporter at O. J. Simpson's mansion or Elian Gonzalez's Miami relatives' house reports breathlessly that nothing is going on. Amid the stasis, a few iconic images recycle endlessly: the Challenger explodes, O. J.'s white bronco cruises down the freeway, the Murrah Building in Oklahoma City stands as an instant ruin, the fireman holds the dead child, Monica Lewinsky hugs President Clinton at the rope line, Clinton points his finger and denies having sex "with that woman," prosecutor Kenneth Starr carries out his garbage and refrains from comment, the hijacked jets smash over and over again into the Twin

Towers. The pundits, barking heads, hunt for amusing or pontifical sidebars, striving to summon the nation to feelings that all of us are supposed to feel, trying to power the display with emotional bursts that the pictures usually do not themselves engender. Only in an ongoing emergency—like the aftermath of the World Trade Center and Pentagon attacks of September 11, 2001—does saturation coverage carry much practical information. Mainly, emotions flow: grief, horror, anger, fear. No wonder steady viewers grow numb.

Yet stasis may be not so much a dramatic flaw as an attraction. The spectator's burden of choice is, for once, lifted. You are riveted, your choices made for you. You duck in and out, check on "what's new." Your opinion is polled, your talk radio calls and e-mails solicited. You may feel privileged to be "a witness to history." Instant communities form on the Internet, jokes fly around the world via e-mail. The people you run into share an automatic agenda—even if high on that agenda is disgust with the excess of coverage, expression of that disgust being itself a predictable feature of saturation coverage. The ritual of common preoccupation seems to justify the intensity of the coverage.

What is the larger import of these fitful rituals? War surely benefits. War in real time provides matchless programming, forging a prime emotional link between citizens and states. The public, saturation-bombed with images, is enthralled. During the Gulf War, the first saturation war, Americans found it impossible to tear themselves away from the small screen. During the month of January 1991, 70 percent of the U.S. public responding to a survey said that they were following news about the Gulf "very closely." TV news viewing shot up, and almost 80 percent told a Gallup Poll they were "staying up late" to watch war news. During the week of January 15–21, 1991, CNN spiked to a prime-time rating higher than the major networks and more than ten times its normal viewership. And the effect? There is evidence that media coverage of both the crisis and the war immediately heightened bellicose sentiment—not only among the more attuned, educated, and prowar (Republican, white, and male) but among normally less attentive women and minorities, and those opposed to the war. With ease, the media were able to promote Saddam Hussein from obscurity to full Hitlerian status within a week—only to escort him back to the shadows once the war was over.

Images of immense suffering may induce fellow feelings of a humanitarian and charitable nature, too. Relief funds boom. Communities of concern—for the Kurds, refugee Haitians, Ethiopians, Somalians, Bosnians, Albanian Kosovars, and Afghanis, genocide-struck Rwandans, AIDS sufferers, victims of terrorism—well up, then subside. Not surprisingly, since the torrent trades in evanescence, what develops around the electronic campfire is a fugitive public, reinforcing warlike sentiments or peaceable solidarity for a time, urging collective action, campaigning for human rights in places where suffering takes place within camera range. A fugitive public is more than no public at all. But it does not by itself coalesce into a steady, compelling, transformative movement, nor is it a public that performs the ongoing work of democracy.

If media invisibility detracts from solidarity, this is not to say that the opposite is a sure thing. It is a cliché, one of the media's own favorites, that the media's global reach makes the world transparent and therefore works toward improvements. When governments do decide to take action somewhere, it serves them to point to CNN pictures as the reason why—*See, we had to act*. We have heard a great deal in recent years about this "CNN effect": the fear, or hope, that when CNN turns its cameras toward civil war, famine, or genocide, *there* will be the issue of the week, mobilizing a public concern that disrupts autocracy, summons help for victims, sways political, military, and economic elites, even terminates interventions. Conventional wisdom is convinced that Bill Clinton withdrew from Somalia in 1993 after CNN showed an American corpse being dragged through the streets of Mogadishu. It is frequently claimed that communism broke down because television conveyed the luster of consumer goods, brought news of freedom from West Germany to East Germany, and so on. Television, ABC's Ted Koppel said in 1990, is "Revolution in a Box."

Whether television embarrasses rulers is by no means clear. Television did not restrain the Chinese in and around Tiananmen Square in 1989. It did not restrain Slobodan Milosevic in either Bosnia or Kosovo during the 1990s. "Ethnic cleansing" and the siege of Sarajevo and other Bosnian cities were major news stories in the United States and Europe between 1992 and 1995. Serbian assaults continued, often televised. All the while, threats were brandished, talks went on, agreements were made and violated. Despite all the coverage, at no time during those years was there significant public support for American or European military intervention in Bosnia—an intervention that took place only after three years of slaughter. Bosnia did not matter enough.

Even while they last, concern and support are not the only reactions to images of atrocity and disaster. Bystanders spurred to action are outnumbered by those who fidget and avoid, perhaps taking heart from the fact that they are not afraid to stare for a while at distant catastrophes, feeling combinations of disquiet, guilt, pity, irritation, sorrow, and helplessness. A worldwide community of the somewhat knowledgeable coexists with devastation. Aware of its distance from the theater of suffering, involved in its noninvolvement, the community of the knowing makes itself at home in a world where it is normal that some are slaughtered while others watch pictures of their slaughter.

The torrent triumphs. Evanescence is the rule. When feelings are disposable, media-stoked passions prove evanescent, too. Sentiment is as fitful as coverage. The salience of an issue spikes dramatically, then sinks just as dramatically. Even war fervor can be disposable. George H. W. Bush ended the Gulf War with an approval rating of 89 percent but lost an election with 38 percent of the popular vote twenty months later. In a world where demagogues go prowling, the refusal to be mobilized can be a sort of triumph for democracy— albeit a soft one. In this light, or twilight, the refusal of public opinion to join crusades, whether in favor of war or against Bill Clinton's morals, has its value. Still, the conserving impulse tempers not only the ugliest passions but also the best, leaving elites free to conduct public business behind closed doors. Unhappy is the democracy that has need of demobilization.

Optimists hope that the Internet will transform the torrent fundamentally. Might it be that, as some young people today claim, neither the old media nor their particular images matter so much anymore, that they are obsolete or at least obsolescent? Much is heard about the promise of new media networks in political mobilization—virtual social movements, in a sense. A bit of utopian glow glimmers about the Internet's power to circumvent central authorities and offer far-flung but resource-poor associations the chance to network, coordinate, and focus their energies. Some claim that the more time is spent on the Internet, the less is spent watching television; but the evidence on that is conflicting, while the Internet's potential for spurring democracy is unclear in the extreme. What can we know about the uses of a technology so young? What we do know is that from radio onward, hymns have been sung to the utopian possibilities of every new medium, only to have it absorbed into the torrent.

At present, everything grows on the Web: entertainment and sports, pornography and gambling, shopping shelves and chat rooms, databases and archives. Social protest and popular lobbying are also thriving. There must already be many thousands of worldwide linkages among citizen groups organized by political affinity. Petitions circulate, sometimes internationally. Organizations like the International Campaign to Ban Landmines have surely benefited from Internet connections. Even within a single metropolis, local associations can cluster and interconnect with unprecedented ease. There are linkups for human rights and environmentalist organizations, groups like Amnesty International and Greenpeace, anticorporate protests—but also for neo-Nazis and white supremacists. As early as 1993, a Rush Limbaugh fan was placing a summary of the daily Limbaugh conversation on the World Wide Web. There have been many informal global contacts, relaying news from Bosnia and other republics of the former Yugoslavia, setting up connections among Chinese dissidents and exiles, organizing and circulating magazines for the Iranian diaspora, for American historians and multinational intellectuals, and so on—establishing and maintaining ties among cosmopolitans and fundamentalists alike.

Activists exult in new opportunities. Without doubt, the Internet helps decentralized networks conduct their political work, recruit, raise money, debate tactics and strategies. Demonstrations like the Seattle mobilization at the World Trade Organization meetings (November–December 1999) and the Million Mom March for gun control (May 2000) can be organized in part via the Internet without centralized national groups. How much the electronic "netizen" networks contribute to political outcomes is more difficult to assess, however. Extensive, sometimes respectful (though sometimes alarmist) media treatment of the Seattle; Washington, D.C.; and other demonstrations against business-centered globalization probably contributed to policy debates within the World Bank, the International Monetary Fund, and the G8 governments. But while easy communication aids activist coordination, it does not necessarily pay off in real-world results.

Do Internet users as a whole become more engaged in civic life or politics than nonusers? As of 1999, the answer seems to be no. Do organizations and networks become more exclusive and self-contained when they spring up on the Web, or are they more likely to reach across social and ideological chasms? No one knows.

Reformers nowadays, looking for firm critical ground, also deplore the "digital divide" between the information- (and therefore image-) rich and the information-poor, assuming that narrowing this divide would help equalize opportunity. The haves now have one more thing to have, the have-nots have one less, and without some redistribution democracy cannot flourish. In the first half decade of Internet growth, it surely was true that to those who were image- or information-rich, more was given. American whites and Asians were early acquirers, and the more educated—overlapping with more white—had more access than blacks and Hispanics. Similar gaps appear between the United States and Europe, and between the entire North of the world and the South.

But suppose that, with special investments and the ordinary rhythm of catch-up, the digital divide does narrow. For the weakening of democratic politics there remains no quick digital fix. The torrent of images, sounds, and stories will widen, ever more of its currents sweeping ever more of us along, but neither its volume, speed, nor bandwidth can be counted on to deepen democracy or, for that matter, the quality of feeling or commitment with which people conduct their lives. Many things become imaginable, but the ability to imagine a life outside the torrent is not one of them. The bulking up of "information," equipped with bells and whistles, does not alter this fundamental social reality: fugitive publics are fugitive. The age of disposable feeling accommodates moments of passion—but each hot, breaking, unsurpassed, amazing, overwhelming event fades, superseded by sequels; each "crime of the century" dissolves into the next, only to be recycled in the form of TV collages, magazine and movie-of-the-week "specials," instant books, branded sound bites and video clips, chat groups and instant polls, each cross-referenced to previous spectacles, each assigned meanings by choruses of pundits and focus groups, each instantly labeled *unique, unforgettable.*

4 | Under the Sign of Mickey Mouse & Co.

Everywhere, the media flow defies national boundaries. This is one of its obvious, but at the same time amazing, features. A global torrent is not, of course, the master metaphor to which we have grown accustomed. We're more accustomed to Marshall McLuhan's *global village*. Those who resort to this metaphor casually often forget that if the world is a global village, some live in mansions on the hill, others in huts. Some dispatch images and sounds around town at the touch of a button; others collect them at the touch of *their* buttons. Yet McLuhan's image reveals an indispensable half-truth. If there is a village, it speaks American. It wears jeans, drinks Coke, eats at the golden arches, walks on swooshed shoes, plays electric guitars, recognizes Mickey Mouse, James Dean, E.T., Bart Simpson, R2-D2, and Pamela Anderson.

At the entrance to the champagne cellar of Piper-Heidsieck in Reims, in eastern France, a plaque declares that the cellar was dedicated by Marie Antoinette. The tour is narrated in six languages, and at the end you walk back upstairs into a museum featuring photographs of famous people drinking champagne. And who are they?

Perhaps members of today's royal houses, presidents or prime ministers, economic titans or Nobel Prize winners? Of course not. They are movie stars, almost all of them American—Marilyn Monroe to Clint Eastwood. The symmetry of the exhibition is obvious, the premise unmistakable: Hollywood stars, champions of consumption, are the royalty of this century, more popular by far than poor doomed Marie.

Hollywood is the global cultural capital—capital in both senses. The United States presides over a sort of World Bank of styles and symbols, an International Cultural Fund of images, sounds, and celebrities. The goods may be distributed by American-, Canadian-, European-, Japanese-, or Australian-owned multinational corporations, but their styles, themes, and images do not detectably change when a new board of directors takes over. Entertainment is one of America's top exports. In 1999, in fact, film, television, music, radio, advertising, print publishing, and computer software together *were* the top export, almost $80 billion worth, and while software alone accounted for $50 billion of the total, some of that category also qualifies as entertainment—video games and pornography, for example. Hardly anyone is exempt from the force of American images and sounds. French resentment of Mickey Mouse, Bruce Willis, and the rest of American civilization is well known. Less well known, and rarely acknowledged by the French, is the fact that *Terminator 2* sold 5 million tickets in France during the month it opened—with no submachine guns at the heads of the customers. The same culture minister, Jack Lang, who in 1982 achieved a moment of predictable notoriety in the United States for declaring that *Dallas* amounted to cultural imperialism, also conferred France's highest honor in the arts on Elizabeth Taylor and Sylvester Stallone. The point is not hypocrisy pure and simple but something deeper, something obscured by a single-minded emphasis on American power: dependency. American popular culture is the nemesis that hundreds of millions—perhaps billions—of people love, and love to hate. The antagonism and the dependency are inseparable, for the media flood—essentially American in its origin, but virtually unlimited in its reach—represents, like it or not, a common imagination.

How shall we understand the Hong Kong T-shirt that says "I Feel Coke"? Or the little Japanese girl who asks an American visitor in all innocence, "Is there really a Disneyland in America?" (She knows the one in Tokyo.) Or the experience of a German television reporter sent to Siberia to film indigenous life, who after flying out of Moscow and then traveling for days by boat, bus, and jeep, arrives near the Arctic Sea where live a tribe of Tungusians known to ethnologists for their bearskin rituals. In the community store sits a grandfather with his grandchild on his knee. Grandfather is dressed in traditional Tungusian clothing. Grandson has on his head a reversed baseball cap.

American popular culture is the closest approximation today to a global lingua franca, drawing the urban and young in particular into a common cultural zone where they share some dreams of freedom, wealth, comfort, innocence, and power—and perhaps most of all, youth as a state of mind. In general, despite the rhetoric of "identity," young people do not live in monocultures. They are not monocular. They are both local and cosmopolitan. Cultural bilingualism is routine. Just as their "cultures" are neither hard-wired nor uniform, so there is no simple way in which they are "Americanized," though there are American tags on their experience—low-cost links to status and fun. Everywhere, fun lovers, efficiency seekers, Americaphiles, and Americaphobes alike pass through the portals of Disney and the arches of McDonald's wearing Levi's jeans and Gap jackets. Mickey Mouse and Donald Duck, John Wayne, Marilyn Monroe, James Dean, Bob Dylan, Michael Jackson, Madonna, Clint Eastwood, Bruce Willis, the multicolor chorus of Coca-Cola, and the next flavor of the month or the universe are the icons of a curious sort of one-world sensibility, a global semiculture. America's bid for global unification surpasses in reach that of the Romans, the British, the Catholic Church, or Islam; though without either an army or a God, it requires less. The Tungusian boy with the reversed cap on his head does not automatically think of it as "American," let alone side with the U.S. Army.

The misleadingly easy answer to the question of how American images and sounds became omnipresent is: American imperialism. But the images are not even faintly force-fed by American corporate, political, or military power. The empire strikes from inside the spectator as well as from outside. This is a conundrum that deserves to be approached with respect if we are to grasp the fact that Mickey Mouse and Coke are everywhere recognized and often enough *enjoyed*. In the peculiar unification at work throughout the world, there is surely a supply side, but there is not only a supply side. Some things are true even if multinational corporations claim so: there is demand.

What do American icons and styles mean to those who are not American? We can only imagine—but let us try. What young people graced with disposable income encounter in American television shows, movies, soft drinks, theme parks, and American-labeled (though not American-manufactured) running shoes, T-shirts, baggy pants, ragged jeans, and so on, is a way of being in the world, the experience of a flow of ready feelings and sensations bobbing up, disposable, dissolving, segueing to the next and the next after that— all in all, the kinetic feel that I have tried to describe in this book. It is a quality of immediacy and casualness not so different from what Americans desire. But what the young experience in the video game arcade or the music megastore is more than the flux of sensation. They flirt with a loose sort of social membership that requires little but a momentary (and monetary) surrender. Sampling American goods, images, and sounds, they affiliate with an empire of informality. Consuming a commodity, wearing a slogan or a logo, you affiliate with disaffiliation. You make a limited-liability connection,

a virtual one. You borrow some of the effervescence that is supposed
to emanate from this American staple, and hope to be recognized as
one of the elect. When you wear the Israeli version that spells *Coca-
Cola* in Hebrew, you express some worldwide connection with
unknown peers, or a sense of irony, or both—in any event, a marker
of membership. In a world of ubiquitous images, of easy mobility
and casual tourism, you get to feel not only local or national but
global—without locking yourself in a box so confining as to deserve
the name "identity."

We are seeing on a world scale the familiar infectious rhythm of
modernity. The money economy extends its reach, bringing with it
a calculating mentality. Even in the poor countries it stirs the same
hunger for private feeling, the same taste for disposable labels and
sensations on demand, the same attention to fashion, the new and
the now, that cropped up earlier in the West. Income beckons;
income rewards. The taste for the marketed spectacle and the media-
soaked way of life spreads. The culture consumer may not like the
American goods in particular but still acquires a taste for the media's
speed, formulas, and frivolity. Indeed, the lightness of American-
sponsored "identity" is central to its appeal. It imposes few burdens.
Attachments and affiliations coexist, overlap, melt together, form,
and re-form.

Marketers, like nationalists and fundamentalists, promote "identities," but for most people, the mélange is the message. Traditional
bonds bend under pressure from imports. Media from beyond help
you have your "roots" and eat them, too. You can watch Mexican
television in the morning and American in the afternoon, or graze
between Kurdish and English. You can consolidate family ties with
joint visits to Disney World—making Orlando, Florida, the major
tourist destination in the United States, and the Tokyo and Marne-
la-Vallée spin-offs massive attractions in Japan and France. You can
attach to your parents, or children, by playing oldie music and

exchanging sports statistics. You plunge back into the media flux, looking for—what? Excitement? Some low-cost variation on known themes? Some next new thing? You don't know just what, but you will when you see it—or if not, you'll change channels.

As devotees of Japanese video games, Hong Kong movies, and Mexican *telenovelas* would quickly remind us, the blends, juxtapositions, and recombinations of popular culture are not just American. American and American-based models, styles, and symbols are simply the most far-flung, successful, and consequential. In the course of a century, America's entertainment corporations succeeded brilliantly in cultivating popular expectations for entertainment—indeed, the sense of a *right* to be entertained, a right that belongs to the history of modernity, the rise of market economies and individualism. The United States, which began as Europe's collective fantasy, built a civilization to deliver the goods for playing, feeling, and meaning. Competitors ignore its success at their own peril, financial and otherwise.

THE SUPPLY SIDE

About the outward thrust of the American culture industry there is no mystery. The mainspring is the classic drive to expand markets. In the latter half of the 1980s, with worldwide deregulation, export sales increased from 30 percent to 40 percent of Hollywood's total revenue for television and film. Since then, the percentages have stabilized. In 2000, total foreign revenues for all film and video revenue streams averaged 37 percent—for theatrical releases, 51 percent; for television, 41 percent; and for video, 27 percent.

Exporters benefit from the economies of scale afforded by serial production. American industrialists have long excelled at efficiencies, first anticipating and later developing the standardized production techniques of Henry Ford's assembly line. Early in the nineteenth century, minstrel shows were already being assembled from standardized components. Such efficiencies were later applied to burlesque, melodrama, vaudeville, radio soap opera, comic books, genre literature, musical comedy, and Hollywood studio productions. Cultural formula is not unique to the United States, but Americans were particularly adept at mass-producing it, using centralized management to organize road shows and coordinate local replicas.

If the American culture industry has long depended on foreign markets, foreign markets now also depend on American formulas: Westerns, action heroes, rock music, hip-hop. Globalized distribution expedites imitation. The American way generates proven results. Little imagination is required to understand why global entertainment conglomerates copy proven recipes or why theater owners outside the United States (many of whom are themselves American) want to screen them, even if they exaggerate the degree to which formula guarantees success. In a business freighted with uncertainty, the easiest decision is to copy. Individuals making careers also want to increase their odds of success.

It's a mistake to exaggerate the power of central supply to generate audiences, but the financial rewards of imitation are potentially so great, legions of entrepreneurs everywhere make the effort. All over the world, young filmmakers aspire to become the next Steven Spielberg or George Lucas, with their blatant emotional payoffs and predictable lines.

Around the world, as in the United States itself, America fabricated the templates, first, for Italian and Spanish Westerns, later for Hong Kong kung fu and "action," Europop, French soap operas, and so on. The Hollywood star system also came in for imitation everywhere. Even if, when faced with a choice, people tend to prefer domestically produced television to Hollywood goods, competitors in television, as in film and music, are pulled into America's gravitational field.

American preeminence in the culture industry is nothing new. Hollywood was a major force in European movie theaters by the second decade of the twentieth century. The United States swamped the competition from Britain, France, and Germany in the silent era, gained further with the devastation of Europe in the First World War and further still in the sound period. By 1925, at least 90 percent of all films shown in Britain, Australia, New Zealand, Canada, Brazil, Argentina, Spain, Portugal, and Mexico came from Hollywood; in 1937, at least 65 percent in Britain, Australia, Canada, Brazil, Italy, and Mexico, and at least 75 percent in China, Colombia, and Egypt. Between the world wars, the main Hollywood studios grossed, on average, 35 percent of their revenues outside the United States. They benefited again from the second destruction of their competitors in World War II. American companies were adept at striking deals with foreign distributors, establishing high-powered marketing operations, even buying up theaters. But even theaters not owned by Americans would sooner take chances on American goods than the alternatives.

American industrial advantages have been especially potent in movies and television, where mass promotion is linked to mass production, and language and local traditions are not as significant as in popular music. Compared with European rivals, Hollywood has the tremendous advantage of starting with a huge domestic market. Once the movie or TV show is made, each additional copy is cheap—by local standards, often ridiculously cheap. In the early 1980s, Danish television could lease a one-hour episode of *Dallas* for the cost of producing a single original *minute* of Danish drama. In television exports, Brazilian and Mexican soap operas rival American products; the Japanese remain dominant in the production and distribution of video games; and it is not inconceivable that other export powerhouses will develop. Still, for the moment, American exports predominate.

THE DEMAND SIDE

But the supply-side argument won't suffice to explain global cultural dominance. American popular culture is not uniquely formulaic or transportable. (Indeed, in 1900, 142 special trains transported touring companies of actors and musicians throughout England and Wales every Sunday.) Moreover, availability is not popularity. No one forced Danes to watch *Dallas*, however cheaply purchased. In fact, when a new television entertainment chief took charge in 1981–82 and proceeded to cancel the show, thirty thousand protest letters poured in, and hundreds of Danes (mostly women, many rural) demonstrated in Copenhagen. When the chief's superiors told him he had better rethink his decision, he passed a sleepless night, bowed, and reversed himself. The dominance of American popular culture is a soft dominance—a collaboration. In the words of media analyst James Monaco, "American movies and TV are popular because they're *popular*."

That popularity has much to do with the fusion of market-mindedness and cultural diversity. The United States has the advantages of a polyglot, multirooted (or rather, uprooted) society that celebrates its compound nature and common virtues (and sins) with remarkable energy. Popular culture, by the time it ships from American shores, has already been "pretested" on a heterogeneous public—a huge internal market with variegated tastes. American popular culture is, after all, the rambunctious child of Europe and Africa. Our popular music and dance derive from the descendants of African slaves, among others. Our comic sense derives principally from the English, East European Jews, and, again, African-Americans, with growing Hispanic infusions. Our stories come from everywhere; consider Ralph Waldo Ellison's *Invisible Man*, inspired jointly by Dostoyevsky, African-American folktales, and jazz. American culture is spongy, or in James Monaco's happy term, *promiscuous*. He adds, "American culture simply doesn't exist without its African and European progenitors, and despite occasional outbursts of 'Americanism' it continues to accept almost any input."

To expand in the United States, popular culture had a clear avenue. It did not have to squeeze up against an aristocratic model, there being no wealthy landowning class to nourish one except in the plantation South—and there, slaves were the population that produced the most influential popular culture. Outside the South, from the early nineteenth century on, the market enjoyed prestige; it was no dishonor to produce culture for popular purposes. Ecclesiastical rivals were relatively weak. From the early years of the Republic, American culture was driven by a single overriding purpose: to entertain the common man and woman. Hence Tocqueville's recognition that American artists cultivated popularity, not elevation; fun, not refinement. As Daniel Dayan has put it with only slight exaggeration, European (and traditional) cultures have a superego, American culture does not. What is the market for entertainment if not a market for id?

Think about possible sources of competition, and the American advantage stands out. In the global market, bottom-up outsells top-down. Despite a tradition of popular culture, the main British model was classbound—culture as cultivation, culture as good for you. The head of the BBC's General Overseas Service complained in 1944 that "if any hundred British troops are invited to choose their own records 90 per cent of the choice will be of American stuff," and from then onward Americanization came in for much high-minded abuse. As for Soviet Russia, when it was a major world power, its culture was mainly didactic. (In 1972, Soviet film exports to its captive market in eastern and central Europe were still weaker, proportionately, than Hollywood's exports everywhere else in the world.) Who could produce fun like Americans? Who believed so fervently in colorful spectacle? In 1992, as France debated the establishment of Euro Disneyland outside Paris, as the theatrical director Arianne Mnouch-kin denounced this "cultural Chernobyl" and French intellectuals joined her protest, it was not completely disingenuous for a Disney official to deny the charge of American cultural imperialism by say-ing: "It's not America, it's Disney. . . . We're not trying to sell any-thing but fun, entertainment."

It is to America's advantage as well that commercial work emerges from Hollywood, New York, and Nashville in the principal world language. Thanks to the British Empire-cum-Commonwealth, English is the second most commonly spoken native language in the world, and the most international. (The vast majority of those who speak the leading language, Chinese, live in a single country, and their language, tonal in speech and ideographic on paper, is not well adapted for export.) English is spoken and read as a second language more commonly than any other. Increasingly, the English that is taught and learned, the language in demand, is American, not British. It is the language of business and has acquired the cachet of inter-national media. Of the major world languages, English is the most compressed; partly because of its Anglo-Saxon origins, the English version of any text is almost always shorter than translations in other languages. English is grammatically simple. American English in par-ticular is pungent, informal, absorptive, evolving, precise when called upon to be precise, transferable between written and verbal forms, lacking in sharp distinctions between "high" and "low" forms, and all in all, well adapted for slogans, headlines, comic strips, song lyrics, jingles, slang, dubbing, and other standard features of popular cul-ture. English is, in a word, the most torrential language.

Moreover, the American language of images is even more acces-sible than the American language of words. The global popularity of Hollywood product often depends less on the spoken word, even when kept elementary (non-English-speakers everywhere could understand Arnold Schwarzenegger without difficulty), than on crackling edits, bright smiles, the camera tracking and swooping, the cars crashing off cliffs or smashing into other cars, the asteroids plunging dramatically toward earth. In action movies, as in the Westerns that preceded them, speech is a secondary mode of expression. European competitors cannot make this claim, though Hong Kong can.

It is also an export advantage that "American" popular culture is frequently not so American at all. "Hollywood" is an export platform that happens to be located on the Pacific coast of the United States but uses capital, hires personnel, and depicts sites from many countries. Disney casually borrows mythologies from Britain, Germany, France, Italy, Denmark, China, colonial America, the Old Testament, anywhere. Any myth can get the Disney treatment: simplified, smoothed down, prettified. Pavilions as emblems of foreign countries, sites as replicas of sites, *Fantasia, Pinocchio, Song of the South, Pocahontas, Mulan*—Disney takes material where it can, as long as it comes out Disney's industrialized fun.

Moreover, to sustain market advantages, the Hollywood multinationals, ever thirsting for novelty, eagerly import, process, and export styles and practitioners from abroad. Consider, among directors, Alfred Hitchcock, Charlie Chaplin, Douglas Sirk, Michael Curtiz, Billy Wilder, Otto Preminger, Ridley Scott, Peter Weir, Bruce Beresford, Paul Verhoeven, John Woo, Ang Lee. (The big Hollywood movie of 1996, *Independence Day*, with its rousing nationalist features, was directed by the German Roland Emmerich— a Hollywood fact reminiscent of Louis B. Mayer's decision to celebrate his birthday on July 4.) Consider, among stars, Greta Garbo, Ingrid Bergman, Cary Grant, Anthony Quinn, Sean Connery, Arnold Schwarzenegger, Jean-Claude Van Damme, Mel Gibson, Hugh Grant, Jackie Chan, Kate Winslet, Michelle Yeoh, Chow Yun-Fat, Catherine Zeta-Jones, Antonio Banderas, Penelope Cruz. Hollywood is the global magnet—and (to mix metaphors) the acid bath into which, often enough, talent dissolves. Even the locales come from everywhere, or nowhere. It is striking how many block-busters take place in outer space (the *Star Wars*, *Alien*, and *Star Trek* series), in the prenational past (the *Jurassic Park* series), in the post-national future (the *Planet of the Apes* series, the two *Terminator* films, *The Matrix*), at sea (*Titanic*, *The Perfect Storm*—the latter also directed by a German, Wolfgang Petersen), or on an extended hop-skip-and-jump around the world (the James Bond series, *Mission: Impossible*).

In music, cultural import-export relations can be intricate. What exactly is an "American" style anyway? In the art critic Harold Rosenberg's phrase, the great American tradition is "the tradition of the new." The cultural gates are poorly guarded and swing both ways. American rhythm and blues influenced Jamaican ska, which evolved into reggae, which in turn was imported to the United States, mainly via Britain. "Musicians in the Kingston tenement yards picked up poor reception of New Orleans radio stations," writes music jour-nalist Vivien Goldman, "and retransmitted boogie woogie piano, horn sections, and strolling, striding bass into Jamaica's insidious one drop groove and scratchy skanga-skanga guitar." The Jamaican cus-tom of "toasting," with the disc jockey talking over prerecorded rhythm tracks (a style that in turn derived from African griot "chats"), led to "dub," in which the DJ remixed the song, which in turn evolved into American rap. The "trance-like quality" of dub's "thudding bass" led to "the incantatory, undulating repetitions of ambient and rave music." American punks who imported ska from London in the 1990s were not necessarily aware that it was Jamaican. Mambo, tango, bossa nova, techno—dancing America puts up no obstacles to imported energies. The result is not an American equiv-alent of France's *mission civilisatrice*; arguably it is the opposite, in which American teenagers shimmy through the malls to the rhythms of the wretched of the earth.

No matter. Of Americanized popular culture, nothing more or less is asked but that it be *interesting*, a portal into the pleasure dome.

In the main, an all-too-bearable lightness is what the traffic will bear. Not for American culture the televisual intricacies of Rainer Werner Fassbinder's *Berlin Alexanderplatz* or Dennis Potter's *The Singing Detective*, or the subtlety and inwardness of the great European filmmakers, or the historical scale of Latin Americans, Japanese, and Chinese. Not for American popular culture the presumption of Art with a capital *A*, known colloquially as *artiness*. Playful, expressive, comfortably uplifting—a host of styles and themes converge in what the psychologist Martha Wolfenstein called a *fun morality*: Thou Shalt Have Fun.

THREE FORMULAS

In a world of image-choked markets, sellers signal buyers what to expect. Formula and style are the two principal signals. Three now-global formulas are especially formidable: the Western (with a variant, the road movie); the "action movie," and the cartoon. These hardly exhaust the sum of American products. Among Hollywood's most successful exports are cop stories, horror and caper films, ensemble melodramas (from *Dallas* to *Friends*), fun-in-the-sun frolics (from *How to Stuff a Wild Bikini* to *Baywatch*), and easily diagrammed romantic comedies (*Pretty Woman, What Women Want*). Hollywood also produces less easily exportable genres, like the courtroom drama. But Westerns, action movies, and cartoons are at the core of Hollywood's global appeal. They can be bent, spliced, and blended (recombination being a distinctly American talent). Even cop and spy sagas, science fiction, soap operas, and beach extravaganzas are essentially variations on the three essential types.

Lone Rangers: Freedom and Moral Regeneration

The Western tradition that the literary historian Richard Slotkin calls "regeneration through violence" has been a staple of American popular culture since the hunter-hero myths and captivity narratives of the seventeenth century, mixing primitivism and romance, individualism and patriotism, moral purity and conservative restoration. The Virginian, John Wayne in his cowboy incarnations, Gary Cooper in *High Noon*, the Lone Ranger—each rugged everyman served the community without being roped into it. Each was an outsider without a past, a plainspoken skeptic, a straight shooter who saw through pretense, a friend of the downtrodden—and at the same time, a violent servant of law and order. On the frontier between civilization and wilderness, where the stagecoach ran into raiding Indians or highwaymen, good and evil collided. The avatar of a moral community of equal citizens invariably overcame both Indian barbarism and the unbridled rapacity of railroads and big ranchers. He was a laconic Emerson in buckskins—an American Adam.

The stylized melodrama of civilization taming the wilderness predates the movies, weaving in and out of the actual westward expansion, the legend inseparable from the events. (You did not have to be an American to get behind this iconography. The romantic Western novels of the German Karl May were hugely popular throughout Europe.) The army scout and hunter William Cody rode in celebrity buffalo hunts, appeared in dime novels, starred in plays (during the winters, going back to scouting in the summers), lent his name to his "own" novels, and published a self-mythologizing *Autobiography*. In 1883, he launched his outdoor Wild West show, complete with sharpshooters and animals, promoted as "America's National Entertainment"—a spectacle that in some fashion or other he performed for the next three decades. The Wild West was a stunning success throughout Europe, including France (Cody played for five months at the Exposition Universelle in Paris), Spain, Italy (where he was received by the pope), Austria, Germany, Holland, and Belgium. Among the 2.5 million people estimated to have attended the show during Cody's six months in London in 1887 was Queen Victoria, who arranged for a command performance and marveled in her journal: "All the different people, wild, painted Red Indians from America, on their wild bare backed horses, of different tribes,—cow boys, Mexicans, &c., all came tearing round at full speed, shrieking & screaming, which had the weirdest effect." In 1912, Cody carried his epic into the movies with a one-reeler, *The Life of Buffalo Bill,* followed by a series of reenactments of *Indian War Pictures.*

From the movies' earliest days, Westerns were central. The first big commercial hit was *The Great Train Robbery* (1903). In 1910, more than 20 percent of American movies were Westerns; in 1931– 35, about 17 percent. Between 1939 and 1969, Richard Slotkin writes, the Western was "the most consistently popular and most widely produced form of action film." This popularity carried into television. In 1955–57, Westerns accounted for nearly 15 percent of all prime-time network hours; in 1959, more than 24 percent. They were "consistently among the top-rated TV shows for most of the 1955–70 period." Between the 1957–58 and 1960–61 seasons, prime-time Westerns attracted roughly a third of the entire viewing audience. Westerns weathered urbanization and suburbanization alike. The wide-open range with its rough-hewn towns certified enduring value for people who drove station wagons and lived in split-level, ranch-style houses.

The Western outlasted the frontier by more than seven decades and continues to be relocated and re-created in various formats and incarnations. We are familiar with the gunfighter-type cop who annoys the brass (*Dirty Harry*), the space jockey who freelances (*Star Wars*), and the future cop who revolts (*Blade Runner*). The TV series *60 Minutes* and its investigative offshoots are the Westerns of journalism: every week, the good guy breezes into town, a town where he or she does not belong, uncovers evil, and defends the community.

In the movies, the city became the frontier. Steve McQueen moved off the range and morphed into *Bullitt*; Clint Eastwood, *Dirty Harry*. Harrison Ford's Indiana Jones, roving scourge of Indian surrogates, had license to roam anywhere. Television acquired the cop show, and the wilderness moved to the ghetto.

During the late days of Communism, the most popular television shows in Hungary were two American police dramas, *Kojak* and *The Streets of San Francisco*. I once asked a Hungarian media researcher for an explanation. The regime would not permit careful research, but he thought Hungarians found the casual, informal, approachable American cops much preferable to the regime's.

The Western, in short, is the drama of the most rugged individualist in the service of the community—admirably suited to flatter the hopes of all who yearn to reinvent themselves, to master some social or psychic wilderness and emerge with a satisfied mind.

Apparently opposite but closely related is the road movie, where the hero flees the community not on a horse but in a car, a modern gunfighter testing himself in a mechanized wilderness. Roots are traps. The goal may be as straightforward as escaping the law or as ambitious as "finding yourself," but either way, you cast loose and make yourself up as you go along, refusing to play by the rules. The protagonists may be innocents falsely accused (*I Was a Fugitive from a Chain Gang, The Fugitive*), criminals in full criminality (*Bonnie and Clyde, Badlands, Natural Born Killers*), seekers (*Easy Rider*), or runaways (*The Defiant Ones, O Brother, Where Art Thou?*). They may be male-bonded or coupled, even female (*Thelma and Louise*). From Walt Whitman through Woody Guthrie, Bob Dylan, and Bruce Springsteen, the road has drawn the lyricist, too. The hero may have been "born to be wild" or may desperately discover that "freedom's just another word for nothing left to lose." The road can be an ocean, a desert, a river. But ultimately, the setting matters less than the yearning. In 1989, an East German student told historian Paul Buhle that the night the Berlin Wall came down she dreamed of Route 66.

Of course, the Route 66 she dreamed of no longer existed, having been bypassed by Interstate 40. She was dreaming of the American TV series of the early 1960s.

Action Movies: Soft-Core Apocalypse

The so-called action movie displays a harsher, more cynical attitude. Dependent on technical advances in computerization, cinematography, and makeup, its ballet of destruction represents a breakdown of the Western's melodramatic clarity. In a world so indiscriminately brutal that weathering its assaults and frictions, or even feeling fright, is an achievement, it offers the pleasure of nihilistic transcendence. Action movies come in many varieties: rogue cop adventure, Vietnam vet revenge, futurist hot pursuit, Eastern martial arts, and battle epic, among others. What they have in common is kinetic shock.

Delivering the disposable sensation, the jolt of fear, the rageful satisfaction of revenge, the action movie is the quintessential *now* phenomenon. The imperative is to jab, startle, and batter a spectator who has become used to being jabbed, startled, battered. This need to raise the stakes explains the remarkable casualness of the action movie's gory images. Spasms of graphic mayhem litter the screen like punctuation marks. Motives and moral consequences are likely to be dispensable fluff, the plot a sprint from one bloodbath to the next. When Hollywood censorship lifted and Sam Peckinpah made screen blood spurt in slow motion in *The Wild Bunch* (1969), he was subverting the tidy ritualistic shoot-out of the conventional Western. But out of last year's formalist departure Hollywood brews next year's formula. With *The Godfather* (1972), gruesome slaughter was on its way to becoming ritualized choreography.

One generation later, even directors lionized for *auteurist* excellence take pride in performing assault and battery on the human image, topping each other in maimings and disfigurements. Grisliness and offhand apocalypse abound. If Martin Scorsese made blood flow with shootings and stabbings in *GoodFellas* (1990), by 1995, in *Casino*, he was forcing a character's head into a vise and squeezing it until his eye started to pop out. But all the grotesquerie cannot be traced simply to improvements, if that's the right word, in special effects; neither is it simply a product of the lifting of movie censorship—which by itself explains why gore is permitted, but not why there is so much of it. If everything can be shown, still, why bother showing it? Nor can violence in the real world account for the violence of the media, for movies and videos are far more hideous than the streets. Facing a jaded audience, the filmmakers up the dosage.

The gory, explosive, and slasher styles draw to the cineplex the demographic segment most eager to get out of their houses: teenagers. These films are box-office successes virtually everywhere they show. Four films produced by one man (*Die Hard* 1 and 2, *Lethal Weapon* 1 and 2) grossed a total of $1 billion worldwide. *Rambo* was a success in places where the American war in Vietnam was far from popular—Vietnam, for example. John Rambo was not simply a reincarnation of the Western hero, not just character, not just redemption, not John Wayne; he was vengeance, a human wrecking ball, a destroyer of worlds. The teenage soldiers-cum-murderers who dressed up in Rambo regalia from Afghanistan to Bosnia knew which Rambo it was they wanted to emulate: the no-nonsense killer. The *Rambo* grunt, the Schwarzenegger one-liner, the *Die Hard* machine-gun burst evidently speak to a take-no-prisoners sensibility that appeals to adolescent boys everywhere.

Around the world, these films and the comparable video games and heavy metal music domesticate brutality. Unable to name modern dangers exactly, young people—males, especially—don't know whether to crave or fear the end of days. Often they feel their masculinity is wounded. Aggression comes easily to them. Action movies and their equivalents in video games and sound are rehearsals. They are the Dolbys of emotional noise amid the mess and inconclusiveness of everyday life. To lead the audience to feel intensely without risk, they administer homeopathic doses of shock. A pile of bodies is no longer shocking. You go to test your toughness and feel the thrill of momentarily losing it—in a comfortable seat, with popcorn. The butcher knives, blood spatters, tire squeals, and humdrum executions are neither exactly realistic nor tragic. The beings who die never really lived. They can be "blown away" so painlessly because they were cartoons in the first place. Life is fluff; such is the way of the world. Move on.

Entertainment certainly has as one of its purposes the muffling of the knowledge of mortality, and the paradox is that this knowledge can be muffled by blowing life away close-up. Action movies, heavy metal, gangsta rap, violent video games, and the other forms of mortality kitsch express a giddy sense of the weightlessness of existence. To behold human images casually "taken out" is to become inured to a world of casual violence and murky threat. During these artificially darkened moments, we know we are all foam on the torrent. The notion of sensitivity training gives rise to worldly mirth, except among the people who practice it, but a strong strain in popular culture amounts to insensitivity training. Few viewers maim or kill because of what they find at the movies, but they do learn to tolerate a world that maims and kills. The relentless cuts, the gruesomeness, and the one-liners offer the experience of the kinetic sublime—a cutting loose from the terrestrial gravity of everyday life into a stratosphere of pure motion, suspense, and release. Whoever gets snuffed, however many bodies pile up, the spectator always survives. Censors like to speak of gratuitous violence, but the adjective misses the point. Violence is the purpose of the show. As cigarettes are instruments for the delivery of nicotine, an "action movie" or violent video game is an occasion for the delivery of controlled bursts of adrenaline. No wonder they are reviewed as if they were pharmaceuticals.

The purveyors of casual violence, gore, and threat, when pressed, take a walk on the demand side and offer a predictable alibi: suppliers deliver only the goods demanded. They claim that their products provide catharsis. But these overnight Aristotelians are as foolish as they are self-serving. The action spectator feels neither pity nor terror for the victims. If the movies were cathartic, violent crime ought to have declined steadily over recent decades as gory movies multiplied. Until the recent downturn (probably caused by an aging population, a strong economy, more imprisonment, better police work, and early deaths of young criminals), that didn't happen.

But if the industry is disingenuous, the Puritans who fight media violence are no closer to the truth. The would-be censors generally do not wonder why the media are saturated with casual aggression—what's in it for the customers. The censorious impulse is not known for its curiosity. It does not wonder what the noise is silencing, why so many people—not only Americans, not only teenagers—might take pleasure in skimming the surface of death. The campaigners believe they know what screen violence does: it invites imitation in the real world. But brutality plays on-screen virtually everywhere on earth without generating epidemics of copy-cat carnage. Demonic Hollywood is a handy issue for politicians who prefer to avoid palpable social failure: poverty, inequality, guns. To blame human wickedness on images is the moralistic recourse of a society that is unwilling to condemn trash on aesthetic grounds. Since the market expresses the only value worth valuing, moral condemnation is untenable unless junk entertainment is believed to have murderous consequences. It isn't bad enough that the movies are ugly. To be judged bad, they have to do bad. The campaign against virtual violence is as shallow as the images it condemns.

Cartoons: Ceremonies of Innocent Wackiness

Next to the not-so-noble savagery of the terrorist and the slasher, Hollywood offers packaged innocence. The Disney-based cartoon and the various Disneylands are in the business of producing adorableness. In movies, comic books, television shows, theme parks, stories, musical theater, and their many accoutrements, Disney assembles smoothness. At the turn of 2001, the corporation bearing the founder's name was bringing in $22 billion in annual sales; its market value was some $52 billion. *Toy Story* had broken movie records in Shanghai, packing in 1 million customers in a city of 13 million. According to Disney CEO Michael Eisner, per capita spending on Disney products in the United States was $65. In Japan, where Disney artifacts are for sale at tourist shrines, it was $45. In denunciatory France, the figure was equally $45. The Disney style of cheery, chirpy fun is arguably America's most potent export in popular culture.

Walt Disney built an empire of pleasantries. He was ruthless—willing to break unions and lead an anti-Communist panic—but not least, he was talented. He was not the first movie cartoonist or best draftsman, but he was the first with a musical soundtrack, first to add voices and sound effects (*yelp! squeal! smack!*), first with Technicolor, and first to produce a full-length animated feature. As critic Richard Schickel has pointed out, he was jokey and an efficient story editor. Efficiency was essential to his success. The Henry Ford of cartoons, he achieved productivity by assembly-line methods, dividing the labor among several teams of animators. Like General Motors, he improved his product with regular model changes.

Disney knew about *synergy* before it became a corporate cliché. As early as 1927, he understood cross-promotion, licensing a chocolate-coated marshmallow candy bar featuring his cartoon character Oswald the Lucky Rabbit. In the 1950s, he was the first Hollywood chief to jump into the small screen and produce a weekly television show. His ABC *Disneyland* series was essentially a stupendously successful, ongoing ad for his new theme park in Anaheim, California. Later, the company Mickey Mouse spawned bought its own cable network and then ABC. Walt Disney was early to grasp the saturation principle. No one better understood how to pump product at high volume and speed into the growing media stream. A classic monopolist, wherever possible he built his own conduits, filled them with Disneyness, and excluded the competition. His little world promoted his little world.

But again, no supply-side advantages fully explain the demand side. Surely it matters that Disney was (and as a company remains) relentlessly upbeat, offering cozy feeling—not ecstatic but family-friendly. The enterprises are deeply shallow and shallowly clean. The parks are fenced-in, centrally cast utopias, flawed by neither conflict nor challenge. Everywhere, the cartoons are not only accessible but dubbed into local languages for local convenience. But there must be more to the demand side.

In the early 1970s, during Salvador Allende's socialist regime, Chilean writer Ariel Dorfman and his Belgian collaborator Armand Mattelart published *How to Read Donald Duck*, a pamphlet charging Disney with propaganda—justifying capitalist greed, displaying smugness toward backward savages, and so on. In Europe, the pamphlet became sufficiently renowned that the Disney corporation charged copyright violation and the U.S. Customs impounded imports. A decade later, in exile in the United States, Dorfman felt compelled to ask what *bound* people to Disney. Why did they enjoy what they were not compelled to enjoy? Surely not because the cartoons fronted for American imperialism. He recalled meeting a slum dweller in Chile who, having heard that Dorfman was crusading against comic books, photo novels, sitcoms, and the rest of industrialized fiction, pleaded: "Don't take my dreams away from me."

In his sequel, *The Empire's Old Clothes* (1983), Dorfman delivered one of the most striking passages in the whole bulky history of ruminations on popular culture. What, he asked, explained the *hold* of cartoonish fiction, especially the products of America's culture industry, even among people battered by American power? Here he came to a conclusion so unexpected (for a man of the left) that he interrupted his own writing to ask, "Did I write that?"

American mass culture appealed to the child the audience would like to be, the child they remembered, the child they still felt themselves at times to be.... In spite of resistance from national cultures and diverse subcultures which have rejected homogenization, in spite of overwhelming elite and intellectual criticism of these works of fiction, the infantilization that seems to be such an essential centerpiece of mass media culture may be grounded in a certain form of human nature that goes beyond historical circumstances. The way in which American mass culture reaches out to people may touch upon mechanisms embedded in our innermost being.

"Human nature ... beyond historical circumstances ... innermost being"—strong claims, but Dorfman was undoubtedly right. Different societies treat childhood differently, but what is universal is the child's biological dependency, playfulness, and naïveté. America, child of the West, youngest of civilizations, is singular in its affirmation of childishness, and is both cherished and despised for it, but the appeal of its cartoon childishness is undeniable. Cartoon characters are incarnations of an innocence that can never be dispelled. Their large heads are the heads of newborns, their smooth faces signs of perpetual immaturity. Life has not yet weathered them or bent their bodies. Cartoons, offering vaguely adult activities in the trappings of childish bodies, appeal to the universal experience of having been a child in a world run by adults. Moreover, as Dorfman wrote, Mickey Mouse "joins power and infantilization." He "lords it over everybody" while his smile "disarms all criticism." The innocent mouse, "like the mass culture into which he was born, automatically reconciles the adult and the child by appealing to" our fundamental biology—"the fact that humans are instinctually conditioned to protect their young and are prepared by nature to react well to anything that resembles juvenility." So Mickey Mouse appeals to minds and

hearts everywhere by "addressing our most tender feelings for our progeny and for the future."

Disney's harmless hijinks also play on the pleasure that a democratic age finds in twitting authority. Disney's adults, like Scrooge McDuck, are pleasingly foolish, foils for fun-loving disobedience. The forces of badness get their lumps—there is always the prospect of justice—yet no one gets punished severely. Disney enshrines the little guy who thumbs his nose at power, the little gal who gets the glass slipper. Rebellion amounts to growing pains, inevitable, painless, and harmless—that is to say, fun.

Then why *shouldn't* people everywhere revel in Disney's animated innocence? Or George Lucas's cartoonish space fables? Why shouldn't live action physical comedy appeal as well? From Chaplin and Laurel and Hardy to Jerry Lewis and Jim Carrey, clowning combines childish insouciance and wildness, suggesting the joys of surmounting social convention—for a while. I once asked a Chinese student what Chinese viewers think when they watch the Academy Award ceremonies. "We think Americans are wild and crazy people," she said. Years later, during the popular National Basketball Association broadcast in China, a Beijing university student wearing jeans and a T-shirt said on the subject of Dennis Rodman: "I couldn't accept this from a Chinese player, but he's an American, so we expect it." Americans may look like cartoon savages, "wild and crazy people," but they are not only cast as the world's pleasure principle; they are its projective screen, its global outlaw, buffoon, and marshal wrapped up in one.

LAVISHNESS, INFORMALITY, AND ENERGY

Let's not neglect the obvious. Made-in-America media celebrate material excess: lavish costumes, voluptuous bodies, taut musculature, streets lined with sports cars, technical wizardry, and extravagant landscapes. There are of course exceptions in the raw, jittery, low-budget look of "independent" films (increasingly distributed or owned by giant corporations), but these are not the blockbusters. Pride of profitability goes to the star vehicle where, even in the absence of a glamorous venue, the production is so lush as to constitute an advertisement for lavishness all by itself. As a Hollywood slogan has it, all the money is on the screen: money to burn.

Music-video, slick-magazine glamour is alluring to people everywhere who would rather not accept their lot and imagine they may not have to: the uprooted and ambitious, the middle classes in poor countries, city dwellers not long off the land, eager to dream big about living large. The *Baywatch* beach, the MTV nightclub, the New York of *Sex and the City*, and so on, offer glimpses of plenitude no less enviable for their imperfections. Even antiglamour has its glamour. No one has ever stated the ambiguity of the American powerhouse hero better than critic Robert Warshow, who wrote of "the gangster as tragic hero" that "he is what we want to be and what we are afraid we may become." If American images were nothing more than celebrations of good fortune, they would be unwatchably tedious. The wealthy and powerful must risk crashing and burning. There must be snakes in Eden—for every Southfork Ranch, a J. R. Ewing; for every John F. Kennedy, a Lee Harvey Oswald. One moment, here is wealth; the next moment, it bursts into flames, smashes into an iceberg, collides with an asteroid. Viewers revel in the display of luxury and remember that material goods are disposable. Stuff is fleeting. Grandeur is embattled. In the end, it is ordinary you who are enviable, safe in your seat.

Lavishness alone would not export so successfully. There must be transgressions, and usually they must be capped by happy endings. Forces of evil must get their comeuppance. The roustabout must vanquish the stuffed shirt, the pretty woman humanize the driven rich man. In the person of no-nonsense Indiana Jones (Harrison Ford), winsome everyman (Tom Hanks), schlemiel (Woody Allen), raffish commoner (Leonardo DiCaprio in *Titanic*, Julia Roberts in *Erin Brockovich*), everyman and -woman square off against the pompous, the ignorant, the cruel and autocratic, and while they do not always prevail, they are always good company. "Make my day," "Read my lips"—this is how to speak American, damn it. When Errol Flynn's Robin Hood, who has dumped a slaughtered deer on Prince John's banquet table, tells the sheriff of Nottingham that the Saxons are "overtaxed, overworked, and paid off with a knife, a club, or a rope," Maid Marian objects: "Why, you speak treason." "Fluently," comes Robin Hood's reply, standing for all the roguishness and physical prowess, the honorable disrespect, that makes the American hero recognizable everywhere as an icon of justice. How fitting that Flynn was born in either Tasmania or Ireland—he claimed both at various times—while Michael Curtiz, director of *The Adventures of Robin Hood* (1938), came from Hungary, and the story, of course, from England.

Yet when the hero transgresses or *subverts*—to use the cultural studies buzzword—it is in the interest of restoring righteous order. For this reason, the land of law and lawyers is chock-full of courtroom dramas, and even though they are not generally export favorites, they have won a reputation for the defense of the little guy. In 1991, Belgrade students who had been beaten by riot police after an opposition rally, then arrested, tortured, and subjected to a show trial, and who still had the audacity to ask for a defense lawyer, were told: "You have been watching too many American films!" (Obviously the policeman knew his American films too.) Indeed, this seems to have been a Serbian theme. "President Milosevic will win this election," said one of his leading supporters nine years later. "This is not Hollywood." The editor of a "hip, glossy magazine" in Beijing who sued her employer for firing her told a reporter, "We've seen a lot of Hollywood movies—they feature weddings, funerals and going to court. So now we think it's only natural to go to court a few times in your life."

The individual refusing to take no for an answer, fighting city hall, fluently speaking treason, or at least seeking a day in court, flourished in the 1960s. The counterculture romanticized Indians, America's losers. Youth culture discovered the pleasures of injury and frustration: "A hard rain's gonna fall." "Hello darkness, my old friend." "I can't get no satisfaction." "This is the end." Rock music let dark stars shine. At the movies, transgression might lead to unhappy or at least ambiguous outcomes; it might even get you killed (*Bonnie and Clyde, Easy Rider, Midnight Cowboy*). In the 1970s, a new wave of American filmmakers imported alienation from Europe. Downer films like *The Godfather, The Parallax View, Three Days of the Condor, Nashville, Network,* and *Chinatown,* among many others, gave the advantage to malevolent forces, and if the good guys did manage some sort of victory in the end, they had to pull it out of a hat. After a period of adjustment, the studios found the market in rebellion. Hollywood enfolded counter-Hollywood. Mainstream and rivulet were equally American, the categories sometimes hard to distinguish. As dissident movements spread around the world, American popular culture was taken to heart by dissidents everywhere, encouraging them in not-always-predictable ways. Independent-minded girls admired Madonna's sly music videos and took her songs as anthems of autonomy. When Václav Havel was a dissident in Czechoslovakia, he found antiestablishment values in Michael Jackson's extravagant music video "Thriller." The America of freedom and rights fought with the America of arrogant wealth not only in American life itself but on the screens of the multiplex. In many countries, *America* would come to signify not napalm—or not *only* napalm—but black power, feminism, gay liberation, the right to be different.

Popular culture "means" what its users think and feel it means. For minority populations everywhere, American movies and music can be taken up as cultural counterweights against the local powers. French teenagers of North African origin listen to American music and adopt American slang. I've seen the word *Bronx* spray-painted on a wall in Amsterdam, where no doubt it affirms the down-home "badness" of young people who have never been anywhere near the terrestrial Bronx but have taken to heart some images from movies or videos.

In a way, there is no paradox here. The whole package of individualism, antiauthoritarianism, and rambunctiousness in American media is the fruit of its fundamental commitment to popularity. Here is the not-so-hidden secret at the heart of American media: because they have no other goal than to be popular, they are eminently marketable by mighty corporations that have no cultural commitment whatsoever. As CBS's vice president for television research once told me: "I'm not interested in culture. I'm not interested in pro-social values. I have only one interest. That's whether people watch the program. That's my definition of good, that's my definition of bad." The executive relished putting the matter so unguardedly, but he spoke for the entirety of the corporate mission. In and around these corporations are dotted exceptional entrepreneurs committed to and knowledgeable about the culture that is their business to promote and circulate. But even the guerrilla fighters must eventually pass the unforgiving test of profitability—and not just passable profitability but the competitive superprofitability that impresses Wall Street investors.

So the disrespectful, lavish, energetic American torrent flows on and on, appealing to ideals of action and self-reinvention, extending the comforts of recognition to the uprooted. In a world of unease and uprooting, the American images, sounds, and stories overlap nations and global diasporas. Cultivating and nourishing desires, unifying but flexible, everywhere they leave behind deposits of what can only be called a civilization—not an ideology, or a system of belief, but something less resistible, a way of life soaked in feeling, seeming to absorb with equal conviction traces of every idea or, for that matter, the absence of all ideas. It has a clear field. In this time, one-world ideologies are decidedly flimsy. With socialism largely discredited, and each world religion checked by the others, the way of life with the greatest allure turns out to be this globalizing civilization of saturation and speed that enshrines individuals, links freedom to taste, tickles the senses. How odd, but inescapable, that insofar as there are unifying symbols today, they should be the undemanding ones—not the cross, the crescent, or the flag, let alone the hammer and sickle, but Coke and Mickey Mouse.

At least for now.

AN END TO CULTURE?

I have been arguing that American culture is a complex collaboration between venal, efficient suppliers and receptive, fickle consumers. The suppliers were already well understood by Alexis de Tocqueville, with his emphasis on efficiency and convenience; the consumers by Georg Simmel, with his emphasis on the hunger for feeling and the taste for the transitory. The suppliers built a machine for delivering cultural goods; the consumers acquired a taste for them. What was true when commercial American culture poured across the country in the twentieth century remains true as it pours through the world today. The preeminence of America's styles and themes is not rule from on high. To take it that way is to misunderstand its soft power.

What I have been calling the demand side is not necessarily clamor or hunger. It is more a compound of interest, liking, tolerance—and enthusiasm. There are fanatics who talk and write feverishly about the *Stars Wars* movies, auctioning and purchasing rare merchandise, going so far as to take a day off from work to buy a movie ticket to see the debut of the *trailer* for Episode I, *The Phantom Menace*; there is the wider circle of millions who look forward less passionately to the next installment; and an even wider one of more or less curious, possibly halfhearted customers keeping up with their crowds. The multiplex is filled with American films because the

United States was first to produce a culture of comfort and convenience whose popularity was its primary reason for being. All in all, American popular culture is popular because (and to the extent that) its sleek, fast, fleeting styles of entertainment—its *commitment* to entertainment—dovetail with modern displacement and desire.

Odds are, more and more people in the twenty-first century will live the sort of existence that primes them for American-style popular taste. Unless they retrench—and there will be many religious, political, and nationalist movements trying to get them to do exactly that—each person will be multiple. Each will feel disordered and restless. Each will be comfortable relating to, feeling with, trying out the most accessible repertory of stories and sounds, cutting and pasting, surfing and clipping. Each will sprout multiple auxiliary relationships to figures who never breathed. Each will enjoy as second nature the experience of being absorbed in a fiction, as described by philosopher Catherine Wilson: "I am neither wholly myself, for I am not experiencing and operating in my 'everyday' world, but nor am I other than myself." The "I" who both is and is not "myself" has a particular history and memory, a particular body, particular likes and dislikes, but is also at home with many imagined others. Postmodernists purport to believe that, beneath the levels of role and disguise, there is no one at home, that the postures and roles "go all the way down," and to some extent they are right; there is no going back to a self whose boundaries and intentions are unambiguous. We are, now, "ourselves" but not only ourselves, increasingly in contact with spirits drawn from the media swirling around us, many of them American in inspiration if not in ownership.

There is no going back to the forest clan or the village. There is no repealing the technologies that spray images on our walls, graft stories onto our screens, sing songs into our headphones. There is no diversion from the seduction and clamor, the convenience and irritation of media. There is no avoiding the spread of American-style pop—its coupling of irreverence and brutality; its love of the road and its degradation of the word; its light rock and heavy metal. This amalgam flows through the world for worse and for better, inviting, in unknowable proportions, immigration, emulation, and revulsion. Where the flow goes, there follows a fear that American marketing exudes a uniform "McWorld"—and brings, in its wake, with dialectical certainty, destructive "Jihads."

Yet for all the fear of standardization, American pop does not erase all the vernacular alternatives, all the local forms in which artists and writers give forth their styles and stories. The emergence of a global semiculture coexists with local sensibilities. It does not simply replace them. As the Norwegian media theorist Helge Rønning suggests, it's plausible to suppose that globalized, largely American pop has become, or is in the process of becoming, almost everyone's second culture. But there is a legitimate fear of standardization. For all the many reactions worldwide to American serials, for example— in Copenhagen, it was fashionable to watch *Beverly Hills 90210* as a joke—and for all the cultural hybridization, American exports in all their seductiveness do seize attention. Just as languages die out, so is culture vulnerable to ecological simplification. Especially in the movies, where the cost of entry is high, Hollywood's premium style—its so-called high production values, its preference for the glib, the slick, the sentimental, the mechanistic and mindless, its disinterest in inwardness, its outright hostility to complication—threatens to diminish the cultural repertory of makers and audiences alike. Drowning language in gaudy and grotesque images, the mainstream Hollywood movie is driven by a hideous zero-sum principle of the senses, as if in imitation of Marshall McLuhan's most simple-minded idea—the belief that when artistic work plays on one sensory capacity (sight), it is obliged to sacrifice a previously dominant sense (the capacity for language).

True, the reach of American media has its limits. True, the linguistic range of "classic Hollywood cinema" was largely poor, too. True, its impoverishment failed to abort (and even, in some cases, succeeded in inspiring) the great generation of Ingmar Bergman, Federico Fellini, Michelangelo Antonioni, Luchino Visconti, Jean-Luc Godard, François Truffaut, Eric Rohmer, Alain Resnais, Akira Kurosawa, Yasujiro Ozu, and Kenji Mizoguchi in the 1950s and 1960s, and later, Werner Herzog, Alain Tanner, Rainer Werner Fassbinder, and Bernard Tavernier. Today, though, despite the multiplex boom, there are often fewer theaters to show the best work for more than a few days. Having been freed of the heavy hand of state censorship only to be deprived of state subsidy, the central and eastern European movie industries more than a decade after the fall of Communism are in a state of collapse. Small countries that make a handful of films a year drown in American blockbusters.

Still and all, the exceptions matter. There are other currents in global circulation. Some are as banal as Hollywood's, and no less serviceable for everyday purposes. But in recent years, we have seen extraordinary un-Americanized productions: from England, Mike Leigh's and Ken Loach's naturalism; from Poland, Krzysztof Kieslowski's existentialism; from Finland, the Kaurismäki brothers' comedy; from France, Emile Zonka's working-class tragedy; from Iran, Abbas Kiarostami's fables; from Taiwan, Edward Yang's family dramas; from Hong Kong, Wong Kar-Wai's thrillers and Chekhovian tales—and doubtless many others—scrambling for the niches left in the corners of the American-dominated mass market, often benefiting from national broadcast and cable financing (Britain's Channel 4, France's Canal +). Hollywood has limits, if not exactly borders.

As for the media as a whole, what could stop the flood but a catastrophic breakdown of civilization? (In Steven Spielberg's *A.I.*, not even global warming and the total immersion of Manhattan wipe out the media.) Why would the beat not go on? Too much desire and too much convenience converge in the nonstop spectacle; too much of the human desire to play, to test and perfect oneself, to feel, to feel good, to feel with others, to feel conveniently; too much of the desire for sensory pleasure, for a refuge from calculation, for a flight from life, or from death, or from both. The media have been gathering force for centuries. Why should their songs and stories cease to generate enthusiasm and anxiety, production and consumption, celebrity and irony, fandom and boredom, criticism and jamming, paranoia and secession? Why would a society in which people have the time to indulge their fancies this way repeal these options? The media will sweep down, their flow continuous and widening, bearing banalities and mysteries, achievements and potentials, strangeness and disappointments—this would appear to be our complex fate.

I am not proposing that anyone cease trying to launch better work. Surely there will be—there *deserve* to be—fights over who gets to harness media power, over censorship, over improving contents and broadening access. Conservatives will want today's colossal controllers to keep control but clean up the sewage. Liberals will want new tributaries to flow and to bend the stream in their preferred directions. Techno-utopians will agree with the liberal law professor who writes of digital on-line sharing: "The result will be more music, poetry, photography and journalism available to a far wider audience. . . . For those who worry about the cultural, economic and political power of the global media companies, the dreamed-of revolution is at hand. . . . It is we, not they, who are about to enter the promised land." But these apparently different ideas share an ideal: more media, more of the time.

I cannot pretend to offer a definitive balance sheet on our odd form of life immersed in images, sounds, and stories. Nor can I suggest a ten-point program for revitalization or a list of preferable activities. I have tried to confront the media as a whole, to reconceive their onrushing immensity, and to explain how they became central to our civilization. To fans, critics, paranoids, exhibitionists, ironists, and the rest, to reformers of all stripes, I would propose taking some time to step back, forgoing the fantasies of electronic perfection, leaving behind the trend-spotting gurus and pundits who purport to interpret for us the hottest and latest. I propose that we stop—and imagine the whole phenomenon freshly, taking the media seriously not as a cornucopia of wondrous gadgets or a collection of social problems, but as a central condition of an entire way of life. Perhaps if we step away from the ripples of the moment, the week, or the season, and contemplate the torrent in its entirety, we will know what we want to do about it besides change channels.

Notes

10   *McLuhan's glib formulation:* "Cogito Interruptus," originally published 1967, reprinted in Umberto Eco, *Travels in Hyperreality*, trans. William Weaver (New York: Harcourt Brace, 1986), esp. pp. 233–35.

11   *Johan Huizinga: Homo Ludens: A Study of the Play Element in Culture* (Boston: Beacon, 1955 [1944]), p. x).

1. Supersaturation, or, The Media Torrent and Disposable Feeling

13   *one English visitor:* Peter Mundy, quoted by Geert Mak, *Amsterdam*, trans. Philipp Blom (Cambridge, Mass: Harvard University Press, 2000), p. 109.

the grandest Dutch inventories: Simon Schama, *The Embarrassment of Riches: An Interpretation of Dutch Culture in the Golden Age* (New York: Knopf, 1987), pp. 313–19. Schama notes that research in the relevant archives is "still in its early days" (p. 315).

scanty and fixed: Many bourgeois Dutch houses also featured a camera lucida, a mounted magnifying lens trained on objects in the vicinity. Because the lens was movable, motion could be simulated—distant objects being brought nearer and sent farther away. But because the apparatus was mounted in a fixed location, the range of objects in motion was limited to those actually visible from the window. (Svetlana Alpers, personal communication, October 8, 1999.)

15   *Raymond Williams:* "Drama in a Dramatised Society," in Alan O'Connor, ed., *Raymond Williams on Television* (Toronto: Between the Lines, 1989 [1974]), pp. 3–5. *Flow* comes up in Williams's *Television: Technology and Cultural Form* (New York: Schocken, 1975), pp. 86 ff. *Blaise Pascal: Pensées,* trans. W. F. Trotter (www.eserver.org/philosophy/pascal-pensees.txt), sec. 2, par. 142.

16   *In 1995:* Robert D. Putnam, *Bowling Alone: The Collapse and Revival of American Community* (New York: Simon and Schuster, 2000), p. 222, citing John P. Robinson and Geoffrey Godbey, *Time for Life: The Surprising Ways Americans Use Their Time,* 2nd ed. (University Park: Pennsylvania State University Press, 1999), pp. 136–53, 340–41, 222.
     France: This April 2001 figure for individuals fifteen and older comes from Mediamat (Mediametriewww.mediametria.fr/television/mediamat_mensuel/2001/avril.html).
     One survey of forty-three nations: Putnam, *Bowling Alone,* p. 480, citing Eurodata TV (*One Television Year in the World: Audience Report,* April 1999).
     one major researcher: John P. Robinson, "I Love My TV," *American Demographics,* September 1990, p. 24.
     Sex, race, income: Robert Kubey and Mihaly Csikszentmihalyi, *Television and the Quality of Life: How Viewing Shapes Everyday Experience* (Hillsdale, N.J.: Lawrence Erlbaum Associates, 1990), pp. 71–73.
     Long-term users . . . and the like: UCLA Center for Communication Policy, *The UCLA Internet Report: Surveying the Digital Future,* November 2000, pp. 10, 17, 18, 14 (www.ccp.ucla.edu).

17   *national survey of media conditions . . . satellite service:* Donald F. Roberts, *Kids and Media @ the New Millennium* (Menlo Park, Calif.: Henry J. Kaiser Family Foundation, 1999), p. 9, table 1. There were 3,155 children in the sample, including oversamples of black and Hispanic children, to ensure that results in these minority populations would also be statistically significant. As best as a reader can discern, this was a reliable study, with a margin of error of no more than plus-or-minus five percentage points. Since the results for younger children, ages two to seven, come from parents' reports, they may well be conservative, since parents may be uninformed of the extent of their children's viewing or may be underplaying it in order not to feel ashamed before interviewers.
     The uniformity: Ibid., p. 11, tables 3-A, 3-B, 3-C.

18   *How accessible:* Ibid., pp. 13–15, tables 4, 5-A, 5-B, 6.
     TV in their bedrooms: In general, fewer western European or Israeli children than Americans have TVs in their bedrooms, but 70 percent in

Great Britain do. Next highest in Europe is 64 percent in Denmark. The lows are 31 percent in Holland and 24 percent in Switzerland. Leen d'Haenens, "Old and New Media: Access and Ownership in the Home," in Sonia Livingstone and Moira Bovill, eds., *Children and Their Changing Media Environment: A European Comparative Study* (London: Lawrence Erlbaum Associates, 2001), p. 57.

18   *As for time:* Roberts, *Kids and Media*, pp. 21–23, tables 8-C, 8-D.
exposure . . . varies inversely with class: The same point applies to differences in media use throughout the prosperous world. As the economist Adair Turner writes: "European Internet penetration lags the US by 18 to 24 months. When cars or television sets were first introduced, the lag was more like 15 years. . . . The shortness of the lag also suggests that social concern about a 'digital divide,' whether within or between nations, is largely misplaced. . . . Time lags between different income groups in the penetration of personal computers, Internet connections or mobile phones are much shorter, once again because all these products are cheap. . . . At the global level the same scepticism about a digital divide should prevail. Africa may lag 15 years or so behind US levels of PC and Internet penetration, but it lags more like a century behind in basic literacy and health care." Adair Turner, "Not the e-conomy," *Prospect* (London), April 2001 (www.prospect-magazine.co.uk/highlights /essay_turner_april01).

19   *western European children:* Johannes W. J. Beentjes et al., "Children's Use of Different Media: For How Long and Why?" in Livingstone and Bovill, eds., *Children and Their Changing Media Environment*, p. 96.

21   *We root for them:* Donald Horton and R. Richard Wohl, "Mass Communication and Para-Social Interaction: Observations on Intimacy at a Distance," *Psychiatry* 19, no. 3 (1956), pp. 215–29, and Herbert J. Gans, *The Urban Villagers* (New York: Free Press, 1962), pp. 187–96.

22   hyperreal . . . *"almost real":* Eco, *Travels in Hyperreality*, pp. 8, 30; Jean Baudrillard, *Simulacra and Simulation*, trans. Sheila Faria Glaser (Ann Arbor: University of Michigan Press, 1994 [1981]).

24   *Raymond Williams:* "Drama in a Dramatised Society," p. 5.

25   *"a supernatural instrument":* Marcel Proust, *The Captive*, in *Remembrance of Things Past*, trans. C. K. Scott Moncrieff and Terence Kilmartin (New York: Random House, 1981), vol. 3, p. 24.
we have the right: I paraphrase this capsule summary of the culture of capitalism from Leonard Michaels, "The Personal and the Individual," *Partisan Review* 68, no. 1 (winter 2001), www.bu.edu/partisanreview/ archive/2001/1/michaels.html.
"extensions of man": Marshall McLuhan, *Understanding Media: The Extensions of Man* (New York: McGraw-Hill, 1964).

27   *In a scene: Don Quixote*, pt. I, chap. 23. On reading aloud in the Spanish
Golden Age, see Roger Chartier, "Reading Matter and 'Popular' Read-
ing: From the Renaissance to the Seventeenth Century," in Guglielmo
Cavallo and Roger Chartier, eds., *A History of Reading in the West*, trans.
Lydia G. Cochrane (Amherst: University of Massachusetts Press, 1999),
pp. 269–78.

    Pilgrim's Progress: Ian Watt, *The Rise of the Novel* (Berkeley: University
of California Press, 1957), p. 50.

28   *David Riesman: The Lonely Crowd*, abridged ed. (New Haven: Yale University Press, 1961 [1950]), p. 96.

    Jim Bridger: Lawrence W. Levine, *Highbrow/Lowbrow* (New York:
Oxford University Press, 1988), p. 18.

    "hardly a pioneer's hut": Alexis de Tocqueville, *Democracy in America*, ed.
Phillips Bradley (New York: Vintage, 1960), vol. 2, p. 58. How much
these volumes were read Tocqueville did not report, although he did
go on charmingly: "I remember that I read the feudal drama of *Henry
V* for the first time in a log cabin."

    Uncle Tom's Cabin: Richard Ohmann, *Selling Culture: Magazines, Mar-
kets, and Class at the Turn of the Century* (London and New York: Verso,
1996), p. 21.

    "refuge" . . . "a new way": Riesman, *The Lonely Crowd*, p. 96.

29   *contemporary housewives:* Janice Radway, *Reading the Romance: Reading,
Patriarchy, and Popular Culture* (Chapel Hill: University of North Car-
olina Press, 1984).

    In 1865: Ohmann, *Selling Culture*, p. 29.

    *Richard Butsch: The Making of American Audiences: From Stage to Televi-
sion, 1750–1990* (Cambridge: Cambridge University Press, 2000),
pp. 295, 297.

    nightly TV audience: Brian Lowry, "Turn Off the Set? Not if Media Can
Help It," *Los Angeles Times*, April 18, 2001.

    Butsch's computations: Calculated from Butsch, *The Making of American
Audiences*, pp. 296–301 and, for 1998, table 750, sec. 14, *2000 Census
Report* (counting individual workers without education beyond high
school).

32   *Siegfried Kracauer: Die Angestellten*, p. 304, in David Frisby, *Fragments
of Modernity: Theories of Modernity in the Work of Simmel, Kracauer and
Benjamin* (Cambridge, Mass.: MIT Press, 1986), p. 170.

    Blaise Pascal: Pensées, sec. 2, par. 171, par. 141.

33   *Marx in 1843:* "Contribution to the Critique of Hegel's *Philosophy of
Right:* Introduction" (1843), in Robert C. Tucker, ed., *The Marx-Engels
Reader* (New York: Norton, 1972), p. 12. Emphasis added.

    By 1867: Karl Marx, *Capital*, pt. I, chap. 1, sec. 4, in Tucker, ed., *The
Marx-Engels Reader*, pp. 216, 217.

34   *Marx tended to think:* Ibid., pt. 3, chap. 7, in Tucker, ed., *The Marx-Engels Reader*, p. 237.
      "real conditions of life": Karl Marx and Friedrich Engels, "Manifesto of the Communist Party" (1848), in Tucker, ed., *The Marx-Engels Reader*, p. 338.
37   *"the power ... human condition":* Georg Simmel, *The Philosophy of Money*, 2nd enlarged ed., ed. David Frisby, trans. Tom Bottomore and David Frisby (London: Routledge, 1990 [1907]), pp. 67, 211.
      "Man is ... between people": Ibid., pp. 211, 228, 232, 298.
      "essentially intellectualistic ... unrelenting hardness": Georg Simmel, "The Metropolis and Metropolitan Life" (1903), trans. Edward A. Shils, in Donald N. Levine, ed., *Georg Simmel: On Individuality and Social Forms* (Chicago: University of Chicago Press, 1971), pp. 325, 327, 326. In this essay, Simmel emphasizes the impact of life in the city. In *The Philosophy of Money* (p. 255), he writes that "cynicism and a blasé attitude" are "almost endemic to the heights of a money culture ... the results of the reduction of the concrete values of life to the mediating value of money." In practice, this is a distinction without a difference; a money culture is distinctly urban, and vice versa. In my discussion of blaséness, I mix elements of both analyses.
38   *"intellectualistic ... aversion":* Simmel, "Metropolis," pp. 326, 327, 329, 332.
      "cynicism ... 'market price' ": Simmel, *Philosophy of Money*, p. 256.
39   *the blasé person ... "the cure":* Ibid., pp. 256, 257.
      "Not only ... particularity": Ibid., pp. 297–98.
40   *The mask never melts:* This sentence is adapted from an unpublished letter to me from Christopher Z. Hobson.
      "rationalistic ... unpsychological": Simmel, *Philosophy of Money*, p. 94.
      historic misunderstandings: Against this orthodoxy, Rousseau, Goethe, and the Romantics draw the opposite conclusion: that they feel, therefore they exist. Indeed, hard neuroscience now confirms their view that feelings are fundamental, that, in an evolutionary sense, they precede thought—that reason has its heart. See Antonio Danasio, *Descartes' Error* (New York: Putnam, 1994) and *The Feeling of What Happens: Body and Emotion in the Making of Consciousness* (San Diego: Harcourt Brace Jovanovich, 1999), esp. pp. 18, 41–42. On pp. 41–42, the neurologist Danasio writes: "Emotion probably assists reasoning, especially when it comes to personal and social matters. . . . [C]ertain levels of emotion processing probably point us to the sector of the decision-making space where our reason can operate most efficiently. . . . Well-targeted and well-deployed emotion seems to be a support system without which the edifice of reason cannot operate properly. These results and their interpretation [call] into question the idea of dismissing emotion as a luxury or a nuisance or a mere evolutionary vestige."
41   *The idea spreads:* Charles Taylor, *Sources of the Self: The Making of the*

> *Modern Identity* (Cambridge, Mass.: Harvard University Press, 1989), pp. 368–69, 374.

41 *management problem:* On "emotion rules" in the management of feeling in public, see Arlie R. Hochschild, *The Managed Heart* (Berkeley: University of California Press, 1983).

in much of the West: In one German village of the seventeenth century, for example, guilt seems to have been experienced—in the words of historian David Sabean—as "not so much a feeling as a condition." Emotion followed directly from external pressures, as the sensation of coldness follows from nightfall. "The internal condition of the heart," Sabean writes, "arose from a situation that was external to the individual." God made you pious, and the powers-that-be made you afraid or respectful. David Warren Sabean, *Power in the Blood: Popular Culture and Village Discourse in Early Modern Germany* (Cambridge: Cambridge University Press, 1984), pp. 34, 47.

42 *Owen Barfield: History in English Words* (London: Faber and Faber, 1962 [1926]), pp. 169–70.

"moral sentiments": Adam Smith, *The Theory of Moral Sentiments* (Oxford: Clarendon Press, 1976 [1759, 1790]), which begins: "How selfish soever man may be supposed, there are evidently some principles in his nature, which interest him in the fortune of others, and render their happiness necessary to him, though he derives nothing from it except the pleasure of seeing it" (p. 9). The Smith who placed such emphasis on fellow-feeling is obviously not the flinty Smith beloved of rugged individualists.

Novels . . . were schools for sentiment: Watt, *The Rise of the Novel.*

Lord Chesterfield's volume of letters: C. Dallett Hemphill, "Class, Gender, and the Regulation of Emotional Expression in Revolutionary-Era Conduct Literature," in Peter N. Stearns and Jan Lewis, eds., *An Emotional History of the United States* (New York: New York University Press, 1998), pp. 34–41.

43 *Alexis de Tocqueville: Democracy in America,* vol. 2, pp. 50, 52, 54, 62–63. The "sentiment" that falls away in the democratic arts is deep feeling, not sentimentality.

44 *Groucho Marx:* Quoted in Geoffrey O'Brien, "The Triumph of Marxism," *New York Review of Books,* July 20, 2000, pp. 8, 10.

45 *Georg Simmel . . . David Frisby:* "Berliner Gewerbe-Ausstellung (Berlin Trade Exhibition)," *Die Zeit* (Vienna) 8, July 25, 1896, in Frisby, *Fragments of Modernity,* p. 94.

Writing in 1904: Simmel, "Fashion" (1904), in Levine, *Georg Simmel,* pp. 296, 303.

46 *Michel Foucault: Discipline and Punish* (New York: Pantheon, 1977), a

translation by Alan Sheridan of *Surveiller et punir*, which would more properly be translated "Surveillance and punishment."

46 *filled public spaces:* A superb catalog of turn-of-the-century representations spreading throughout the commercial sections of great cities is William Leach, *Land of Desire: Merchants, Power, and the Rise of a New American Culture* (New York: Pantheon, 1993).

William Wordsworth: The Prelude, bk. 7, "Residence in London," lines 201–3, 212, 232–33, 238–39 (1850 edition).

47 *Theodore Dreiser: Sister Carrie* (New York: Modern Library, 1997 [1900]), pp. 127, 12–13.

This vivid commotion: Again, there are historical precedents. The novelty of huge electrical signs should not be allowed to obscure the fact that in medieval Paris, shop signs "projected far into the streets, obstructed the traffic and blocked the long vistas so pleasing to the Baroque, absolutist mentality" (whereupon, in the seventeenth century, according to a contemporary English account, Louis XIV ordered shop-keepers "to take down all their signs at once, and not to advance them above a Foot or two from the Wall."). Wolfgang Schivelbusch, *Disenchanted Night: The Industrialization of Light in the Nineteenth Century*, trans. Angela Davies (Berkeley: University of California Press, 1988), pp. 84–85.

Traditional signs: Is it an accident that Ferdinand de Saussure produced his influential idea of a sign as a combination of a present "signifier" and an absent "signified" amid the proliferation of actual signs? (Student notes on his lectures were published posthumously, as *Cours de linguistique générale*, in 1916.)

48 *Times Square:* See Leach, *Land of Desire*, pp. 47–48, 338–48, and *One Hundred Years of Spectacle*, a work-in-progress by Marshall Berman.

neon lights: These were patented in 1910. http://dmla.clan.lib.nv.us/docs/museums/reno/exneon/neontext.htm.

jarred intellectuals . . . "thirst for life": Siegfried Kracauer in 1928 referred to Paris as "the headquarters of nightlife," where "the illumination is so shrill that one must close one's ears to it." Kracauer, "Ansichtspostkarte," *Frankfurter Zeitung*, May 26, 1930, in Frisby, *Fragments of Modernity*, pp. 141–42.

one editorial booster: Four-Track News 6 (February 1904), p. 121, quoted in David Nasaw, *Going Out: The Rise and Fall of Public Amusements* (New York: Basic, 1993), p. 8.

O. J. Gude: "Art and Advertising Joined by Electricity," *Signs of the Times: A Journal for All Interested in Better Advertising* 3 (August 1912) and 9 (October 1912), pp. 246–47, quoted in Leach, *Land of Desire*, pp. 47, 48.

49 *an advertising journal:* "Be It So, Electrical Advertising Has Only

Begun," *Signs of the Times* (December 1912), quoted in Leach, *Land of Desire*, p. 47. Italics in the original.

49   *such imposing displays:* Leach, *Land of Desire*, p. 47.

   collective spectacles: Michael McGerr, *The Decline of Popular Politics* (New York: Oxford University Press, 1986), and Michael Schudson, *The Good Citizen* (Cambridge, Mass.: Harvard University Press, 1995).

50   *low-risk access:* On the transcendent promise of advertisements, see Jackson Lears, *Fables of Abundance: A Cultural History of Advertising in America* (New York: Basic, 1994).

51   *Neal Gabler: Life the Movie: How Entertainment Conquered Reality* (New York: Knopf, 1998), pp. 60–61.

   spirit of information: The pleasures of being informed, in touch with the world, are emphasized in Michael Schudson's pioneering account of the rise of the penny press, in *Discovering the News* (New York: Basic, 1978), pp. 43–60.

   What Simmel called: Philosophy of Money, p. 484.

54   *logic of individualism:* But of course inexorability is easiest to spot after the fact. Dick Tracy's two-way wrist radio appeared in a comic strip in 1946, but at this writing, despite the shrinking size of cell phones, industry has not yet caught up with fancy.

   "Give today a soundtrack": A subsequent billboard proposes, or demands, "Satisfy lust" and "Be inspired," and depicts a mobile phone and the company's name: Siemens.

   The Walkman story: John Nathan, *SONY: The Private Life* (Boston: Houghton Mifflin, 1999), pp. 150–52, 155, and Michael Bull, *Sounding Out the City: Personal Stereos and the Management of Everyday Life* (Oxford: Berg, 2000), p. 5.

55   *the Internet pioneer:* Leonard Kleinrock, "What Is Nomadicity?" introduction to "Nomadic '96: The Nomadic Computing and Communications Conference" ("The First Industry-Wide Conference Devoted to the Exciting New Technologies of Nomadic Computing!"), March 13–15, 1996, San Jose, California. Professor Kleinrock of UCLA, according to his handout, "led the effort to become the first node on the ARPANET [the predecessor to the Internet] in 1969" and "is at the forefront of efforts to create the technologies and infrastructures necessary to enable nomadic computing and communications." "Most of us are nomads," he writes. "We need support for various devices, applications and services as we move from place to place. The loss in productivity without such support is vast, as are the advantages to be found with proper nomadic support." Note that, as usual in the business sales environment, Kleinrock begins with the economic incentive for all-around information access. Raymond Williams was getting at the same phenomenon with the clumsy term *mobile privatization*. Given the

fact that he used the term in 1975 (*Television: Technology and Cultural Form*, p. 26), he was dead on. What he did not anticipate was the multiplication of electronic means by which connectedness would outgrow central headquarters.

56   *Jean-Paul Sartre: Critique de la Raison Dialectique* (Paris: Gallimard, 1985 [1960]), pp. 361ff.
       Walkmanned Londoners: Bull, *Sounding Out*, pp. 50, 52, 96, 17.

57   *"arsenal of mobile technology":* Ibid., p. 75.
       technological sublime: Howard P. Segal, *Technological Utopianism in American Culture* (Chicago: University of Chicago Press, 1985).
       techgnosis: Erik Davis, *Techgnosis* (New York: Harmony Books, 1998).

58   *Kunitake Ando:* Reuters, "Sony Plans Web Walkman," May 15, 2000, http://www.pcworld.com/pcwtoday/article/0,1510,16704,00.html.
       In the year 2000: Pew Research Center survey, on-line, spring 2000.
       So did 63 percent: Alan Travis, "Britons Grasp Net and Web Phones," *Guardian*, January 24, 2001.

59   *the trill of the cell phone:* Neither were the commercial signs that crowded into sight a century ago. As William Leach writes (*Land of Desire*, p. 48): "Not everyone was pleased by these intrusions. Reform groups in many cities saw the signs as aesthetic nuisances and as threats to real estate values. 'The abuses,' admitted Emily Fogg Mead, 'are much in evidence. ... The weary traveler becomes impatient at the staring street-car "ads," at the gaping signs and, above all, at the desecration of rocks and cliffs and beautiful scenery.' One such traveler was the sociologist Edward Ross, who, on a railroad trip through the Pacific Northwest in 1912, saw a sign—'Mrs. Scruber's Tooth Powder'—displayed against a background of shaggy pines. 'Had we passengers felt proper resentment, we would have avoided that tooth powder to the end of our days,' he wrote [in 1901]. But, idolators of 'enterprise' that we are, we never think of boycotting those who fling their business in our faces at inopportune moments. Urban businesses, he continued, seem to have carte blanche to do what they wish with the public space: 'In the city, every accessible spot where the eye may wander, frantically proclaims the merits of somebody's pickles or Scott Whiskey.' But 'why,' Ross asked, 'should a man be allowed violently to seize and wrench my attention every time I step out of doors, to flash his wares into my brain with a sign?' " Ross was one of the founders of American sociology. Little did he know!
       Devices to block mobile phones: Lisa Guernsey, "Taking the Offensive Against Cell Phones," *New York Times*, Circuits Section, January 11, 2001.

60   *Soundtracking:* For this felicitous term I am indebted to J. Bottum, "The Soundtracking of America," *Atlantic Monthly*, March 2000.

60   *choose not to hear:* Aristotle noted this fact. Don Gifford, *The Farther Shore: A Natural History of Perception, 1798–1984* (New York: Atlantic Monthly Press, 1990), p. 54.

61   *Milan Kundera's words: Testaments Betrayed,* trans. Linda Asher (New York: HarperCollins, 1995), pp. 235–36.
     Industry . . . Muzak Corporation: Cited in Simon C. Jones and Thomas G. Schumacher, "Muzak: On Functional Music and Power," *Critical Studies in Mass Communication* 9 (1992), pp. 158–59. My discussion of Muzak is heavily indebted to this article, which Fred Turner called to my attention.
     "By 1946" . . . melody: Ibid., pp. 159–60, citing J. Hulting, "Muzak: A Study in Sonic Ideology" (M.A. thesis, University of Pennsylvania, 1988).

62   *"a hint of nostalgia . . . security of home":* Jones and Schumacher, "Muzak," p. 161.
     In the 1950s: David R. Yale, "The Politics of Muzak: Big Brother Calls the Tune," *Student Musicologists at Minnesota 4,* pp. 80–103.
     By the 1980s: Jones and Schumacher, "Muzak," pp. 162–64.
     Airports: Airports have also discovered the virtues of installing another source of sound, namely an airport version of the TV news, which hums along reassuringly on its own timetable, impervious to flight delays and personal disruptions. Despite the declining attention to television news, news remains the residual commons, whereas any particular choice of entertainment might feel exclusive. The screen tuned to the news converts the gate area to a domestic commons, like a bar deploying sports events. See Adam Hochschild, "Taken Hostage at the Airport," *New York Times* Op-Ed Page, October 26, 1996.

63   *J. Bottum:* "Soundtracking."

64   *woofer-heavy:* Indeed, it may be more advisable than generally understood to obscure the humdrum bass notes and minor chords that crowd the modern soundscape whether one thinks one hears them or not. According to the psychologist Stephen W. Porges (personal communication, July 3, 2000), the human brain is hard-wired to interpret low frequencies as the sounds of predators, spurring the tension of an automatic fight-or-flight reaction. The infusion of everyday life by deep bass notes may therefore produce a characteristic low-level state of alarm. According to Toby Lester of the *Atlantic,* while major thirds formed by distinct notes that combine in the built environment produce happiness, certain minor chords, notably the minor third, can be counted on to produce bad moods. Christian musical theorists of the Middle Ages believed that particular chords had definite symbolic content, the augmented fourth in particular being known as the *diabolus in musica*; it

turns out that they had science on their side. "Mapping," "This American Life," Public Radio International, September 4, 1998.

65   *nutcracking:* Alfred Harbage, *Shakespeare's Audience* (New York: Columbia University Press, 1941), p. 112. Harbage deduces: "If such sounds as this could provide the major annoyance (like coughing and paper-rustling now), a standard of silence may be inferred little inferior to ours."

Frances Trollope: Levine, *Highbrow/Lowbrow: The Emergence of Cultural Hierarchy in America* (New York: Oxford University Press, 1988), p. 25.

A New York journalist: George G. Foster, *New York in Slices: By an Experienced Carver* (New York: W. F. Burgess, 1849), p. 120, and Foster, *New York Naked* (New York: n. p., n. d.), p. 144, quoted in Robert W. Snyder, *The Voice of the City: Vaudeville and Popular Culture in New York* (New York: Oxford University Press, 1989), p. 7.

66   *A French reporter . . . "your infernal neck":* Levine, *Highbrow/Lowbrow*, pp. 27, 30.

sacralized space . . . those of the middle class: Ibid., pp. 104–46 and 219–31; Kathy Peiss, *Cheap Amusements: Working Women and Leisure in Turn-of-the-Century New York* (Philadelphia: Temple University Press, 1986); Snyder, *Voice of the City*; Nasaw, *Going Out*; Lizabeth Cohen, *Making a New Deal: Industrial Workers in Chicago, 1919–1939* (Cambridge: Cambridge University Press, 1990), pp. 123ff.

Jonathan Crary: Suspensions of Perception: Attention, Spectacle, and Modern Culture (Cambridge, Mass.: MIT Press, 1999), pp. 1–79. The quotes are from pp. 49, 17, and 16, respectively, the second and third drawn from James Cappie, "Some Points in the Physiology of Attention, Belief, and Will," *Brain* 9 (July 1886), p. 201, and Oswald Külpe, *Outlines of Psychology* (1893), trans. Edward Bradford Titchener (London: Sonnenschein, 1895), p. 215. Italics in the original.

"the bringing of the consciousness" . . . "leisure time": Crary, *Suspensions of Perception*, p. 77.

67   *the locomotive:* Many examples of this theme can be found throughout Leo Marx, *The Machine in the Garden: Technology and the Pastoral Ideal in America* (New York: Oxford University Press, 1964).

the right to privacy: Samuel D. Warren and Louis D. Brandeis, "The Right to Privacy," *Harvard Law Review*, vol. 4, p. 195 (December 1890).

ABC installed: Lisa de Moraes, "The Latest Ad Campaign From Tinkletown," *Washington Post*, July 18, 2000.

69   *Mike Searles:* Quoted in Allan Casey, "Make Your School an Ad-free Zone," *Adbusters* 28 (winter 2000), p. 67, and http://adbusters.org/campaigns/commercialfree/tour/1.html.

hiring celebrities: For American advertising's increasing use of celebrities throughout the twentieth century, I am indebted to research by Sue Collins.

69 *"unique selling proposition"*: Rosser Reeves, *Reality in Advertising* (New York: Knopf, 1961), passim.

2. Speed and Sensibility

72 *between 36 and 107:* Robert V. Bellamy, Jr., and James R. Walker, *Television and the Remote Control: Grazing on a Vast Wasteland* (New York: Guilford, 2000), pp. 38–44.
a study conducted in 2000: Pew Research Center study, 2000.
the telephone: Stephen Kern, *The Culture of Time and Space, 1880–1918* (Cambridge, Mass.: Harvard University Press, 1984), pp. 271–77.

74 *James R. Beniger: The Control Revolution: Technological and Economic Origins of the Information Society* (Cambridge, Mass.: Harvard University Press, 1986), p. vii.
James Truslow Adams: The Tempo of Modern Life (Boston: Albert and Charles Boni, 1931), pp. 85, 90.

76 *Michael Schudson:* Personal communication.
"now this": On the "now this" snippet mode in television news, see Neil Postman, *Amusing Ourselves to Death: Public Discourse in the Age of Show Business* (New York: Penguin, 1986), pp. 99–100.
Edward Luttwak: Turbo-Capitalism: Winners and Losers in the Global Economy (New York: HarperCollins, 1999).
Charles H. Ferguson: High Stakes, No Prisoners: A Winner's Tale of Greed and Glory in the Internet Wars (New York: Times Books, 1999), p. 51.

77 *Zaki Laïdi: La Tyrannie de L'Urgence* (Montreal: Editions Fides, 1999), p. 21.
Paul Virilio: Speed and Politics: An Essay on Dromology, trans. Mark Polizzotti (New York: Semiotexte, 1986), p. 47.
seventeenth-century Holland: Simon Schama, *The Embarrassment of Riches: An Interpretation of Dutch Culture in the Golden Age* (New York: Knopf, 1987).
eighteenth-century England: Neil McKendrick, John Brewer, and J. H. Plumb, *Birth of a Consumer Society* (London: Europa, 1982).
eight-hour working day: Already in 1848, French workers had demanded "the revolution of three eights"—eight hours of work, eight hours of sleep, eight hours of leisure time. Virilio, *Speed and Politics*, p. 28.

78 *consumers too:* See Lawrence Glickman, *A Living Wage: American Workers and the Making of Consumer Society* (Ithaca: Cornell University Press, 1997), and Gary Cross, *An All-Consuming Century: Why Commercialism Won in Modern America* (New York: Columbia University Press, 2000).
they did not want: On General Motors's idea of annual model changes and "trading up," as opposed to Henry Ford's idea of an unvarying

black sedan to be sold at a progressively lower price, see Alfred Sloan, *My Years with General Motors* (New York: Macfadden, 1965), pp. 273–74.

78   *They would rather reward:* Gary Cross, *Time and Money: The Making of Consumer Culture* (London and New York: Routledge, 1993), p. 131.
In Cross's view: Ibid., pp. 82–87, 207 ff.

79   *Colin Campbell: The Romantic Ethic and the Spirit of Modern Consumerism* (Oxford: Basil Blackwell, 1987), pp. 86, 87. See the useful discussion by Jean-Christophe Agnew, "Consumer Culture in Historical Perspective," in John Brewer and Roy Porter, eds., *Consumption and the World of Goods* (London: Routledge, 1993), pp. 24–26.
"He's brilliant": Sharon Waxman, "King of the World Wild Web: Young Seth Warshavsky Knows What Makes People Click," *Washington Post,* January 6, 1999.

80   *working more hours:* See Juliet Schor, *The Overworked American* (New York: Basic, 1991) and the critique by James Gleick, *Faster: The Acceleration of Just About Everything* (New York: Pantheon, 1999), pp. 139–47.

81   *Plutarch: Life of Pericles,* trans. John Dryden (classics.mit.edu/Plutarch/pericles.html).
St. Augustine: Confessions, trans. Albert C. Outler, bk. 8, chap. 4, 9; bk. 10, chap. 35, 57; bk 4, chap. 15, 31; bk. 5, chap. 1; bk. 9, chap. 6, 12.

82   *the English language:* Eric Partridge, *Origins: A Short Etymological Dictionary of Modern English* (New York: Greenwich House, 1983), p. 648.
In England: Robert Levine, *A Question of Time* (New York: Basic, 1997), p. 57.
The German: Jacob Grimm and Wilhelm Grimm, *Deutsches Wörterbuch* (Leipzig: Verlag von S. Hirzel, 1899), vol. 9, p. 296.
Benedictine monks: Michael Young, *The Metronomic Society: Natural Rhythms and Human Timetables* (Cambridge, Mass.: Harvard University Press, 1988), p. 202.
Lewis Mumford: Technics and Civilization (New York: Harcourt Brace, 1934), pp. 13–17.

83   *Recent surveys:* M. Bornstein and H. Bornstein, "The Pace of Life," *Nature* 259 (1976), pp. 557–59, and M. H. Bornstein, "The Pace of Life: Revisited," *International Journal of Psychology* 14 (1979), pp. 83–90, cited in Levine, *A Question of Time,* p. 16.
desperate fascination: Charles Dickens, *Dombey and Son,* quoted in Raymond Williams, *The Country and the City* (New York: Oxford University Press, 1973), p. 159.

84   *Walter Benjamin:* "Some Motifs in Baudelaire," in *Charles Baudelaire: A*

224   *Notes*

Lyric Poet in the Era of High Capitalism (London: NLB, 1973 [1939]),
pp. 159–61.

85   *It took sixty-seven years . . . Internet:* Robert D. Putnam, *Bowling Alone:*
The Collapse and Revival of American Community (New York: Simon and
Schuster, 2000), p. 217, table 2, drawing on Sue Bowden and Avner
Offer, "Household Appliances and the Use of Time: The United States
and Britain Since the 1920s," *Economic History Review* 47 (November
1994), p. 729, and the *Statistical Abstract of the United States.* The esti-
mate on the Internet is taken from pp. 169 and 223, citing "64.2 Million
American Adults Regularly Use the Internet," Mediamark press release
(May 12, 1999), at www.mediamark.com/mri/docs/press_99.htm.

87   *In 1916:* F. T. Marinetti et al., "The Futurist Cinema," http://www.
unknown.nu/futurism/cinema.html.
     Tinsel ages spawn: Writing about the related tendency to think that cul-
ture in general was better during a bygone age, Patrick Brantlinger has
used the term *negative classicism. Bread and Circuses: Theories of Mass*
Culture as Social Decay (Ithaca: Cornell University Press, 1983).

89   *Arthur Penn:* "Bonnie and Clyde: An Interview with Arthur Penn," in
John G. Cawelti, ed., *Focus on Bonnie and Clyde* (Englewood Cliffs, N.J.:
Prentice Hall), 1973, p. 16.
     George W. S. Trow: My Pilgrim's Progress (New York: Pantheon, 1999),
pp. 21, 22. (I've altered the order of some segments—my own creative
editing.)

91   *video games outgross:* Seth Stevenson, "Why Are Video Games for Adults
So Juvenile?" *Slate.com,* April 19, 2001.

93   *For Capra:* Quoted in Evan William Cameron, *Sound and the Cinema:*
The Coming of Sound to American Film (Pleasantville, N.Y.: Redgrave,
1980), p. 82.

95   *J. C. Herz: Joystick Nation: How Videogames Ate Our Quarters, Won Our*
Hearts, and Rewired Our Minds (Boston: Little, Brown, 1997), p. 140.
     French impressionists: Richard R. Brettell, *Impression: Painting Quickly in*
France, 1860–1890 (New Haven: Yale University Press, 2000), writing
of paintings "done in such a way as to *look* as if they were painted
quickly" (p. 17).

96   *David Carson: The End of Print: The Graphic Design of David Carson* (San
Francisco: Chronicle Books, 1995).
     Kiku Adatto: "Sound Bite Democracy: Network Evening News Presi-
dential Campaign Coverage, 1968 and 1988" (Research Paper R-2, Joan
Shorenstein Barone Center for Press, Politics, and Public Policy, June
1990) and "The Incredible Shrinking Sound Bite," *New Republic,* May
29, 1990, pp. 20–23.
     By 2000 . . . candidates: According to research by the Center for Media
and Public Affairs (www.cmpa.com/Mediamon/mm111200.htm).

97   *Chris Matthews:* Quoted in Paul Farhi, " 'McLaughlin': Still Something
      to Shout About?" *Washington Post*, March 10, 2000.
      In 1824: Thomas Jefferson to David Harding, in Andrew A. Lipscomb
      and Albert E. Bergh, eds., *The Writings of Thomas Jefferson*, memorial
      ed. (Washington, D.C.: Thomas Jefferson Memorial Association, 1903–
      4), vol. 16, p. 30.
      In 1924: Literary Digest, August 9, 1924.
98   *fiction reviews:* The United States is not alone. London's *Guardian* offers
      a cheeky weekly feature called "The digested read . . . Condensed in the
      style of the original . . . Too busy to read the hot books? Let us read
      them for you." In the midst of this section appears a pull quote: "And
      if you really are pressed: The digested read, digested . . ."—followed by
      about twenty words of summation of the summation.
      1936 . . . and 2001: For the four most recent dates, all ten were findable,
      but in 1996, we discarded two children's books that made the list. For
      1936, numbers 2, 5, 6, and 9 could not be unearthed anywhere despite
      visits to the New York University library, the New York Public Library,
      the Strand, and various other used-book stores.
      Taking four sentences: The following discussion is largely drawn from my
      "The Dumb-Down," *Nation*, March 17, 1997, p. 28.
100   *Ernest Hemingway:* This point was put to me by Neil Postman.
101   *methodological objections:* These were made to me by Richard Rothstein,
      personal communication, April 28, 1997.
      $2 to $3: Data courtesy of Joan Shelley Rubin, drawing on *Publishers
      Weekly* and other sources.
      Jennifer Kelley: For the *Times Magazine*, data are for the first Sunday
      issue of October; for *National Geographic*, the October issue.
102   *Geoffrey Nunberg:* For the *Times*, Professor Nunberg used the lead sen-
      tences of prominent front-page news stories, drawing one from each of
      forty consecutive issues from October 1 of the indicated year. For *Sci-
      ence*, he used full-length research articles from the time they began in
      1916, taking the first full sentence from each page in issues from
      autumn of the indicated year, until about forty were collected. Geoffrey
      Nunberg, Xerox Palo Alto Research Center and Department of Lin-
      guistics, Stanford University, personal communication, April 21, 1997.
      I am grateful to Professor Nunberg not only for the original research
      but for permission to reproduce his findings here.
103   *Nunberg writes:* Geoffrey Nunberg, *The Way We Talk Now* (Boston:
      Houghton Mifflin, 2001).
104   *Sony was the first:* John Nathan, *SONY: The Private Life* (Boston: Hough-
      ton Mifflin, 1999), p. 109–10.
      Robert M. Solow: But Solow adds this qualification: "I will feel better
      about the endurance of the productivity improvement after it survives

its first recession." Louis Uchitelle, "Productivity Finally Shows the Impact of Computers," *New York Times*, March 12, 2000, Business Section, citing research by Federal Reserve economists Stephen D. Oliner and Daniel E. Sichel. Their conclusion: "Information technology has been the key factor behind the improved productivity performance."

105   *the argument for productivity increases:* See the excellent discussion of the productivity debate in Nicholas Garnham, "Information Society Theory as Ideology: A Critique," *Information, Communication, and Society* 3, no. 2 (2000).

106   *American Airlines:* Barney Wurf, "Information Age Anthology," www.dodcorp.org/antch209.htm#47. The resulting company, Caribbean Data Services, the largest "informatics" employer in Barbados, opened a second office in the Dominican Republic in 1987, paying half the wages.

43 million: Alex Pham, "E-tailers' Prime Time Is During Office Hours," *Los Angeles Times*, December 18, 2000. On-line shopping "keeps employees at their desks," said one researcher. "They don't have to take a two-hour lunch to go out and shop." Some research says that employers don't have to worry. "At home, people will surf more casually," said another researcher. "It's a much more focused initiative at work. People are squeezing this in between things."

distraction may be just what they need: As it happens, just as I was finishing this chapter, during a stupendous lightning storm in the Hudson Valley, my telephone went out, so for one working day (aside from one twenty-minute round-trip to a pay phone to call the repair office), I lacked the distractions of telephone and e-mail. I think my output improved, at least in quantity per day. The reader will have to be the judge of quality.

P.S. It is too good a coincidence to believe, but as I was writing the previous paragraph the phone repairman showed up and made the repair. I take my leave from the reader now to collect a day's worth of e-mail and voicemail messages.

Harvard Divinity School: Fox Butterfield, "Pornography Cited in Ouster at Harvard," *New York Times*, May 20, 1999. According to a 1999 survey by the market research firm Vault.com, 42 percent of employers "actively monitor their workers' Internet activity," up from 31 percent the previous year. (Pham, "E-tailers' Prime Time.") Many companies market on-line computer surveillance equipment; one Web site claims: "With Spector, you will be able to SEE what your kids and employees have been doing online and offline." (http://people.ne.mediaone.net/rizun/Spy/spy.htm.) Still more surveillance potential is built into software. According to a report in *Wired*, "any manager who purchases network-operating software is probably getting built-in snoop features. In an office hardwired with a server-based local area network managed by software such as Microsoft LAN Manager, a technically inclined boss or network administrator can turn any employee workstation into a covert surveillance post." (John Whalen, "You're Not Paranoid: They Really Are Watching You," *Wired*, March 1995.)

107 *as drugs spread:* At least before the dot-com bubble burst, there were reports of growing use of cocaine, Ecstasy, and GHB among young professionals. A programmer who upped his prescribed Ritalin dosage said, "There's always been an anarchist technophile drug-use thing that seems to go together." P. J. Huffstutter and Robin Fields, "The Dirty Little Secret of the Dot-Com World," *Los Angeles Times*, Sunday, October 1, 2000.

109 *Berndt Ostendorf:* "Why Is American Popular Culture So Popular? A View from Europe" (Odense, Denmark: Oasis, 2000), pp. 35–36. See also Todd Gitlin, "Prime Time Ideology: The Hegemonic Process in Television Entertainment," *Social Problems*, February 1979, pp. 251–66.

111 *Some working women:* See Arlie Hochschild, *The Time Bind* (New York: Metropolitan, 1997).
Some people use a Walkman: Michael Bull, *Sounding Out the City: Personal Stereos and the Management of Everyday Life* (Oxford: Berg, 2000), pp. 58–60.

112 *more likely to graze:* Bellamy and Walker, *Television and the Remote Control*, pp. 126–37.
Men tend to surf: Jupiter Communications with Media Tetrix, "It's a Woman's World Wide Web," cited in Laurie L. Flynn, "Internet Is More Than Just Fun for Women," *New York Times*, August 14, 2000. According to one analyst of on-line behavior, "Women are interested in a more efficient experience—getting on-line and getting off. Men are more interested in technology for technology's sake, and in the more random aspects of Net surfing."

113 *Action movies get faster:* Mark Kingwell, "Fast Forward," *Harper's Magazine*, May 1998, p. 45.

114 *Samuel Taylor Coleridge . . . "bicycles":* Quoted in Richard Altick, *The English Common Reader* (Chicago: University of Chicago Press, 1957), pp. 370, 369 (quoting *Publishers' Circular*, October 1, 1890, p. 1154), pp. 374–75.
semicolonless: Michael Kinsley, editor of *Slate*, has written that he programmed his computer to eliminate semicolons. E. J. Dionne, "Under Observation," *Washington Post* Magazine, November 24, 1996, p. 12.

115 *Joseph Schumpeter's: Capitalism, Socialism, and Democracy* (New York: Harper, 1942), p. 84.

116 *Karl Marx's: The Communist Manifesto.* I am indebted to Marshall Berman's inspiring treatment of Marx's theme in *All That Is Solid Melts into Air* (New York: Simon and Schuster, 1982).

3. Styles of Navigation and Political Sideshows

121   *simplification:* See the excellent discussion of television's bias toward simplification in Jeffrey Scheuer, *The Sound-Bite Society: Television and the
American Mind* (New York: Four Walls Eight Windows, 1999), pp. 61–
90.
Neal Shapiro: Interview with a *Dateline* producer who wishes to remain
anonymous, August 30, 1998. Once, when he told her to slice something out of one of her pieces, and she said, "I can't do that," he
retorted, "I'll find somebody who can."
onset of the Gulf War: An earlier version of the following discussion
appeared as "On Being Sound-Bitten: Reflections on Truth, Impression, and Belief in a Time of Media Saturation," *Boston Review*, December 1991, pp. 15–17.

122   *horrified by the war:* I remain horrified, but in the light of what I came
to learn about Saddam Hussein's weapons of mass destruction, I sub-
sequently decided I made the wrong judgment. But that is neither here
nor there for purposes of this tale.

124   *"He manned":* Dotson had asked me for a photo of myself at a demonstration. I had told him that I had not been in the business of getting photo-
graphed at antiwar demonstrations, and the picture of me with Stone,
shot by a college photographer—and not a barricade within a hundred
miles—was the closest I could come. Contrary to Dotson's voice-over, I
was not a student at Berkeley until 1974. Inventing spurious barricades,
even if figurative ones, enabled him to construct his frame, his summary
of 1960s radicals, once simplistic and wild, now complicated and tame.
This was also his approach to his two other interviewees.

125   *struggle for control:* Thus French sociologist Pierre Bourdieu has
denounced the *"structural corruption"* of television, whose competition
for market share leads it to deploy quasi-intellectual "fast-thinkers" as
purveyors of "cultural 'fast food'—predigested and prethought." In a
tract widely debated in France in 1996, Bourdieu challenged expert
chatterers to cease what he called "collaboration . . . with the powers
that be." Pierre Bourdieu, *On Television*, trans. Priscilla Parkhurst Fer-
guson (New York: New Press, 1998 [1996]), pp. 17, 29, 59, 62 (Bourdieu's italics).

127   *as many as 95 percent:* R. Jeffrey Smith and Evelyn Richards, "Numerous
U.S. Bombs Probably Missed Targets; Not All Munitions Used in Gulf
Are Smart," *Washington Post*, February 22, 1991, p. A25; Tom Wicker,
"Military Control of War News Left Truth a Casualty," *New York
Times*, March 21, 1991, p. A22.

129   *"a vast festive diaspora":* Daniel Dayan, "Television: Le Presque-Public,"
unpublished paper, 2000.

129   *"soap operas . . . getting fatter"*: A Usenet quote from rec.arts.tv.soaps, in Nancy K. Baym, *Tune in, Log On: Soaps, Fandom, and On-line Community* (Thousand Oaks, Calif.: Sage, 2000), p. 36. Spelling corrected.

      the connoisseur: But as Pierre Bourdieu reminds us, all fans think of themselves as connoisseurs. All taste, being relative, is also distaste. Pierre Bourdieu, *Distinction: A Social Critique of the Judgment of Taste*, trans. Richard Nice (Cambridge, Mass.: Harvard University Press, 1984 [1979]).

      "If I read a book": Quoted in Thomas Wentworth Higginson, "Emily Dickinson's Letters," *Atlantic*, October 1891.

130   *Proust: Time Regained*, trans. Andreas Mayor, in *Remembrance of Things Past* (New York: Vintage, 1982 [1927]), vol. 3, p. 928.

      Actress Hélène Rolles . . . "experience emotions": Dominique Pasquier, "Teen Series' Reception: Television, Adolescence, and Culture of Feelings," *Childhood: A Global Journal of Child Research* 3 (1996), pp. 352, 354. My italics.

132   *Dawg Pound Dawgs:* See Susan Faludi, *Stiffed* (New York: Morrow, 1999), chap. 4.

133   *a homeless world:* See Peter L. Berger, Brigitte Berger, and Hansfried Kellner, *The Homeless Mind: Modernization and Consciousness* (New York: Random House, 1973). But nostalgia campaigns often fail. A case in point: the reintroduction of "Old Coke" bottles in 1999.

      more than it was: The stardust effect persists even in the post-1960s era when stars enjoy playing down (or *playing* at playing down) their status. In this antiheroic time, cool is produced systematically by being underproduced: shaky cameras, washed-out look, grainy film, ragged sound, sloppy dress, et cetera. In his introduction to *Rolling Stone: The Photographs* (New York: Simon and Schuster, 1989), Tom Wolfe nicely observes how the rock era star delights in posing (and being posed) in oh-shucks guises—rumpled in bed, hair uncombed, or without makeup.

      "I shook hands": The knowing star is acutely aware, even appreciative, of the passions of fans (she had better be), but also knows how absurd they are. When I met Jane Fonda at her home in 1980, she joked that she was collecting her fingernails for fans—she was mocking not only herself but fandom itself.

      the aura rub off: See the many examples of fans' excitement about visiting the sets of TV series in Nick Couldry, *The Place of Media Power: Pilgrims and Witnesses of the Media Age* (London: Routledge, 2000), chap. 4.

134   *"powerless élite"*: Francesco Alberoni, "The Powerless Elite: Theory and Sociological Research on the Phenomenon of the Stars," in Denis McQuail, ed., *Sociology of Mass Communications* (London: Penguin, 1972), pp. 75–98.

      Stalkers: A milder form of star tribute was paid by a twenty-year-old

Dutch hacker who sent around an e-mail attachment that purported to be a photo of the Russian tennis princess Anna Kournikova but that, when opened, turned out to be a virus that clogged computer servers around the world. The young resident of a Dutch town called Sneek explained that he did this "just because I am a big fan of hers. She deserves some attention, doesn't she?" (Andrew Osborn, "Hacker Launched Anna Bug 'as a Warning,'" *Guardian*, February 15, 2001.)

137   *misrepresentation scandals:* There are textual reliability panics as well, memorably in 1981, when reporter Janet Cooke was fired by the *Washington Post* and stripped of her Pulitzer Prize when the child heroin addict she had profiled turned out to be fictional.

ethical agonizing: But arguably the most influential simulation is one that has rarely been questioned and continues to this day without scandal: networks in the United States and Britain regularly display animated cartoons to diagram military fantasies of all sorts—notably, anti-missile missiles successfully destroying incoming missiles, the sort of interceptions that, in real-world tests, regularly fail. Here, television represents what the government would like to happen. We might surmise that these jolly cartoons have influenced the poll findings showing that most Americans believe missile defense to be feasible, or even that it is already in place. For example, according to a Roper Center poll of September 2000, 58 percent of those surveyed thought the United States "currently has . . . a missile defense system to protect against nuclear attacks," as against 28 percent who thought it did not. (Roper Center On-Line, September 22, 2000.) In March 2001, 64 percent thought missile defense exists, as against 21 percent who did not. (Roper Center On-Line, March 13, 2001.) These figures were kindly furnished to me by Joel Klein.

139   *movies romanticized crime:* David Nasaw, *Going Out: The Rise and Fall of Public Amusements* (New York: Basic, 1993), pp. 174–85, and Herbert Blumer, *Movies and Conduct* (New York: Macmillan, 1933).

140   *African-American prisoners:* Robert M. Entman and Andrew Rojecki, *The Black Image in the White Mind: Media and Race in America* (Chicago: University of Chicago Press, 2000), p. 82.

Gulf War coverage: Jarol B. Manheim, "Strategy Public Diplomacy: Managing Kuwait's Image During the Gulf Conflict," in W. Lance Bennett and David W. Paletz, eds., *Taken by Storm* (Chicago: University of Chicago Press, 1994), pp. 131–48.

Patriot missiles: Theodore Postel, "Lessons of the Gulf Experience with Patriot," *International Security* 16, no. 3 (winter 1991–92), pp. 119–71.

Political campaign coverage: On the horse race, see, for example, Thomas E. Patterson, *Out of Order* (New York: Knopf, 1993).

Television violence: A useful summary is W. James Potter, *On Media Violence* (Thousand Oaks, Calif.: Sage, 1999), pp. 25–42, especially table

3.1, p. 26. Most conclusions about the effects of TV violence are limited to short-run, measurable effects under laboratory conditions.

141 *News framing:* In a huge literature on agenda-setting, one outstanding experimental study is Donald Kidder and Shanto Iyengar, *News That Matters: Television and American Opinion* (Chicago: University of Chicago Press, 1987).

Television news significantly influences: Shanto Iyengar, *Is Anyone Responsible?* (Chicago: University of Chicago Press, 1991).

Television news convinces viewers: Ibid.

most research: The current consensus was stated firmly by Umberto Eco in 1967: "variability of interpretation is the invariant law of mass communication" (*Travels in Hyperreality*, trans. William Weaver [New York: Harcourt Brace, 1986], p. 141). Against the argument that media violence causes real-world violence, see Marjorie Heins, *Not in Front of the Children: "Indecency," Censorship, and the Innocence of Youth* (New York: Hill and Wang, 2001), chap. 10, and Todd Gitlin, "Imagebusters," *American Prospect* 5, no. 16 (December 1, 1994), and "Imagebusters, The Sequel," *American Prospect* 5, no. 17 (March 21, 1995).

Neal Gabler: Life the Movie: How Entertainment Conquered Reality (New York: Knopf, 1998), pp. 8, 97.

142 *an addiction:* Influential efforts in this direction are Jerry Mander, *Four Arguments for the Elimination of Television* (New York: William Morrow, 1978), and Marie Winn, *The Plug-in Drug: Television, Children, and the Family* (New York: Viking, 1985). I have flirted with some of these fears myself in "On Drugs and Mass Media in America's Consumer Society," in Hank Resnik, ed., *Youth and Drugs: Society's Mixed Messages*, OSAP Prevention Monograph-6, U.S. Department of Health and Human Services, Public Health Service, Alcohol, Drug Abuse, and Mental Health Administration, Office for Substance Abuse Prevention, 1990, pp. 31–52.

143 *"narcotizing dysfunction":* Paul F. Lazarsfeld and Robert K. Merton, "Mass Communication, Popular Taste, and Organized Social Action," in Lyman Bryson, ed., *The Communication of Ideas* (New York: Harper and Brothers, 1948), pp. 95–118.

144 *"If you relax":* Wilson Bryan Key, *Media Sexploitation* (New York: Signet, 1976), p. 8.

"Bridge over Troubled Water": Ibid., pp. 138–44.

145 *Stanley Cavell:* "The Fact of Television," in his *Themes Out of School: Effects and Causes* (Chicago: University of Chicago Press, 1984), pp. 267, 268 (first published in *Daedalus*, fall 1982).

146 *not drowning but waving:* I owe this delicious sentence to the British television documentary producer Adam Curtis, in conversation, May 2, 2001.

146 *"status-conferring effect"*: Lazarsfeld and Merton, "Mass Communication, Popular Taste, and Organized Social Action," p. 97.

an improvised shrine: Jane Gross, "Small Gestures of Grief for a Young Man Larger Than Life," *New York Times*, July 22, 1999. Among the letters left outside the Manhattan home of John Kennedy, Jr., were some addressed to his uncle Robert, as if John would serve as an emissary, a sort of postman to the dead. (Personal communication, Jane Gross.)

147 *Daniel Boorstin: The Image: A Guide to Pseudo-Events in America* (New York: Vintage, 1962).

CDs over the Internet: Amy Harmon, "Unknown Musicians Finding Payoffs Through the Internet Jukebox," *New York Times*, July 20, 2000.

Commercial radio broadcasting: Erik Barnouw, *A Tower in Babel: A History of Broadcasting in the United States to 1933* (New York: Oxford University Press, 1972), pp. 110ff.

sexually deviant types: See Joshua Gamson, *Freaks Talk Back: Tabloid Talk Shows and Sexual Nonconformity* (Chicago: University of Chicago Press, 1998).

148 relatability: A producer of *The Real World* used this term during a radio talk show in which I participated, "Which Way L.A." KCRW, Santa Monica, September 13, 1999. Dave Eggers brilliantly catches the glimmer of postures and performances in this images-within-images world in his description of auditioning for *The Real World*. See *A Heartbreaking Work of Staggering Genius* (New York: Simon and Schuster, 2000), pp. 147–208.

Josh Harris: Douglas Rushkoff, "Look at Me: The Flipside to Internet Voyeurism," *Guardian Online*, February 22, 2001, p. 14, from which the description of Josh Harris is quoted. Harris went into business to sell self-surveillance equipment, along with Internet access, to imitators, several thousands of whom were said to have signed on. For the sequel, see Tanya Corrin, "Now you see me . . . ," *Observer Review*, April 8, 2001, pp. 1–2.

Ana Voog: All quotes from www.anacam.com.

149 Beverly Hills 90210: "Which Way L.A."

151 *"inside-dopester":* David Riesman, *The Lonely Crowd*, abridged ed. (New Haven: Yale University Press, 1961 [1950]), p. 182.

152 *Tarantino has said:* Quoted in Jeff Dawson, *Quentin Tarantino: The Cinema of Cool* (New York: Applause Books, 1997), pp. 80–81.

153 Saturday Night Live: In his Ph.D. dissertation, "Apprehending Politics: The Contextualized Role of News Media Engagement in the Individual Political Development of 'Generation X'ers' " (New York University Department of Culture and Communication, 2001), pp. 206–12, Marco Calavita finds that *Saturday Night Live* is a common marker of consciousness for those born after 1960. Mark Crispin Miller denounced

the *SNL* attitude as "the hipness unto death" in *Boxed In* (Evanston, Ill.: Northwestern University Press, 1988), pp. 3–27.

153   *culture jammer:* Naomi Klein writes (*No Logo: Taking Aim at the Brand Bullies* [New York: Picador, 1999], p. 281): "The term 'culture jamming' was coined in 1984 by the San Francisco audio-collage band Negativland."

154   *photomontagists:* Dawn Ades, *Photomontage*, revised and enlarged ed. (London: Thames and Hudson, 1986).
      "semiotic Robin Hoodism": Klein, *No Logo*, p. 280.
      Hocus Focus: Judith Coburn, "Up Against the Wall: Hocus Focus Rewrites Apple's Ad Campaign," *Village Voice*, December 2–8, 1998, www.villagevoice.com/issues/9849/coburn.shtml. For some of the images, see www.hocusfocus.org/notes.html.

155   *the demonstrator:* Todd Gitlin, *The Whole World Is Watching: Mass Media in the Making and Unmaking of the New Left* (Berkeley: University of California Press, 1980).
      his own videotape: In Israeli-occupied southern Lebanon, Hezbollah cameramen shot videotapes of guerrilla actions and sent them to Israeli television and Lebanese and Western wire services. According to Hezbollah commander Sheikh Nabil Quok, "By the use of these films, we were able to control from a long distance the morale of a lot of Israelis." " 'Seventy-five percent of Hezbollah's war was the videotapes,' said an experienced official with the UN peacekeeping troops in the area." John Kifner, "Guerrillas Used Media to Amplify Strikes Against Israel," *International Herald Tribune*, July 20, 2000.
      electronic sit-in: Amy Harmon, " 'Hacktivists' of All Persuasions Take Their Struggle to the Web, *New York Times*, October 31, 1998.
      One hacked Mexican . . . "coca leaves": All hacked sites accessed through www.2600.com, the site of *2600: The Hacker Quarterly*, published by Eric Corley (a.k.a. "Emmanuel Goldstein," Big Brother's nemesis in *1984*) in New York.

156   *Jon Johansen:* Carl S. Kaplan, "Compressed Data: Trial Involving DVD Software and Copyrights Set to Begin," *New York Times*, July 21, 2000. The judge found against Corley. John Sullivan, "Judge Halts Program to Crack DVD Film Codes," *New York Times*, August 18, 2000.
      hackers' convention: July 13–16, 2000. For the program, see www.h2k.net.

157   *"I think everyone":* Quoted in Klein, *No Logo*, p. 284.
      the bright light: Mander, *Four Arguments*, pp. 154ff.

158   *Plato warned: The Republic*, bk. 7.
      Wordsworth: "The Prelude," bk. 7, lines 701–2, 709–10 (1805–6 edition).
      Walt Whitman: "Starting from Paumanok," in *Leaves of Grass*.
      Heidegger: Rüdiger Safranski, *Martin Heidegger: Beyond Good and Evil*, trans. Ewald Osers (Cambridge, Mass.: Harvard University Press,

1998), p. 331, quoting Heidegger, *Gesamtausgabe: Ausgabe letzter Hand*, vol. 55, p. 84.

158   *European Cup . . . his moves:* Safranski, Martin Heidegger, p. 428.
      "National TV-Turnoff Week": www.tvfa.org/turnoff.html.

159   *Nietzsche's . . . recommendation: The Gay Science,* par. 329.
      Ask people to give up: Personal tales of secession remain frequent features of the press. As I revise, for example, I come across Mark Tran, "Life Outside the Box" ("Has TV taken over your life? Perhaps it's time to do what Mark Tran did—bin it"), *Guardian*, Section G2, February 21, 2001.
      1997 figures: Statistical Abstract of the United States, tables 921, 60. Source: Television Bureau of Advertising, *Trends in Television*, 1997. This is the latest year accessible at this writing.
      autonomy: David Riesman's discussion of autonomy in pt. 3 of *The Lonely Crowd* is still germane.

160   *Joseph Turow . . . "rifles": Breaking Up America* (Chicago: University of Chicago Press, 1997), pp. 56, 64, 66, 53.

161   *giant corporations:* See Michael J. Piore and Charles F. Sabel, *The Second Industrial Divide: Possibilities for Prosperity* (New York: Basic, 1984). On the consumer side, see Michael J. Weiss, *The Clustering of America* (New York: Harper and Row, 1988).
      Herbert Marcuse: One-Dimensional Man (Boston: Beacon Press, 1964), p. 90.
      criticism merely confirms: This is the argument of Marcuse's influential essay "Repressive Tolerance," in Marcuse, Barrington Moore, Jr., and Robert Paul Wolff, *A Critique of Pure Tolerance* (Boston: Beacon, 1965).
      forced . . . to be free: The phrase is from Rousseau's *Social Contract.* Indeed, in his *Discourse on the Sciences and Arts*, he throws down the gauntlet and brandishes the first powerful modern declaration of abolitionism.

162   *Mander's second book: In the Presence of the Sacred* (San Francisco: Sierra Club Books, 1991).

163   *John Zerzan . . . "technological progress":* "The Mass Psychology of Misery," "Society," and "Technology," from *Future Primitive and Other Essays* (Brooklyn; Autonomedia in conjunction with *Anarchy: A Journal of Desire Armed*, 1994), on-line at www.spunk.org/library/writers/zerzan.
      "Can we justify . . . dreams?": John Zerzan, "Culture," www.spunk.org/library/writers/zerzan.

165   *the media . . . have invited tolerance . . . antiauthoritarian sentiments:* David Riesman made the case that mass media induced tolerance in *The Lonely Crowd*, pp. 192ff. The argument that television has contributed to

equality and antiauthoritarianism was made by Joshua Meyrowitz in *No Sense of Place* (New York: Oxford University Press, 1985).

165 *Jeffrey Scheuer: The Sound Bite Society*, esp. pp. 121ff.

Bowling Alone: Putnam's original article, published in the *Journal of Democracy* in 1994, is revised and elaborated in his book, subtitled *The Collapse and Revival of American Community* (New York: Simon and Schuster, 2000). The enormous attention paid to Putnam's thesis, despite the fact that it was originally published in an obscure journal, surely reflects more than the clever metaphor of the title, more, too, than a media feeding frenzy; it reflects a widespread anxiety, at least among the educated classes, about the condition of American democracy, not only the declining rate of voting but the apparent erosion of the associational life that is today, in keeping with the supreme resonance of economic metaphors, known as "social capital."

After scrutinizing many statistics: Similar correlations between more TV watching and less social involvement of all sorts—volunteering, churchgoing, club meetings, community projects, letter writing, et cetera— show up in other countries as well. Putnam, *Bowling Alone*, p. 234.

166 *In the 1970s:* Ibid., p. 238.

surveys from 1994 and 1995: These correlations held up, in statistically significant form, when other factors—including education, age, sex, income, and race—were held constant. Personal communication, Robert D. Putnam, August 29, 2000. The DDB Needham Life Style surveys, the source of these data, did not ask about voting per se. However, as Putnam says, registration "is probably a reasonably good proxy" for voting. I am grateful to Professor Putnam for checking his data in response to my query, for the figures on television and voting are not in his book. The basic data are accessible, however, on his Web site, www.BowlingAlone.com.

The additional hour a day: Putnam, *Bowling Alone*, pp. 224–25 (his figures for habitual and selective viewing run from 1979 through 1993), 230–31 (Putnam's italics), 228–29.

167 *events of overt political import:* These are among the cases discussed in Daniel Dayan and Elihu Katz, *Media Events: The Live Broadcasting of History* (Cambridge, Mass.: Harvard University Press, 1992).

During the year of the Lewinsky scandal: These figures were generously shared with me by Andrew Tyndall of the *Tyndall Report* (personal communication, February 28, 2001).

168 *During the first six days:* Figures from the Center for Media and Public Affairs, cited in Howard Kurtz, "The Times' Left-Hand Man," *Washington Post*, July 26, 1999.

John Seigenthaler, Jr.: He was speaking to the fellows of the Media Study

Center at a briefing at MSNBC headquarters, Secaucus, New Jersey, October 19, 1998.

169 *a 2000 audience survey:* Pew Center, "Biennial News Consumption Survey" (www.people-press.org/media00rpt.htm).

ratings remain relatively *low:* Most of the time, CNN, MSNBC, and Fox News total less than 1 percent of households with access to those channels, roughly 700,000 households nationally. On January 21, 1998, when the Lewinsky story broke, the three cable news networks together spiked up to about 1.6 percent of total cable-accessible households, and on September 11, 1998, when the Starr report was published, to 1.9 percent. (Nielsen Media Research figures, cited in "Lewinsky: Why News Networks Would Miss Her," *New York Times,* November 9, 1998.) The total numbers are diminutive, but, for those networks and their advertising revenue, the increments are huge. The significance of CNN reports is greatly amplified by conventional newsrooms, where monitors are tuned to cable news at all hours of the day and night.

the public distinguishes: During the entire year of Clinton-Lewinsky, as watchdogs and pundits nipped at the presidential underwear, exposed it, analyzed and fretted about it, and in the process stained themselves, the public attitude toward the media was consistent, and it was not flattering. Just after the first week of coverage, early in 1998, 80 percent of the public called the scandal coverage "excessive," 71 percent "embarrassing," 67 percent "biased," 60 percent "irresponsible," and 57 percent "disgusting." Sixty-five percent thought the Clinton-Lewinsky story "not important enough to deserve the level of coverage it has received." Sixty-three percent opposed journalistic speculation, 44 percent of them "strongly." Eighty-one percent said that the heavy coverage was driven "more by the desire to attract a large audience than by the goal of getting to the bottom of the story." The figures after seven months of saturation coverage were similar. Forty-eight percent said they weren't paying attention anymore, while 7 percent wanted more. (January–February figures from Media Studies Center, "News Media Coverage of the Investigation of President Clinton" [New York, 1998], and www.freedomforum.org/newsstand/1998/2/6release-method.asp, p. 3. August figures from Freedom Forum and Newseum *News* 5, no. 8 [September 1998], pp. 1–2.)

170 *January 1991:* Shanto Iyengar and Adam Simon, "News Coverage of the Gulf Crisis and Public Opinion," in W. Lance Bennett and David L. Paletz, eds., *Taken by Storm: The Media, Public Opinion, and U.S. Foreign Policy in the Gulf War* (Chicago: University of Chicago Press, 1994), p. 167.

CNN spiked: Daniel C. Hallin and Todd Gitlin, "The Gulf War as

Popular Culture and Television Drama," in Bennett and Paletz, eds., *Taken by Storm*, p. 149.

171 *heightened bellicose sentiment:* Iyengar and Simon, "News Coverage," pp. 167, 182.

172 *communism broke down:* Comparable effects have also been imputed to radio and popular music. Cassettes of Ayatollah Khomeini played a significant part in the 1979 Islamic revolution against the shah of Iran (Annabelle Sreberny-Mohammadi and Ali Mohammadi, *Small Media, Big Revolution: Communication, Culture, and the Iranian Revolution* [Minneapolis: University of Minnesota Press, 1994]).

Bystanders spurred: Stanley Cohen, *States of Denial* (London: Blackwell, 2001), and Luc Boltanski, *Suffering and Distance: Morality, Media, and Politics*, trans. Graham Burchell (Cambridge: Cambridge University Press, 1999).

173 *Bush ended the Gulf War:* Marvin Kalb, "A View from the Press," in Bennett and Paletz, eds., *Taken by Storm*, p. 5.

Unhappy is the democracy: The strongest defenses of demobilization pertain not to democracy at all, but to totalitarian societies, where withdrawal from public activity and refusal to trust the media may be the most that most decent people can do. In a society that demands total mobilization, a refusal to be mobilized (or what German intellectuals like Karl Jaspers called *internal emigration* during the Nazi years) microscopically weakens the regime, shores up the crumbling morale of the dissidents, and, at most, can be seen as building up dissident networks that might someday constitute the kernels of a free "civil society." The Hungarian writer George Konrád called this stance *antipolitics*, and Václav Havel referred to something similar under the heading "the power of the powerless," making the point that, in a system of totalist thought, a refusal to accept orthodox definitions, an insistence on acting as if one was free, is essential—a sort of self-fulfilling prophecy. (George Konrád, *Antipolitics* [New York: Harcourt Brace Jovanovich, 1984], Václav Havel, *The Power of the Powerless*, ed. John Keane [New York: M. E. Sharpe, 1990]). Without question a spirited demobilization from official orthodoxies did play a major part in the destruction of Communism in 1989–90. But the mesh of free association that went under the name "civil society" proved largely negative—refusals to support the old order, not the construction of a new one. "Civil society" was too thin to withstand the collapse of its enemy, the Communist state. It was a necessary condition for active democracy, not a sufficient one. The aftermath of Communism was not so much a revitalized society of public participation as a normalization of self-interested and elite politics.

evidence on that is conflicting: For an early argument that computer use, including the Internet, has little effect on television watching, see Steve

Coffey and Horst Stipp, "The Interactions Between Computer and Television Usage," *Journal of Advertising Research* 37, no. 2 (March 1997), pp. 61–67.

174   *Extensive, sometimes respectful media treatment:* After I published an article in the *Washington Post* ("Shouts Lead to Murmurs," April 17, 2000, Outlook Section, p. 1) defending the Washington demonstrators of April 2000 and arguing that their sloganeering still motivated reformers, I received a number of letters and phone calls from within the World Bank confirming this view.

   easy communication: Naomi Klein, "Cries in the Street in L.A.," *Nation*, September 4–11, 2000.

   As of 1999: Putnam, *Bowling Alone*, pp. 170–71, citing Pippa Norris, "Who Surfs? New Technology, Old Voters, and Virtual Democracy," in Elaine C. Kamarok and Joseph S. Nye, eds., *democracy.com: Governance in a Networked World* (New York: Hollis; 1999), pp. 71–94; Pippa Norris, "Who Surfs Café Europa? Virtual Democracy in the U.S. and Western Europe," paper presented at the Annual Meeting of the American Political Science Association (Atlanta, September 1999). Putnam notes that "once we control for the higher education levels of Internet users, they are indistinguishable from nonusers when it comes to civic engagement," and adds that the fact that growing numbers of people are diving into the Net proves "little about the *effects* of the Net, because of the likelihood that Internet users are self-selected in relevant ways." Putnam's italics.

   Do organizations and networks: This question is debated by Cass Sunstein, Michael Schudson, Jay Rosen, and others in a symposium, "Is the Internet Bad for Democracy?" *Boston Review*, Summer 2001, pp. 4–19.

175   *the first half decade of Internet growth:* Between December 1998 and August 2000, the divide closed somewhat, but still left blacks and Hispanics less wired than whites and Asians, even controlling for income and education. UCLA Center for Communication Policy, *The UCLA Internet Report: Surveying the Digital Future*, November 2000 (www.ccp.ucla.edu).

4. Under the Sign of Mickey Mouse & Co.

Parts of this chapter appeared in earlier versions in "World Leaders: Mickey, et al.," *New York Times*, Arts and Leisure Section, May 3, 1992, and "The Unification of the World Under the Signs of Mickey Mouse and Bruce Willis: The Supply and Demand Sides of American Popular Culture," in Joseph Man Chan and Bryce McIntyre, eds., *In Search of Boundaries: Communication, Nation-States, and National Identities* (Westport, Conn.: Ablex, 2002).

177 *America's top exports:* Economists Incorporated for the International Intellectual Property Alliance, Executive Summary, 2000_SIWEK_EXEC.pdf. Thanks to Siva Vaidhyanathan for his discerning analysis of these statistics.

178 *a German television reporter:* This story is told by Berndt Ostendorf in "What Makes American Popular Culture So Popular: A View from Europe" (Odense, Denmark: Oasis, 2000).
Just as their "cultures": I benefited from a discussion about the overuse of the term *culture* with Kevin Robins, March 2, 2001.

181 *In the latter half of the 1980s:* National Technical Information Service, *Globalization of the Mass Media* (Washington, D.C.: Department of Commerce, 1993), pp. 1–2, cited in Edward S. Herman and Robert W. McChesney, *The Global Media: The New Missionaries of Corporate Capitalism* (London: Cassell, 1997), p. 39.
In 2000: Calculated from *Schroder's International Media and Entertainment Report 2000*, p. 37. Courtesy of David Lieberman, media business editor of *USA Today*.

182 *minstrel shows:* Ostendorf, "What Makes American Popular Culture So Popular?" pp. 16–18, 47.
when faced with a choice: Herman and McChesney, *Global Media*, p. 42. See also Tapio Varis, "Values and the Limits of the Global Media in the Age of Cyberspace," in Michael Prosser and K.S. Sitaram, eds., *Civic Discourse: Intercultural, International, and Global Media* (Stamford, CT: Ablex, 1999), vol. 2, pp. 5–17. During one week in the spring of 2001, not one of the fifty top-rated British TV shows was American.
competitors . . . are pulled: Jeremy Tunstall, *The Media Are American: Anglo-American Media in the World* (New York: Columbia University Press, 1977), pp. 50–51.

183 *By 1925 . . . Egypt:* Ibid., p. 284, drawing on William Victor Strauss, "Foreign Distribution of American Motion Pictures," *Harvard Business Review*, 1930, and U.S. Department of Commerce, *Review of Foreign Film Markets*, 1937.
Between the world wars: Ruth Vasey, *The World According to Hollywood, 1918–1939* (Madison: University of Wisconsin Press, 1997), p. 7.

184 *142 special trains:* Cyril Ehrlich, *The Music Profession in Britain Since the Eighteenth Century* (London: Oxford University Press, 1985), p. 56. Thanks to Peter Mandler for this reference.
thirty thousand protest letters: Personal communication, Henrik Christiansen, former chief of entertainment for Danish television (and previously head of news), September 1998.
James Monaco: "Images and Sounds as Cultural Commodities," p. 231, from an article I clipped a long time ago but without noting from which magazine I'd clipped it.

185   *Monaco's happy term:* Ibid., p. 231.
      American culture was driven: Library shelves groan with histories of pop-
      ular American culture, but fundamental works worth singling out
      include Henry Nash Smith, *Virgin Land: The American West as Sym-
      bol and Myth* (Cambridge, Mass.: Harvard University Press, 1950);
      Richard Slotkin, *Regeneration Through Violence: The Mythology of the
      American Frontier, 1600–1860* (Middletown, Conn.: Wesleyan Uni-
      versity Press, 1973); John G. Cawelti, *Adventure, Mystery, and Ro-
      mance: Formula Stories as Art and Popular Culture* (Chicago: University
      of Chicago Press, 1976); and Michael Denning, *Mechanic Accents:
      Dime Novels and Working-Class Culture in America* (London: Verso,
      1987).
      Daniel Dayan: Personal communication, July 20, 2000.
      The head of the BBC's General Overseas Service: Quoted in Asa Briggs,
      The War of Words (London: Oxford University Press, 1970), p. 567–68.
      Americanization: Dick Hebdige, *Hiding in the Light* (London: Routledge/
      Comedia, 1988), pp. 52–76. There were exceptions, however. In the
      Noel Coward–David Lean film *Brief Encounter* (1946), the Trevor How-
      ard character raves about the merits of Donald Duck as a distraction
      from the war.
      Soviet film exports: Tunstall, *Media Are American*, p. 62.
186   *a Disney official:* Quoted in Todd Gitlin, "World Leaders: Mickey, et
      al." *New York Times*, Arts and Leisure Section, May 3, 1992, p. 1.
      American English in particular: Tunstall, *Media Are American*, pp.
      127–8.
187   *Louis B. Mayer's decision:* Neal Gabler, *An Empire of Their Own: How the
      Jews Invented Hollywood* (New York: Crown, 1988), p. 3.
188   *Harold Rosenberg: The Tradition of the New* (New York: Grove, 1961).
      Rosenberg was referring to modernism in the arts, but he might equally
      well have meant popular culture.
      "Musicians in the Kingston tenement yards": Vivien Goldman, "One Drop
      of Mighty Dread: How Jamaica Changed the World's Music,"
      CommonQuest 4, no. 3 (2000), pp. 23, 22, 25.
      American punks: Ibid., p. 27. American food has been and continues to
      be shaped by a similar hybridization, which is the point of the joke
      about the tourist who walks up to a stranger in New York and asks
      where he can get a pizza. The stranger points to a Chinese restaurant.
      Perplexed, the tourist walks into the restaurant and says hesitantly to a
      waiter, "Is it really true that you serve pizza?" "Of course," is the
      answer, "what size would you like, and what topping? We have mush-
      room, pepperoni—" "Excuse me," says the tourist, "but I don't under-
      stand why a Chinese restaurant serves pizza." The waiter replies, "For
      all our Jewish customers!"

189 *Martha Wolfenstein:* "The Emergence of Fun Morality," in Eric Lar-
     rabee, ed., *Mass Leisure* (Glencoe, IL: Free Press, 1958), p. 86.
190 *William Cody:* Joy S. Kasson, *Buffalo Bill's Wild West: Celebrity, Memory,
     and Popular History* (New York: Hill and Wang, 2000), pp. 11–53, 81,
     83, 90, 256–62.
191 *first big commerical hit:* Richard Slotkin, *Gunfighter Nation: The Myth of
     the Frontier in Twentieth-Century America* (New York: Atheneum, 1992),
     p. 231.
     In 1910: Edward Buscombe, ed., *The BFI Companion to the Western*
     (London: André Deutsch, 1988), p. 24, cited in Kasson, *Buffalo Bill's
     Wild West*, p. 256.
     Between 1939 and 1969 . . . viewing audience: Slotkin, *Gunfighter Nation*,
     pp. 256, 348.
192 *Paul Buhle:* Personal communication, 1990.
197 *According to Disney CEO:* "The Mighty Bucks of Michael Eisner," *Busi-
     ness and Investing* online (http://scoop.crosswinds.net/books/eisner.
     html).
198 *Chilean writer Ariel Dorfman:* Dorfman and Mattelart, *How to Read
     Donald Duck* (New York: International General, 1975). Their inter-
     pretations were often ingenious, though they were strictly textual—
     assuming, like most literary analysis, that the meanings absorbed by the
     reader are obvious, transparent. *How to Read Donald Duck* would be
     more fruitfully read as an argument about form, not content: a protest
     against distraction and in favor of an alternative way of life, socialist
     revolution.
199 *"American mass culture . . . innermost being":* Ariel Dorfman, *The Empire's
     Old Clothes: What the Lone Ranger, Babar, and Other Innocent Heroes Do
     to Our Minds* (New York: Pantheon, 1983), pp. 3–4.
     "joins power" . . . "for the future": Ibid., pp. 203–4.
200 *a Beijing university student:* Elizabeth Rosenthal, "In Beijing Students'
     Worldview, Jordan Rules," *New York Times*, June 16, 1998.
201 *Robert Warshow: The Immediate Experience: Movies, Comics, Theatre, and
     Other Aspects of Popular Culture* (New York: Atheneum, 1971 [1962]),
     p. 131.
202 *courtroom dramas:* Ostendorf, "What Makes American Popular Culture
     So Popular?" p. 11.
     Belgrade students: John Sweeney, "Red Mussolini puts his faith in storm-
     troopers," *Observer*, March 17, 1991, p. 13.
     "President Milosevic": Steven Erlander, "Milosevic, Trailing in Polls,
     Rails Against NATO," *New York Times*, September 20, 2000.
     "We've seen a lot of Hollywood movies": Elizabeth Rosenthal, "Chinese
     Test New Weapon From West: Lawsuits," *New York Times*, June 16,
     2001.

203 *Václav Havel:* "Thriller," in *Living in Truth*, ed. Jan Vladislav (London: Faber and Faber, 1987), pp. 158–63.

204 *CBS's vice president:* Arnold Becker, quoted in Todd Gitlin, *Inside Prime Time* (New York: Pantheon, 1983), p. 31.

206 *Catherine Wilson:* "Vicariousness and Authenticity," in Ken Goldberg, ed., *The Robot in the Garden: Telerobotics and Telepistemology in the Age of the Internet* (Cambridge, Mass: M.I.T. Press, 2000), p. 81.

207 *"McWorld":* The most impressive articulation of this position in recent years is Benjamin Barber, *Jihad vs. McWorld* (New York: Times Books, 1995). But see the critique by Fareed Zakaria, *New Republic*, January 22, 1996, pp. 27ff.
     Marshall McLuhan's most simple-minded idea: Understanding Media (New York: Mentor, 1964), p. 23.

208 *there are often fewer theaters:* The fine Swiss director Alain Tanner told me in 1983 that in recent years three-quarters of the art houses of Paris had closed, and that, even with the advantage of the government subsidy he received, he doubted he would have launched his career in fiction films if he had been starting out in the 1980s.

209 *liberal law professor:* Eben Moglen, "Liberation Musicology," *Nation*, March 12, 2001, p. 6.

Acknowledgments

I wish to thank Nick Couldry, Adam Curtis, Daniel Dayan, Dylan Evans, H. J. Krysmanski, Deborah Meier, Mark Crispin Miller, Dave Morley, Kevin Robins, and Siva Vaidhyanathan for conversations, alerts, and prods, and Carl Bromley, Marco Calavita, Annie Dutoit, Jennifer Kelley, and Erik Vroons for research assistance. I owe much to Marco Calavita, Daniel Dayan, Joshua Gamson, Michael Schudson, Fred Turner, and Ed Vulliamy for reading and criticizing the manuscript.

I gained stimulus as well as time to write (not to mention much pleasure from excellent provisions) from my stay at the Freedom Forum's Media Studies Center in New York (thanks especially to Lawrence McGill and Robert Snyder) and at the Bellagio Center of the Rockefeller Foundation (thanks especially to Gianna Celli).

I received useful reactions to lectures on these themes at the Rutgers University Department of Communication, the Medill School of Journalism at Northwestern University, the National Humanities Center, Ryerson University, the University of British Columbia, the Chinese University of Hong Kong, the Bavarian-American Institute of Munich, the John F. Kennedy Institute of the Free University of Berlin, the Institute of Sociology at the University of Münster, the Media Communication and Cultural Studies Association conference in Loughborough, the University of Westminster Department of Communication, Goldsmiths College of the University of London, the City University of London, the London School of Economics, and the American University of Paris.

Tom Engelhardt, master editor, found the book buried in the manuscript, discerned some sense in my babblings and intuitions, and, if that was not enough, proposed countless specific improvements. Sara Bershtel thought I could make still more sense; I hope she was right. Shara Kay devised the title. Ellen Levine and her staff helped in many ways.

Laurel Cook made life bearable—blessed, in fact. Shoshana, Justin, and Fletcher Haulley, my stepchildren, frequently reminded me that the world was not coming to an end.

Index

About the Author

Todd Gitlin, one of America's most prominent public intellectuals, is the author of eight previous books, including *The Twilight of Common Dreams: Why America Is Wracked by Culture Wars* (1995), *The Sixties: Years of Hope, Days of Rage* (1987), *Inside Prime Time* (1983), and the award-winning novel *Sacrifice* (1999). A frequent contributor to magazines and newspapers, he lectures widely at home and abroad on contemporary culture and history, and has held the chair in American civilization at the École des Hautes Études en Sciences Sociales in Paris. He is the North American editor of the Web site openDemocracy.net and a member of the editorial boards of *Dissent*, *The American Scholar*, and *The Journal of Human Rights*. He is a professor of culture, journalism, and sociology at New York University and lives in the city where he grew up, New York, with his wife, Laurel Cook.